The Haynes Automotive
Heating &
Air Conditioning
Systems Manual

by Mike Stubblefield and John H Haynes

Member of the Guild of Motoring Writers

The Haynes Repair Manual
for automotive heating and air conditioning systems

(6W5 – 1480)

ABCDE
FGHIJ
KLMNO
PQRST 2

AUTOMOTIVE
PARTS &
ACCESSORIES
ASSOCIATION MEMBER

Haynes Publishing Group
Sparkford Nr Yeovil
Somerset BA22 7JJ England

Haynes North America, Inc
861 Lawrence Drive
Newbury Park
California 91320 USA

Acknowledgements

We are grateful for the help and cooperation of Chrysler Corporation, Ford Motor Company, General Motors Corporation, Mac Tools, Inc., Snap-On Tool Corporation, Robinair Division of Sealed Power Corporation and Everco Industries, Inc. for their assistance with technical information, certain illustrations and photos.

A book in the **Haynes Automotive Repair Manual Series**

Printed in the USA

ISBN 1 56392 071 9

Library of Congress Catalog Card Number 88-83195

Contents

Preface

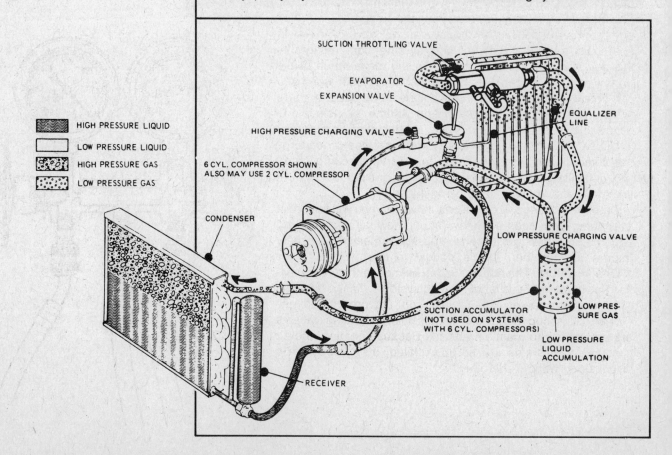

There was a time when every good mechanic understood the basic systems of the automobile pretty well. But that time has passed. The days of the renaissance repairman are over. As systems have become more complicated, the investment in training and tools necessary to service the entire range of automotive technology found on a typical modern vehicle has widened to the point that no one actually "fixes cars" anymore. Instead, most modern mechanics specialize. Today, we have engine builders, front end specialists, tune-up specialists, transmission specialists, etc. Unfortunately, this approach has created an aura of "black magic" around the more esoteric of these topics.

Automotive air conditioning is certainly one subject that is poorly understood by nearly all do-it-yourselfers and a lot of professsionals as well. The reasons for this situation come down to motivation, money and knowledge.

Unlike performance-related topics such as degreeing a cam, rejetting a carburetor, etc., air conditioning theory, service and troubleshooting is, frankly, pretty dry stuff. A well maintained air conditioning system won't make

HIGH PRESSURE LIQUID

LOW PRESSURE LIQUID

HIGH PRESSURE GAS

LOW PRESSURE GAS

SUCTION THROTTLING VALVE

EVAPORATOR

EXPANSION VALVE

HIGH PRESSURE CHARGING VALVE

EQUALIZER LINE

6 CYL. COMPRESSOR SHOWN ALSO MAY USE 2 CYL. COMPRESSOR

CONDENSER

LOW PRESSURE CHARGING VALVE

LOW PRES-SURE GAS

SUCTION ACCUMULATOR (NOT USED ON SYSTEMS WITH 6 CYL. COMPRESSORS)

LOW PRESSURE LIQUID ACCUMULATION

RECEIVER

a vehicle faster. But it will make it more comfortable. Unfortunately, performance — not comfort — is what gets young mechanics going. Consequently, they don't usually grow up saying "I want to be an air conditioning technician."

Then there are the special tools. Even if you are the kind of person who is attracted to air conditioning work, the tools needed to diagnose, repair and maintain a typical system are highly specialized and expensive. They're so specialized, in fact, that they can't be used for much else. Only a professional who chooses the field as a career can justify the kind of investment it takes to become an air conditioning specialist.

Another reason air conditioning seems so mysterious is that little useful knowledge of the basics is readily available. Lots of books explain how to service specific systems, but few bother with the underlying principles of operation. This is unfortunate, because a good grasp of basic theory can enable a mechanic to understand any air conditioning system.

If carefully read and understood, this book should help any mechanic understand the fundamentals of air conditioning systems. It begins with a discussion of basic air conditioning theory, followed by a description of each of the components found in typical heating and air conditioning systems. Any real comprehension of what follows after that is only possible if the first two chapters are read and understood. The rest of the book is devoted to routine maintenance, service procedures, repairs and troubleshooting.

Only two things are *not* included in this volume: 1) removal and installation procedures and 2) compressor overhauls. For specific air conditioning and heating system component removal and installation procedures, refer to the Haynes Owner's Workshop Manual for the vehicle in question. If — after using this book to troubleshoot an air conditioning system — you conclude that the compressor is malfunctioning, we recommend that you remove it and install a rebuilt unit. There are several reasons for this. First, time is money. The money you will save by rebuilding the compressor yourself is more than offset by the money you will have to invest in specialized tools that may not work on other compressors. In this day of rebuilt components, it doesn't make much sense to rebuild a critical component like the compressor when you can obtain a rebuilt one for a few dollars more. Second, there simply is not enough space in this volume to include the overhaul procedure for every air conditioning compressor available. And, frankly, we don't want to provide procedures that someone might attempt to use for a particular compressor, only to find later that the unit was a newer, or older, or different version of the "typical" unit we included.

Other than these two omissions, however, you will find most everything you need to know about how air conditioning systems work, how to maintain them, service them, troubleshoot them and repair them in this modest volume.

One final note: The astute reader will notice that little mention has been made so far of heating systems. That's because — aside from heater core replacement (covered in Haynes Owners Workshop Manuals when possible) — heating systems are pretty easy to maintain and fix. Because heating and air conditioning systems are so interrelated, it's impossible to discuss one without the other.

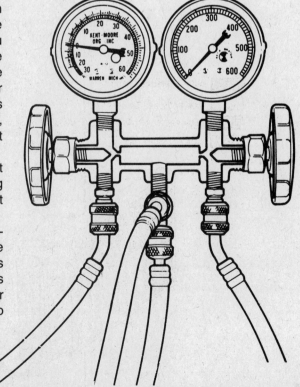

1 Basic theory of air conditioning system operation

Automotive air conditioning is generally regarded as one of the two most significant contributions by American automotive engineering to the evolution of the automobile (the automatic transmission is the other). At first, air conditioning was an expensive option found only on the most luxurious automobiles. As time went on, it became more available, and affordable, to the general motoring public. Today, air conditioning systems are such a widely used option that we seldom give them much thought, until they break and we have to fix them. And that's what this book is all about — how to keep A/C systems operating and how to fix them when they break. The heating system has also been included in this volume because it is an integral part of most modern automotive "climate control" systems. In many instances, it's impossible to work on the air conditioning system without working on the heating system as well.

But before we get into maintaining or servicing either system, it's essential that you know the principles of air conditioning and heating system operation. This chapter provides a clear description of these principles. Make sure you understand them clearly before you try to maintain, diagnose or repair the air conditioning or heating system in your vehicle. Neglecting the material in this first chapter could get you into trouble later.

The comfort zone

Studies have shown that most people feel comfortable in a relatively narrow temperature zone of about 70 to 80° F **(see illustration)**. When the effect of humidity is taken into consideration, this range becomes a little wider. Humidity is simply the amount of moisture in the air. When the air has absorbed as much moisture as it can, the relative humidity is said to be 100%. If the humidity is relatively high, say 70%, we may still feel comfortable down in the mid-60's; if the humidity is low enough, say 30%, we can even tolerate the low 90's without much discomfort. The actual amount of humidity varies in accordance with the temperature, because warm air holds more moisture than cold air.

What this means in practical terms is that you can feel just as cool when the temperature is 80°F and the relative humidity is 30% as when the temperature is 70°F and the relative humidity is 90%.

The key to whether you feel hot or cold is the ability of your body perspiration to evaporate quickly and easily. If the air is dry, perspiration evaporates quickly and the heat leaving the body makes it feel cool. But when the moisture content of the air is high, perspiration cannot evaporate as rapidly, so less body heat is removed and you feel warmer.

Most automotive air conditioning and heating systems are integrated into a "climate control" system that controls the temperature, humidity and air circulation by cooling the air inside the passenger compartment when it's hot outside and heating it when the outside air is cold. We'll look at typical air conditioning and heating system components and controls in Chapter Two. In this chapter, we examine the underlying physical phenomena which enable all air conditioning and heating systems to accomplish these tasks.

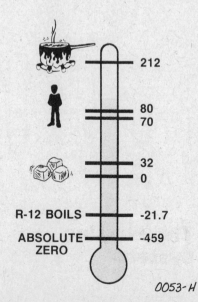

212

80
70

32
0

R-12 BOILS — -21.7

ABSOLUTE ZERO — -459

0053-H

Most people feel comfortable in a relatively narrow temperature zone between 70 and 80°F

Heat

Without heat, a heating system would be impossible, and air conditioning would be unneccesary. What, exactly, is heat? Here's what the American Heritage Dictionary has to say about heat:

"1. A form of energy associated with the motion of atoms or molecules in solids and capable of being transmitted through solid and fluid media by conduction, through fluid media by convection, and through empty space by radiation."

The dictionary goes on to define other meanings for heat, but the one above best characterizes heat for the purposes of this discussion. Fancy terms like "conduction," "convection" and "radiation" notwithstanding, the gist of the above definition is that *heat is basically energy*.

When viewed in its broadest sense, energy takes many forms, manifests itself in many ways and can be transformed from one form to another in many complex ways. But heat is always there in some way. Let's take a few examples. The sun, obviously, gives off vast quantities of energy, heat being one of the more obvious ones. On a smaller scale, any fire also gives off heat. The connecting rods, crankshaft and drivetrain of an internal combustion engine convert the chemical energy released in the explosion of gasoline vapors into the kinetic energy of the moving automobile, in the process creating a lot of heat because of the friction created by all those moving parts rubbing against one another. And every time the driver applies the brakes to stop the vehicle, the friction generated between the brake pads and rotors, and between the tires and the road, transforms the kinetic energy of the moving vehicle into heat.

But when you hear the word "heat," do you think of kinetic energy, friction, internal combustion, fires or the sun? Probably not. The first thought that crosses your mind is the palpable *effect* of heat on your body when you are in close proximity to a heat source. In other words, the word "heat" makes you think of the *physiological sensation of being hot*. That's because we humans are pretty sensitive to heat, or the absence of it.

Remember, there is a relatively narrow temperature range within which we feel truly comfortable. Put another way, we must have the right amount of heat to feel comfortable. Sure, some people have learned to survive at the extreme edges of this range, but the majority of us like to be in that comfort zone of about 70 to 80° F. In this zone, we feel good. That's why air conditioning and heating systems are so popular in our vehicles, homes and offices. Without them, we would sometimes be uncomfortable.

Before we examine the principles of operation of modern air conditioning systems, let's take a quick look at the basics of the typical heating system, which is considerably simpler than an air conditioning system.

The heating system

The internal combustion engine is nothing more than a big heat pump that converts chemical energy into mechanical energy. The temperature in the combustion chamber ranges from 1200° to 1800°F.

About a third of this heat is actually used for pushing the piston down on its power stroke. Another third escapes out the exhaust system. The remainder is conducted through the cylinder walls and cylinder head into the engine cooling system. The heater harnesses this waste heat generated by the engine to heat the passenger compartment.

Heating and air conditioning

Heat moves from warmer to cooler substances

A basic characteristic of heat is that it always moves from a warmer to a cooler substance (see illustration). For example, place an ice cube in your hand and hold it for a minute. Your hands feel cold and the ice cube starts melting. The heat is transferring from your hands to the ice cube. We will talk more about the movement of heat in the following discussion about air conditioning. Now let's look at the three means by which heat is transferred.

If you place an ice cube in your hand, it quickly starts to feel cold because the heat is transferring from your hand to the ice cube — heat always moves from a warmer to a cooler substance

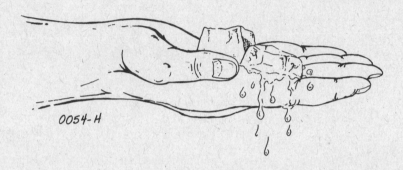

0054-H

Convection, conduction and radiation

Convection (see illustration) is the movement of heat that occurs in liquids and gases when the heated portion rises and is displaced by the cooler portion, creating a circular movement known as a "convection current." Turn on the faucet for the hot water in the shower. Note that it's hot, even though the heater is some distance away. The moving water carries the heat to the shower nozzle. Similarly, when air warmer than the surrounding air is forced into the passenger compartment, it moves up, forcing the cooler air down. This constant displacement of cooler air by warmer air eventually distributes the heated air evenly throughout the passenger compartment.

Conduction (see illustration) is the transfer of heat through a solid material. Pick up a cast iron pan from the stove. Note that the handle is warm. The heat has conducted through the hot metal pan to the cooler handle. Do the same thing with an aluminum pan and you may burn your hand. That's because the rate of transfer depends on the thermal conductivity of the material. And aluminum is a better conductor than cast iron. All "heat exchangers" (devices that transfer heat from a heated liquid to the air, or vice versa) are constructed from metals like aluminum and copper, which are considered the best thermal conductors.

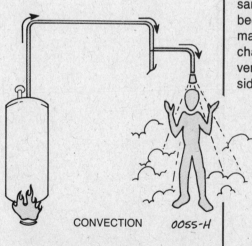

CONVECTION   0055-H

What happens when you turn on the hot water faucet in the shower? Hot water comes out the shower nozzle, even though the hot water heater is some distance away, because the water — or any liquid or gas, for that matter — has the ability to carry heat from one place to another — this phenomenon is known as convection

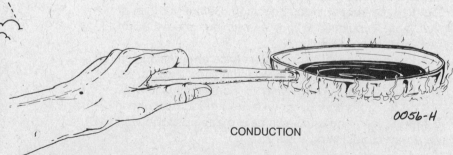

0056-H

CONDUCTION

When you pick up a cast iron pan from the stove, the handle feels warm, even though it's not directly exposed to the flame, because the heat "conducts" through the metal pan to the handle — do the same thing with an aluminum pan, however, and you could burn your hand, because aluminum is a better conductor of heat than cast iron (in other words, the rate of heat transfer depends on the thermal conductivity of the substance)

Radiation **(see illustration)** is the transfer of heat by those waves located in the "infra-red" portion of the "electromagnetic spectrum." Because infra-red waves have wavelengths longer than those of visible light rays, they are invisible. But when you see "heat waves" rolling off a hot asphalt road or the hood of a hot car, that's radiation. The important thing to remember about radiation is that anything that is heated up will give off radiating heat.

Using these three methods of heat transfer, we can describe any heating system. At the heart of the system is a small heat exchanger, commonly known as a heater core. The core is nothing more than a convoluted section of metal tubing through which hot engine coolant is pumped. The heat in the coolant moves through the walls of the tubes and into hundreds of tiny, wafer thin cooling fins attached to the tubing (conduction). An electric fan blows air through the core and heat is transferred from the fins to the cooler air as it passes over them (radiation). This heated air is then forced through a series of ducts and outlets into the passenger compartment, where it warms the air (convection).

0057-H

When you feel the heat on a sunny day, it's because infra-red (invisible) waves from the sun are radiating through space, falling on your vehicle, and heating it up

Air conditioners

Chances are that every vehicle you've ever owned has a heater, but you have probably owned one without an air conditioner. If so, you know what it's like to spend an hour, or a day, confined to the passenger compartment of such a vehicle on a hot day **(see illustration)** When exposed to direct sunlight while parked or driven on a hot day with the windows rolled up, inside temperatures can exceed 140°F. Heat radiated by the sun falls on the metal and glass skin of the roof, body panels and windows, is conducted through the skin and radiated into the passenger compartment. Even heat radiating up off the hot pavement enters the vehicle in a similar fashion. The engine, exhaust system and transmission all shed a huge amount of heat, which also finds its way into the passenger compartment. Even the occupants themselves give off heat. Many modern vehicles have only two roll-down windows, no vent windows and poor ventilation systems. For these vehicles, air conditioning systems aren't just a convenience, they're a necessity. Spending time in one of these vehicles on a hot day with a broken air conditioner is extremely uncomfortable. That's why it's essential that you keep it in top condition. Before you can do that though, you need to know a few things about the principles of air conditioning.

Though you might be able to service an air conditioning system without really understanding how it works, you will have a tough time trying to troubleshoot it when something goes wrong. So take the time to fully understand the following principles before attempting to work on an air conditioning system.

The sun, of course, isn't the only heat source — everything with heat radiates (because it's moving from warmer to cooler substances, remember?). Add up the heat radiating off your vehicle, its engine, the road, etc. and you can see why it gets hot inside the passenger compartment

ENGINE

0058-H

Heating and air conditioning

What is automotive air conditioning?

Automotive air conditioning is the process by which air is cooled, cleaned and dehumidified before entering, or re-entering, the passenger compartment. Basically, an air conditioning system removes heat from the passenger compartment by absorbing it and carrying it outside, where it is released into the atmosphere.

This process is possible because we have learned how to manipulate three simple natural phenomena:

1 Heat transfer
2 The "latent heat of vaporization"
3 The effect of pressure on boiling or condensation

No true comprehension of air conditioning is possible until you understand these three underlying principles because they form the basis of all air conditioning systems.

Heat Transfer

If two materials of different temperatures are placed near each other, the heat in the warmer material will always travel to the colder material until both are the same temperature.

Take, for example, a bottle of warm beer sitting next to a tray of ice cubes on the kitchen counter (see illustration). The colder tray of ice cubes does not transfer its colder temperature to the bottle of beer next to it. Instead, the heat in the beer automatically flows to the ice cube tray.

How much heat? In order to express the amount of heat that transfers from one substance to another, a standard of measurement known as the British Thermal Unit (BTU) has been created. One BTU is equal to the amount of heat required to raise the temperature of one pound of water 0.55°C (1°F) (see illustration). For example, to raise the temperature of one pound of water from 0°C (32°F) to 100°C (212°F), one BTU of heat must be added for each 0.55°C (1°F) rise in temperature, or a total of 180 BTUs of heat. Conversely, in order to lower the temperature of one pound of water from 100°C (212°F) to 0°C (32°F), 180 BTUs of heat must be removed from the water.

0059-H

Heat transfer

What happens if you place a bottle of room temperature beer next to a tray of ice cubes? The bottle of beer cools off because its heat travels from the beer to the ice cubes (not because the cold of the ice cubes is transferred to the beer!)

One British Thermal Unit (BTU) is equal to the amount of heat required to raise the temperature of one pound of water one degree Fahrenheit

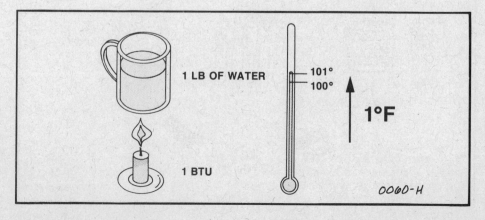

1 LB OF WATER

101°
100°

1°F

1 BTU

0060-H

Latent heat of vaporization

When a liquid boils (changes to a gas), it absorbs heat without raising the temperature of the resulting gas. When the gas condenses (changes back to a liquid), it gives off heat without lowering the temperature of the resulting liquid.

For example, place one pound of water at 0°C (32°F) in a container over a flame. With each BTU of heat that the water absorbs from the flame, its temperature rises 0.55°C (1°F). Thus, after it has absorbed 180 BTUs of heat, the water reaches a temperature of 100°C (212°F). But then a funny thing happens. Even though the flame continues to transfer heat to the water, the temperature of the water remains at 100°C (212°F). It also starts to boil, or change from a liquid to a gaseous state. And it continues to boil until the entire pound of water has passed into the atmosphere as vapor. If, instead of escaping into the atmosphere, the vapor from the whole pound of water were somehow trapped in a container and checked with a thermometer, it too would indicate a temperature of 100°C (212°F). In other words, even though the flame undoubtedly transferred more than 180 BTUs of heat to the water, there could not have been more than an 82°C (180°F) rise in the water's temperature (it went from 32 to 212°F, right?). Where did the rest of the heat go? It was absorbed by the water as it boiled off and disappeared with the vapor. If the vapor contacted cool air, however, the hidden heat would reappear and flow into the cooler air as the vapor condensed back to water. In scientific terms, this phenomenon is known as the ''latent,'' or hidden, heat of vaporization.

Water has a latent heat of vaporization of 970 BTUs and a boiling point of 100°C (212°F). What this means is that as a pound of water reaches a temperature of 100°C (212°F), it will absorb 970 BTUs of heat as it changes to vapor. Conversely, the vapor will give off 970 BTUs of heat in condensing back to water **(see illustration)**.

This remarkable transfer of heat that occurs when a liquid boils or a vapor condenses, is the basic principle of operation for all air conditioning systems.

The amount of heat that a liquid can absorb as it vaporizes is not the only critical characteristic to consider. It must also have a low boiling point. In other words, the temperature at which it boils must be lower than the substance to be cooled.

Water has a latent heat of vaporization of 970 BTUs and a boiling point of 212°F — in other words, as a pound of water reaches a temperature of 212°F, it will absorb 970 BTUs of heat as its changes to vapor; conversely, the vapor will shed 970 BTUs of heat as it condenses back to water

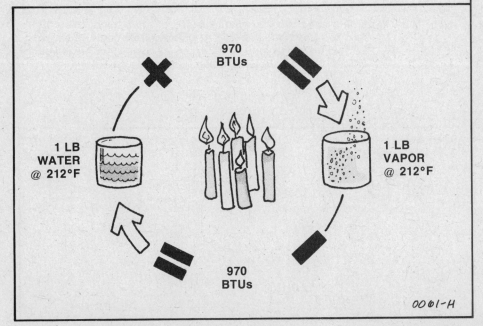

970 BTUs

1 LB WATER @ 212°F

1 LB VAPOR @ 212°F

970 BTUs

0001-H

Heating and air conditioning

Place our bottle of beer, for example, at a room temperature of, say, 21.6°C (70°F) next to boiling water. The heat will flow from the (higher temperature) water to the (cooler temperature) beer. Thus, we get one warm beer, because the boiling point of water is too high.

In order to make practical use of the heat transfer that occurs when a liquid boils, we have to find some liquid with a low boiling point. Refrigerant-12 (or R-12) is the special substance that has been used most widely in motor vehicles until the early 1990's. It boils at -29.85°C (-21.7°F) in an open container. In other words, here's a liquid that will boil, and vaporize, way below the temperature of any passenger compartment this side of Bemidji, Minnesota, and will absorb tremendous amounts of heat without getting any warmer itself.

Recently, however, worldwide concern about depletion of stratospheric ozone caused by substances such as R-12 which contain chlorofluorocarbons (CFCs) has resulted in the introduction of a new non-CFC refrigerant known as R-134a, which is less damaging to the ozone layer. This new refrigerant boils at -26.15°C (-15.07°F), so its heat transfer capabilities are very similar to R-12.

R-134a is being quickly phased in by all manufacturers on new-vehicle air conditioning systems; by 1995, no new vehicles will be equipped with R-12 based systems. However, there are about 300 million vehicles in the US already equipped with R-12-based air conditioning systems, so even though R-12 is being phased out, it will be around for several more years.

We'll get back to R-12 and R-134a in a moment. First, we need to discuss the third principle of air conditioning operation.

Effect of pressure on boiling or condensation

The saturation temperature (the temperature at which boiling or condensation occurs) of a liquid or a vapor increases or decreases in accordance with the pressure to which it is subjected.

In the typical "fixed orifice tube" (we'll discuss that term in the next chapter) air conditioning system, liquid refrigerant (R-12) is stored in the condenser under high pressure. When the liquid R-12 is released into the evaporator by the fixed orifice tube, the resulting decrease in pressure and partial boiling

In its simplest terms, refrigerant absorbs heat from the passenger compartment at the evaporator, transfers it through a tube and sheds it to the outside air at the condenser

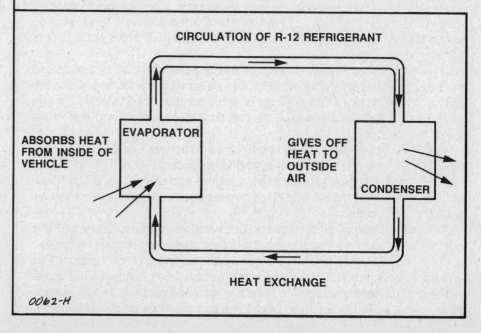

CIRCULATION OF R-12 REFRIGERANT

EVAPORATOR

ABSORBS HEAT FROM INSIDE OF VEHICLE

GIVES OFF HEAT TO OUTSIDE AIR

CONDENSER

HEAT EXCHANGE

0062-H

lowers its temperature to the new boiling point. As the R-12 flows through the evaporator, the passenger compartment air passes over the outside surface of the evaporator coils. As it boils, the R-12 absorbs heat from the air and cools the passenger compartment **(see illustration)**. The heat from the passenger compartment is absorbed by the boiling refrigerant and hidden in the vapor. The refrigeration cycle is now under way. To complete the cycle, three things need to happen:

1 The heat in the vapor must be disposed of
2 The vapor must be converted back to liquid for reuse
3 The liquid must be returned to the starting point in the refrigeration cycle

The compressor and condenser perform these functions. The compressor pumps the refrigerant vapor — which contains the "latent," or hidden, heat — out of the evaporator and suction accumulator drier, then forces it, under high pressure, into the condenser which is located in the outside air stream at the front of the vehicle. The increased pressure in the condenser raises the R-12 condensation or saturation temperature to a point higher than that of the outside air. As the heat transfers from the hot vapor to the cooler air, the R-12 condenses back to a liquid. The liquid, under high pressure now, returns through the liquid line back to the fixed orifice tube for reuse.

But how can heat be transferred from a comparatively cooler vehicle passenger compartment to the hot outside air? The answer lies in the difference between the refrigerant pressure that exists in the evaporator, and the pressure that exists in the condenser. In the evaporator, the suction of the compressor reduces the pressure, and the boiling point, below the temperature of the passenger compartment. Thus, heat transfers from the passenger compartment to the boiling refrigerant. In the condenser, which is pressurized by the compressor, the condensation point is raised above the temperature of the outside air. Thus, the heat transfers from the condensing refrigerant to the outside air. The fixed orifice tube and the compressor simply create pressure conditions that allow the third law of nature to work.

Refrigerant-12

The movement of heat and the change of state of a substance leads us now to Refrigerant-12 (R-12 or Freon), which is the chemical substance dichlorodifluoromethane (CCl_2F_2) used as a "heat carrier" in the air conditioning system.

Why R-12? Because it can change states and carry heat away as required by the air conditioning system and it can do so while remaining within the normal operating temperature range of an air conditioning system. Although water can also change states, R-12 can do it more rapidly and at a much lower temperature.

R-12 is used in earlier automotive air conditioners because of its low boiling point (the point at which evaporation occurs). At any temperature above-21.6°F, R-12 will change state, vaporize and absorb great quantities of heat from inside the vehicle. This creates the "cooling effect" of the air conditioning system.

R-12 was also the preferred medium because manufacturers and the government found it to be among the safest chemical substances for use in the air conditioning system. It is non-toxic (as long as it isn't exposed to an open flame), non-corrosive, odorless, soluble in oil, harmless to natural rubber components and easy to handle when used properly. In large quantities, however, R-12 can discolor chrome and stainless steel components.

Heating and air conditioning

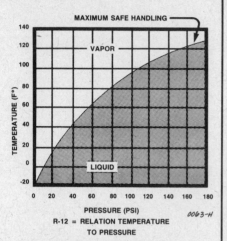

R-12 = RELATION TEMPERATURE TO PRESSURE

The most important characteristic of R-12, or refrigerant, is the relationship it maintains between pressure and temperature: If the pressure of R-12 is low, the temperature will also be low; if the pressure is high, the temperature will also be high — and, as the graph shows, within the 20 to 80 psi range, temperature and pressure vary directly

The pressure-temperature relationship of R-12

At the condenser, the R-12 is at a high temperature and pressure — higher, in fact, than the outside air around the condenser, so the heat in the R-12 flows away, through the condenser tubing and fins and into the outside air — by giving off heat, the R-12 condenses back to a liquid again and the cycle starts all over

When exposed to an open flame, drawn into the engine or detected with a Halide (propane) leak tester, R-12 can turn into phosgene gas, which is poisonous. **You should NEVER inhale phosgene gas!**

But the real drawback of R-12 is that, despite its numerous desirable characteristics, it is a member of the chemical family known as chlorofluorocarbons (CFCs), which consist of one or two carbon atoms surrounded by chlorine and fluorine atoms. Recent scientific studies indicate that the ozone layer of the earth's atmosphere, which absorbs more than 99% of the damaging ultraviolet light emitted by the sun, is being seriously depleted as a result of CFC leakage from air conditioning and refrigeration systems.

Once they escape from air conditioners, CFCs migrate over a 15 to 30 year period up to the stratosphere, some 9 to 30 miles above the earth's surface, and home to the vital ozone layer. When CFCs reach the stratosphere, sunlight splits off highly reactive chlorine atoms, which in turn destroy millions of ozone molecules, allowing more ultraviolet light to reach the earth's surface. Researchers believe that every 1% decrease in ozone in the stratosphere will lead to a 5% to 6% increase in skin cancers. An increase in ultraviolet light can also kill off plankton on the ocean's surface that serve as a food source for other marine life and can decrease the yield of agricultural crops by giving them the equivalent of a sunburn.

Do your part to protect the environment by scrupulous adherence to the Environmental Protection Agency's new regulations for recovering and recycling refrigerant.

The most important characteristic of R-12 is the relationship between pressure and temperature. If the pressure of R-12 is low, the temperature will also be low. If the pressure is high, the temperature will also be high **(see illustration)**.

Within the 20 to 80 psi range, the temperature and pressure of R-12 vary directly. A one psi increase in pressure yields a one degree Fahrenheit change in temperature. So an increase or decrease in R-12 temperature can be obtained by varying the R-12 pressure.

For an air conditioning system to operate at peak efficiency, the R-12 must reach the coldest state (the lowest pressure), at which it can operate without icing, in the evaporator and its warmest (highest pressure) in the condenser. Recall that, in our discussion about latent heat of vaporization, we mentioned that R-12 vaporizes at a low temperature and absorbs great quantities of heat. In the evaporator, the R-12 is under very low pressure. Thus a low temperature is also obtained. This temperature is much lower than the temperature of the air inside the vehicle. Thus, the heat will travel to the colder R-12. As the heat is absorbed, the R-12 vaporizes and carries the heat from the evaporator to the condenser.

At the condenser, the R-12 is at a high temperature and pressure. The temperature of the R-12 is higher than the outside air at the condenser. The heat flows from the condenser to the atmosphere; thus the heat is released outside the vehicle. By giving off heat, the R-12 condenses back to a liquid and the cycle starts over again **(see illustration)**.

These two changes of state — evaporation and condensation — occur during every air conditioning cycle. Heat is absorbed from inside the vehicle by the cold, liquid R-12 flowing through the evaporator. Evaporation takes

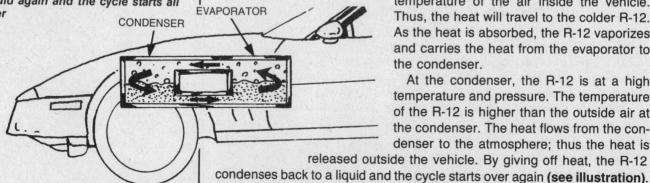

CONDENSER

EVAPORATOR

0064-H

place and the heat-laden R-12 vapors move out of the evaporator to the compressor.

The compressor increases the pressure and the temperature of the R-12 vapors. The vapors are then pumped to the condenser where the heat is transferred to the outside air and condensation takes place (the R-12, while giving off its heat, returns to a liquid form).

At sea level, under atmospheric pressure, R-12 vaporizes at –21.6°F. By pressurizing R-12, it vaporizes at higher temperatures. This is the same process that occurs in radiators. When a pressure cap rated at 15 psi is installed on a radiator, water — which normally boils at 212°F — will boil at about 265°F. Thus, by pressurizing R-12 to between 15 and 30 psi, the point of vaporization can be increased to between 11 and 32°F, which is the desirable level in most evaporators. At even higher pressures (180 to 230 psi), R-12 will condense back into a liquid at temperatures between 130 and 150°F, which is desirable in most condenser units.

There are two major advantages in using R-12. First, it's able to cycle through changes of state within a wide range of temperatures and pressures that exist within the air conditioning system. Second, with R-12, it's possible to use economical air conditioning control devices (which will be discussed in Chapter Two).

If you have read and understood everything in this chapter, you now know how a heater heats and how an air conditioner cools. A heating system simply transfers heat from the hot engine coolant to the passenger compartment through convection, conduction and radiation. An air conditioning system is nothing more than a combination of various mechanical components utilizing a chemical medium, R-12, to absorb heat from inside the vehicle and transfer it to the outside air. The remaining cooler air contains less moisture, adding to the cooling sensation. In effect, one might say that an air conditioning system does not really cool a vehicle, but actually "unheats" it. Now we are ready to discuss the components of heating and air conditioning systems, and how they work together, in more detail.

R-134a

As part of a worldwide effort to protect the ozone layer, the United States joined 75 other countries as a Party to the international treaty known as the Montreal Protocol in 1990. The USA is committed to phasing out R-12 and other ozone-depleting substances by the year 2000. The 1990 Clean Air Act Amendments incorporated this production phaseout date and also addressed the use and emission of these chemicals. President Bush later pledged to halt almost all production of CFCs by the end of 1995. Automobile manufacturers are now in the process of phasing out R-12 and switching to a new refrigerant - known as HFC-134a, or R-134a - which is a hydrofluorocarbon (HFC)-based substance. Because of the absence of chlorine in its molecular structure, R-134a is 95 percent less harmful to stratospheric ozone than R-12.

But R-134a isn't perfect: It's slightly less efficient at transferring heat than R-12: The latent heat of vaporization (the amount of energy required to change from a vapor to a liquid) for R-12 is 36.42 Kcal/Kg @ 0°C; R-134a's latent heat of vaporization is 47.19 Kcal/Kg @ 0°C. In other words, R-134a consumes a little more energy in shedding the heat it has absorbed and transferred from the passenger compartment than does R-12. Practically speaking, this means that the system must operate at slightly higher pressures, and some of the system components - the compressor, the condenser and the evaporator - must be a little more robust and a little larger. It also means that more airflow across the condenser will be necessary, which may result in reduced vehicle performance in heavy traffic.

2 Basic air conditioning and heating system components

Heating system components

Strictly speaking, there are very few components in the heating system — the heater core, the hoses that connect it to the engine's cooling system and an electric blower (fan) that draws air into the heater case and blows it through the heater core.

Other components — such as the water pump and thermostat — are really part of the engine cooling system and their functions are well documented elsewhere. The rest of the heating system — the heater case (or heater box), the blend doors, the dash control assembly, the control valve (if equipped), any temperature sensors, etc. — are really heater *controls*. Typical control components are covered later in this chapter.

The heater core is located under the dash, inside a large (usually plastic) assembly known as the heater case (or heater box). On vehicles with an integrated air conditioning and heating system, this assembly is usually referred to as a heater/evaporator case because the evaporator and the heater are both housed in it. Hoses deliver engine coolant to the heater core and transport it back to the engine. If the heater is equipped with a control valve, it's located in-line in the heater hose. Think of the heater core **(see illustration)** as a small radiator. Like the radiator, the heater core is also a heat exchanger which sheds the engine heat carried by the coolant. It accomplishes this task by conducting the heat through the tubing walls and into thousands of tiny cooling fins. So, like the radiator, the heater core actually helps to cool the engine. But instead of radiating the heat into the outside air, the heater core radiates it into the air inside the heater box, which is blown by an electric fan into the passenger compartment. That's all there is to it. We will look at the heating *system* in more detail in Chapter Three.

Think of the heater core as a little radiator — like a radiator, the core carries engine coolant through its tubing and transfers the heat from the coolant through the tubing walls into cooling fins which shed the heat into the air being blown through the heater case by the blower assembly

Air conditioning components

There are five basic components in every automotive air conditioning system:

1 Compressor
2 Condenser
3 Accumulator or receiver-dryer
4 Expansion valve or orifice tube
5 Evaporator

No air conditioning system, whether it uses R-12 or R-134a, can operate without all five components. On R-134a systems, the compressor, the condenser and the evaporator are physically larger than their counterparts on R-12 systems, but they function in exactly the same way. A number of additional components, whose function is to control and maximize the efficiency of specific systems, are also employed in all systems. We will examine those components in the second half of this chapter. First, let's look at the five primary components in detail.

Compressor

Compressors vary considerably in design but they all perform the same two functions: pumping refrigerant through the system and increasing its pressure and temperature so it will condense and release heat. The following paragraphs will give you a brief idea of how the two basic types of compressors work. Since we aren't going to cover compressor rebuilding, this rudimentary knowledge should suffice.

Compressor clutch

All automotive air conditioning compressors are belt-driven from the engine's crankshaft. An electro-magnetic clutch **(see illustration)** disengages the compressor from the belt when compressor operation is unnecessary, or unwanted.

The clutch is engaged or disengaged both by the control panel on the dash and by the actual demands of the system. In some systems, the clutch con-

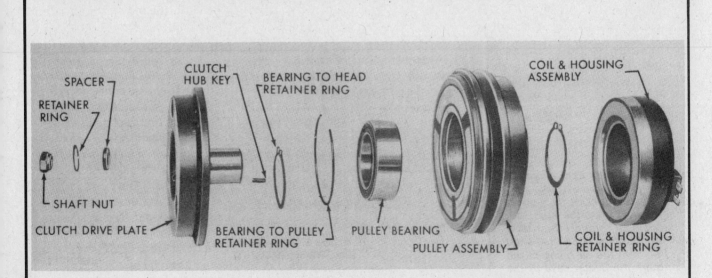

An exploded view of a typical electro-magnetic compressor clutch assembly

stantly "cycles" compressor operation on and off. In others, the compressor runs continuously as long as the system is turned "on."

Older compressors had a "rotating coil" clutch design. The magnetic coil that engages or disengages the compressor is mounted within the pulley and rotates with it. Electrical connections for the clutch operation are made through a stationary brush assembly and rotating slip rings, which are part of the field coil assembly.

A stationary coil design is employed in all contemporary air conditioning compressors. In this type, the magnetic coil is mounted on the end of the compressor and the electrical connections are made directly to the coil leads.

Function

The compressor is the pump that circulates refrigerant through the system. The suction side of the compressor pulls in refrigerant in a low pressure, low temperature form. The refrigerant is then pumped through the compressor to the discharge or outlet side where it's compressed, raising its temperature. It's now ready once more to condense and release heat. The pressurized, heated refrigerant vapor is forced out of the compressor, through the high pressure line, to the condenser.

Operation

Basically, all compressors fall into one of two categories: piston type and rotary vane type. As the name implies, piston type compressors have one or more (up to ten) pistons arranged in either an inline, axial, radial or vee configuration. Rotary vane compressors have no pistons.

Piston-type compressors

Piston type compressors **(see illustration)** go through an intake stroke and a compression stroke for each cylinder. On the intake stroke, the refrigerant from the low side (evaporator side) of the system is drawn into the

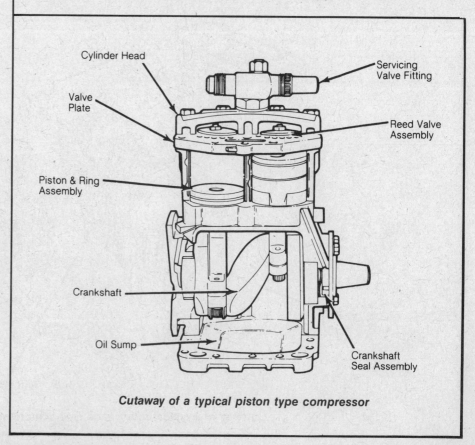

Cylinder Head

Servicing Valve Fitting

Valve Plate

Reed Valve Assembly

Piston & Ring Assembly

Crankshaft

Oil Sump

Crankshaft Seal Assembly

Cutaway of a typical piston type compressor

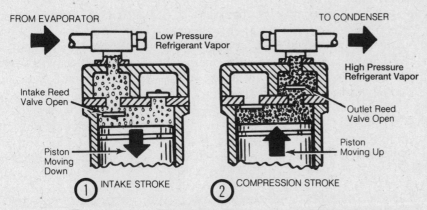

FROM EVAPORATOR

Low Pressure
Refrigerant Vapor

Intake Reed
Valve Open

Piston
Moving
Down

① INTAKE STROKE

TO CONDENSER

High Pressure
Refrigerant Vapor

Outlet Reed
Valve Open

Piston
Moving Up

② COMPRESSION STROKE

Diagram of compressor operation

1 *Intake stroke* - *gaseous refrigerant from low (evaporator) side of system is drawn into compressor through one-way reed valve.*

2 *Compression stroke* - *gaseous refrigerant is compressed into high pressure, high temperature, heat-carrying refrigerant and pushed out one-way reed valve to condenser*

compressor. The intake of refrigerant occurs through reed valves. These one-way valves control the flow of refrigerant vapors into the cylinder.

During the compression stroke, the gaseous refrigerant is compressed. This increases both the pressure and the temperature of the heat-carrying refrigerant. The outlet (discharge) side reed valves then open to allow the refrigerant to move into the condenser. The outlet reed valves may be considered the beginning of the high side of the system.

Rotary vane type compressors consist of a rotor with several vanes and a precisely shaped housing **(see illustration)**. As the compressor shaft rotates, the vanes and housing form chambers. The refrigerant is drawn

Rotary vane type compressors

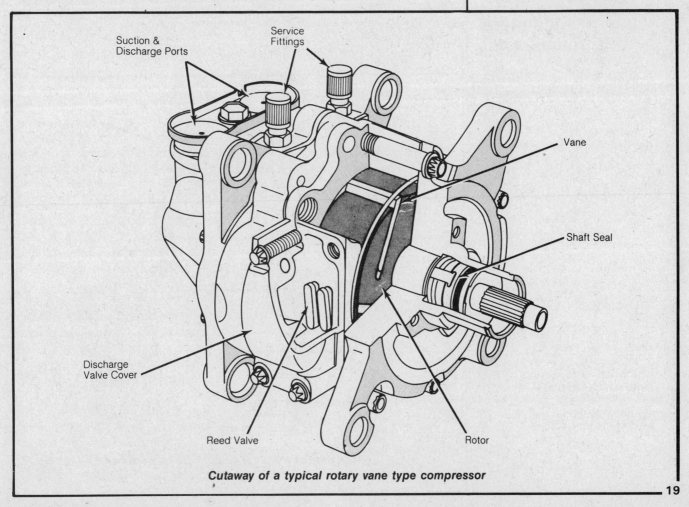

Suction &
Discharge Ports

Service
Fittings

Vane

Shaft Seal

Discharge
Valve Cover

Reed Valve

Rotor

Cutaway of a typical rotary vane type compressor

Heating and air conditioning

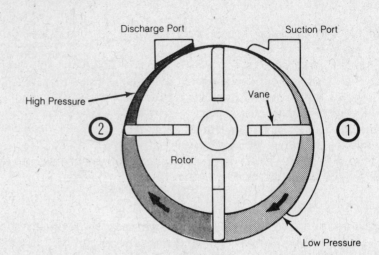

Discharge Port   Suction Port

High Pressure

Vane

Rotor

Low Pressure

Diagram of compressor operation

1 **Intake** — *As a low pressure chamber sweeps by the suction port, gaseous refrigerant from low (evaporator) side of system is drawn through one-way reed valve.*

2 **Exhaust** — *As rotor rotates, chamber decreases in size, compressing refrigerant. As chamber sweeps by discharge port, pressurized refrigerant is expelled through another one-way reed valve and heads for the condenser.*

through the suction port into the chambers, which become smaller as the rotor turns. The discharge port is located at the point where the gas is completely compressed.

The vane type compressor employs no sealing rings. The vanes are sealed against the housing by centrifugal force and lubricating oil. The oil sump is located on the discharge side, so the high pressure tends to force it around the vanes into the low pressure side. This action insures continuous lubrication. Because it depends upon a constant supply of oil, the vane type compressor is susceptible to damage if the system charge is lost. Usually, some sort of protection device is employed to disengage the clutch if system pressure drops too low.

Compressors and liquid refrigerant

It should be noted that compressors CANNOT pump liquid refrigerant (a liquid cannot be compressed). They are designed to operate on refrigerant VAPOR. If liquid refrigerant gets into the compressor, it can damage the reed valves. Moreover, it can also damage the pistons. That's why every system is equipped with either an accumulator or a receiver-drier (both of which are covered later) to absorb excess moisture and protect the compressor. We will discuss liquid refrigerant in the system — how it gets there and how to get rid of it — in detail in Chapters 5 and 6.

Condenser

The condenser (**see illustration**), sometimes referred to as the refrigerant coil, is nothing more than a heat exchanger. It's similar in design to the evaporator, the heater core and the radiator. The condenser is mounted directly in front of the radiator where it can receive the full air flow created by vehicle forward motion and by the engine fan. This configuration affords the maximum surface area for heat transfer within a minimum amount of engine compartment space.

The condenser receives the heated, pressurized refrigerant vapor from the compressor's discharge hose. The refrigerant vapor enters at the top of the condenser and flows through the coils, conducting heat

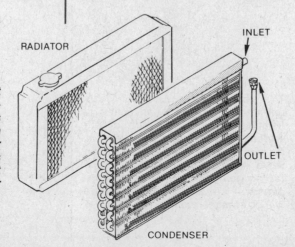

RADIATOR

INLET

OUTLET

CONDENSER

A typical condenser unit (or refrigerant coil) — the condenser looks and works just like a heater core, evaporator or radiator and is always installed right in front of the radiator

through the walls of the tubing and into the cooling fins, then radiating of the fins into the cooler atmosphere.

As the refrigerant vapors are cooled and flow down through the condenser, they gradually condense back into liquid form. At that point where the refrigerant vapors turn to liquid, they shed the greatest amount of heat.

In an air conditioning system that's operating under an average heat load, the condenser will have a combination of hot refrigerant vapor in the upper two-thirds and warm liquid refrigerant which has condensed in the lower third of the coils. This high pressure liquid refrigerant flows out of the condenser and moves to the evaporator.

There are two common methods for storing excess refrigerant and removing moisture from an air conditioning system. The first, which is used by several manufacturers, including Chrysler Corporation, is known as a receiver-drier **(see illustration)**. The receiver-drier is installed in-line on the high side of the system, somewhere between the condenser and the expansion valve. It consists of a tank, a filter, a drying agent, a pick-up tube and, on some units, a sight glass which affords a ''view'' of the system's internal operation **(see illustration)**.

The receiver-drier has several functions. First, it acts as a storage tank for the liquid refrigerant from the condenser until it's required by the evaporator (the evaporator requires a varying amount of refrigerant, depending on operating conditions).

The receiver-drier also protects the system. It contains a drying agent that absorbs moisture from the refrigerant. This agent, which is usually in the form of a silica gel, is known as "desiccant." It is essential that moisture be removed from the system - if allowed to accumulate, it can wreak havoc on air conditioning components and eventually cause system failure. Desiccant replacement will be covered in Chapter 5.

Receiver-drier

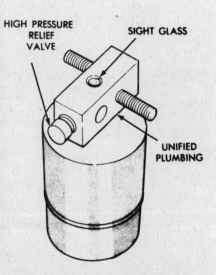

The receiver-drier performs two functions: it acts as a storage tank for the liquid refrigerant until it's required by the evaporator and it protects the system by absorbing moisture from the refrigerant into a "desiccant bag" of silica gel

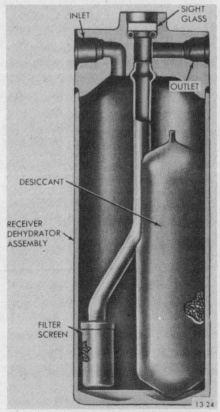

The receiver-drier assembly (this one's from a Chrysler K-car), is always installed on the high side of the system, downstream from the condenser, but before the expansion valve — to locate it, find the metal tubing going in and out of the condenser — the condenser outlet pipe will go straight into the receiver-drier

Heating and air conditioning

Accumulator

General Motors and Ford Motor Company air conditioning systems are equipped with a device that is somewhat different from the receiver-drier. This component is known as an accumulator (**see illustration**).

Unlike the receiver-drier, which is mounted on the high side of the system, the accumulator is located on the low side of the system, usually right at the evaporator outlet. However, its two-fold function — to store excess refrigerant and remove moisture from the system - is the same as that of the receiver-drier. If any liquid refrigerant is passed out of the evaporator, it's stored by the accumulator. Because liquids cannot be compressed, liquid refrigerant can damage the compressor. And, like the receiver-drier, the accumulator also utilizes desiccant to remove moisture from the system (**see illustration**).

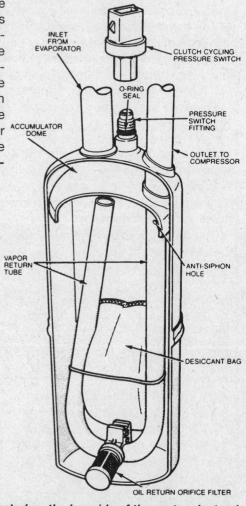

A typical accumulator assembly is not always this easy to see — this one's on a Pontiac Fiero, so it's not obscured by the engine — but, like all accumulators, it's mounted on the firewall right at the evaporator outlet pipe

Although it's located on the low side of the system instead of the high side like the receiver-drier, the accumulator fulfills the same two functions as the receiver-drier: it stores excess refrigerant and removes moisture from the system - when liquid refrigerant comes out of the evaporator, it's stored by the accumulator to prevent damage to the compressor (liquid cannot be compressed)

Moisture in the system

If a component malfunctions or a hose leaks, allowing moisture to contaminate the system, the desiccant must be replaced. In many systems, this can require replacing the accumulator or the receiver-drier, because the desiccant is often non-removable. Some designs, however, permit desiccant removal without junking the entire accumulator or receiver-drier.

But if moisture in the system is suspected, the accumulator or receiver-drier is normally replaced, because moisture combines with refrigerant to form hydrochloric acid, which is highly corrosive to components. And if moisture gathers on the expansion valve or orifice tube (see below), it can freeze, blocking the flow of refrigerant and preventing the cooling action at the evaporator.

System components

To obtain optimal cooling performance from any system, the flow of refrigerant to the evaporator must be controlled and complete evaporation of the liquid refrigerant within the evaporator must be assured. These two tasks are accomplished by a thermostatic expansion valve or a fixed orifice tube.

The thermostatic expansion valve **(see illustration)**, which is located in the line between the receiver-drier and the evaporator (usually right at the evaporator), meters, modulates and controls the flow of refrigerant:
1 **Metering** — A metered orifice within the valve changes the pressure of the incoming liquid refrigerant from high pressure to low pressure.

Controlling refrigerant flow to evaporator

Thermostatic expansion valve

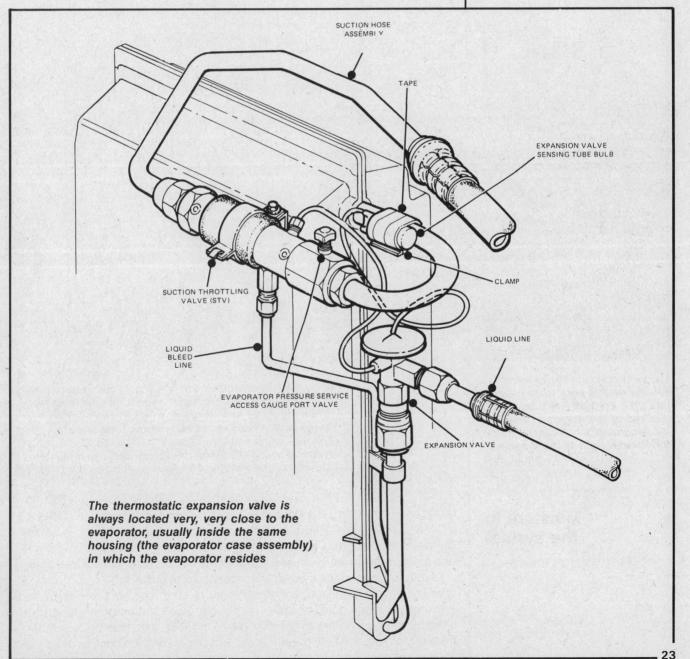

SUCTION HOSE ASSEMBLY

TAPE

EXPANSION VALVE SENSING TUBE BULB

CLAMP

SUCTION THROTTLING VALVE (STV)

LIQUID BLEED LINE

LIQUID LINE

EVAPORATOR PRESSURE SERVICE ACCESS GAUGE PORT VALVE

EXPANSION VALVE

The thermostatic expansion valve is always located very, very close to the evaporator, usually inside the same housing (the evaporator case assembly) in which the evaporator resides

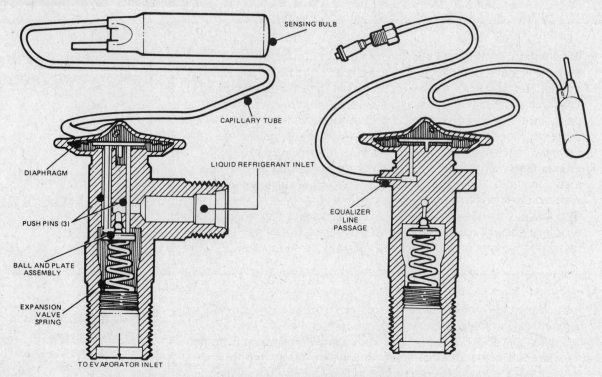

Cutaway of a typical (Ford) thermostatic expansion valve:

1) Regulated by a spring-loaded valve, refrigerant flows through the valve
2) The valve is regulated by a pressure-controlled diaphragm through push pins linking the diaphragm and valve
3) The pressure in the diaphragm chamber varies in accordance with the pressure inside a temperature sensing bulb located close to the evaporator and the capillary tube which links it to the diaphragm chamber
4) An increase in refrigerant temperature at the evaporator outlet increases the pressure in the temperature bulb and tube system, which exerts downward pressure on the expansion valve diaphragm, opening the valve
5) A decrease in refrigerant temperature decreases the pressure in the bulb and tube, lessening the pressure on the diaphragm and allowing the valve to close

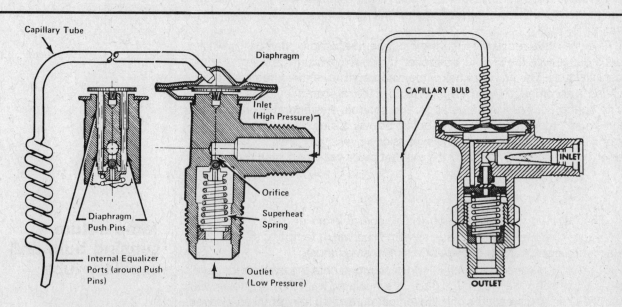

Cutaways of two other typical expansion valves (Volkswagen, with coil end, left; General Motors, with bulb end, right) — note the similarity between these designs and the Ford unit

2 **Modulating** - A thermostatically-controlled valve located inside the expansion valve body fluctuates toward an open or closed position as required to control the liquid refrigerant passing through the orifice. This ensures that the evaporator receives the proper amount of refrigerant. The low pressure created at the expansion valve makes it possible for the liquid refrigerant to vaporize as it passes through the evaporator coils, absorbing heat from the vehicle's interior.

3 **Controlling** - The valve must quickly respond to changes in heat load conditions. As increased heat is sensed, the valve will move toward an open position to increase the flow of refrigerant. Decreased heat loads or increased compressor output volume due to increased engine speed will cause the valve to move toward a closed position, restricting the amount of refrigerant entering the evaporator.

Refrigerant from the receiver-drier enters the expansion valve as a liquid under high pressure. As it passes through the metering orifice in the valve, the refrigerant is forced through the small orifice and sprayed out the other side. The result is a pressure differential, i.e. lower pressure and temperature, which allows the atomized refrigerant to flow through the evaporator and easily vaporize. Because it's at a lower temperature than the interior air of the vehicle, the refrigerant will absorb heat and carry it away from the passenger compartment.

Atomization of low pressure liquid refrigerant

Note: *The following explanation of expansion valve operation is for a typical design used on many air conditioning systems. Though some detail differences may exist between this and other types, the principles are the same.*

Typically, refrigerant flow through the thermostatic expansion valve is controlled by a spring-loaded valve, which, in turn, is controlled by the difference in pressure above and below the valve. Diaphragm movement is transmitted to the valve through operating pins linking the diaphragm plate and the valve.

The pressure above the diaphragm (upper diaphragm chamber) varies in accordance with the pressure supplied by the temperature sensing bulb and capillary tube. The pressure below the diaphragm (lower diaphragm chamber) varies in accordance with the temperature of the refrigerant entering the valve. The spring adjusts valve operation and controls a temperature differential known as "superheat" (see *Valve spring* below). It's important that you understand how this device works. The expansion valve is the "brain" of a receiver-drier type system. So even if it's still not clear yet, keep reading.

Expansion valve operation

The capillary tube, tube end (bulb, coil or plain end) and upper diaphragm chamber form a closed system filled with a temperature-sensitive gas (refrigerant, carbon dioxide or a similar substance).

The capillary tube, coil or plain end is clamped onto the evaporator outlet pipe (or installed in a well in the pipe). It's insulated from the outside air with special tape, so it measures only the temperature of the refrigerant as it leaves the evaporator.

Any increase in refrigerant temperature at the evaporator outlet increases the pressure in the temperature bulb and tube system. This in turn exerts

Temperature sensing bulb and capillary tube

25

Heating and air conditioning

a downward pressure on the diaphragm, opening the valve. Similarly, a decrease in refrigerant temperature decreases the pressure in the temperature bulb system. This lessens the pressure on the diaphragm, allowing the valve to close.

The lower diaphragm chamber reflects the evaporator inlet temperature. A passage in the expansion valve from the outlet passage leads to this chamber. On some valves, an external tube is connected to the refrigerant line between the evaporator and the compressor. These passages allow refrigerant pressure to reach the underside of the diaphragm, balancing the pressure on the upper side of the diaphragm.

Valve spring

A spring below the valve tends to move the valve toward the closed position. It also acts in conjunction with the diaphragm to control valve movement. The spring is preset to provide proper valve action and also allows for a differential of 4 to 16°F between the evaporator inlet and outlet temperatures.

This temperature differential is called "superheat." The few extra degrees of heat ensures that the vapor at the evaporator outlet doesn't contain any droplets of liquid refrigerant when it is returned to the compressor.

The expansion valve spring is preset and cannot be adjusted. It should be noted that late model GM and Ford systems use an expansion tube or orifice tube instead of an expansion valve and do not have the spring and temperature differential feature. That's why the accumulator is located on the outlet side of the evaporator, where it can collect any residual liquid refrigerant that might pass through the evaporator.

Servicing the expansion valve

Expansion valves are preset at the factory, so a defective valve must be replaced with a new one. Expansion valves with a filter screen should have the screen replaced whenever the system is open.

The internally equalized expansion valve (like the units already shown) has a drilled equalizing passage between the outlet chamber and the lower side of the diaphragm. A variation of the internally equalized expansion valve is known as the Suction Throttling Valve, Pilot Operated Absolute, or, simply, STV POA **(see illustration)**. On systems equipped with this design, the equalizer line is attached to a special fitting on the STV unit. The line allows refrigerant pressure to be applied to the lower diaphragm in the same manner as the internally equalized type.

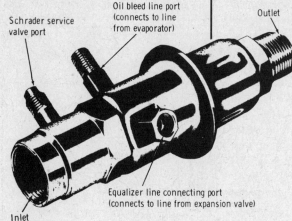

Schrader service valve port

Oil bleed line port (connects to line from evaporator)

Outlet

Equalizer line connecting port (connects to line from expansion valve)

Inlet

This variation of the internally equalized expansion valve is called a suction throttling valve pilot operated absolute (STV POA) — the equalizer line is attached to the STV unit, allowing refrigerant pressure to be applied to the lower diaphragm in the same manner as the internally equalized type

COMPRESSOR

VACUUM ELEMENT

BULB

CONDENSER

POA VALVE

EVAPORATOR

EXPANSION VALVE

EQUALIZER LINE

OIL BLEED LINE

CAPILLARY TUBE

System components

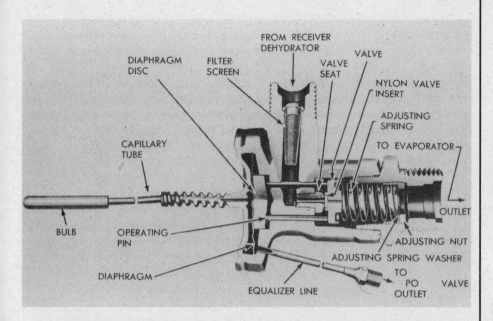

A cutaway of a typical externally equalized expansion valve — this design employs a line and fitting which are connected from the lower side of the diaphragm to a point on the low side hose between the evaporator and the compressor

The externally equalized valve (see illustration) has a line and fitting which are connected from the lower side of the diaphragm to a point on the low side hose between the evaporator and the compressor.

Like other air conditioning system components, expansion valves undergo constant evolution. Manufacturers have introduced a number of different expansion valve designs in recent years. Functionally, the valve described above is typical of many units, including the following variations. Also, operation changes little from one design to another.

Chrysler Corporation "H" valve (see illustration) — First used in 1974, this type gets its name from its distinctive "H" configuration. There are two

Typical configurations

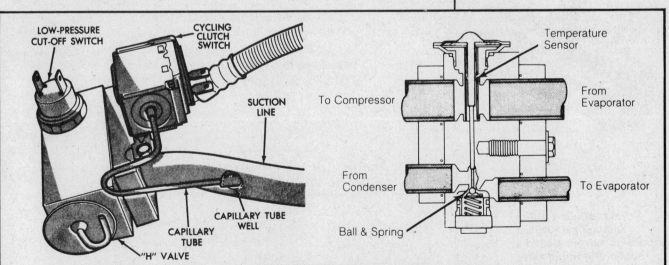

A typical Chrysler "H" valve (left); a cutaway of the same valve (right), which gets its name from the refrigerant passages which form the legs of the "H":

1. One passage, which contains a ball and spring valve, is in the refrigerant line from the condenser to the evaporator.
2. The other passage, which contains the valve's sensing element, is in the refrigerant line from the evaporator to the compressor.

Heating and air conditioning

refrigerant passages which form the legs of the "H." One passage is in the refrigerant line from the condenser to the evaporator and contains a ball and spring valve. The other passage is in the refrigerant line from the evaporator to the compressor and contains the valve's temperature sensing element.

In 1976, Ford Motor Company introduced the combination (or block) type valve, which combines an expansion valve (similar to Chrysler's "H" valve) and the STV into one housing **(see illustration)**. This design puts the operation of these two valves in close proximity for quicker valve response.

In 1980, Ford introduced the mini-combination valve. Its configuration is basically similar to that of the earlier valve, but the "H" expansion valve is smaller and the STV has been redesigned to eliminate the internal piston and separate housing manifold.

The manifold assembly has a manifold block which attaches to the evaporator. The expansion valve and STV are attached to the manifold by short sections of tubing **(see illustration)**.

After 1978, Ford expansion valves have used a ball-and-slotted seat arrangement **(see illustrations)**. The slotted seat keeps the valve from closing completely. A slight amount of

REAR VIEW

EVAPORATOR LIQUID BLEED CONNECTION

EVAPORATOR MANIFOLD PLATE

STV HOUSING MANIFOLD

SUCTION LINE CONNECTION

EXPANSION VALVE

EVAPORATOR OUTLET (SUCTION)

EVAPORATOR MANIFOLD PLATE-TO-EXPANSION VALVE ATTACHING SCREWS

EVAPORATOR INLET

Ford Motor Company's combination, or block, valve combines an expansion valve (similar in design to the Chrysler "H" valve) with the suction throttling valve for quicker valve response

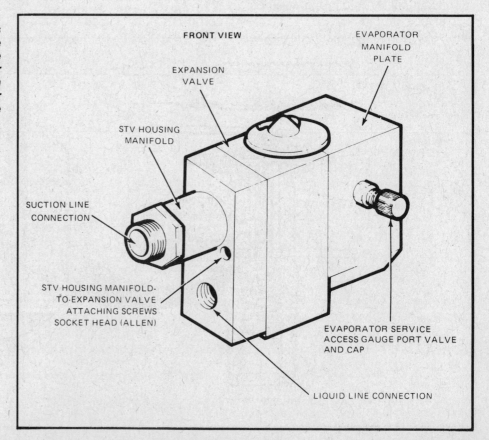

FRONT VIEW

EVAPORATOR MANIFOLD PLATE

EXPANSION VALVE

STV HOUSING MANIFOLD

SUCTION LINE CONNECTION

STV HOUSING MANIFOLD-TO-EXPANSION VALVE ATTACHING SCREWS SOCKET HEAD (ALLEN)

EVAPORATOR SERVICE ACCESS GAUGE PORT VALVE AND CAP

LIQUID LINE CONNECTION

System components

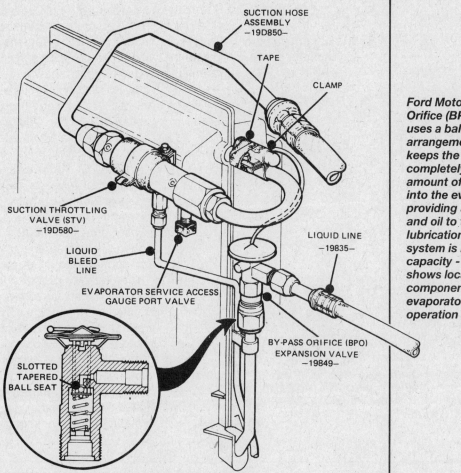

SUCTION HOSE ASSEMBLY —19D850—

TAPE

CLAMP

SUCTION THROTTLING VALVE (STV) —19D580—

LIQUID BLEED LINE

EVAPORATOR SERVICE ACCESS GAUGE PORT VALVE

SLOTTED TAPERED BALL SEAT

LIQUID LINE —19835—

BY-PASS ORIFICE (BPO) EXPANSION VALVE —19849—

Ford Motor Company's By-pass Orifice (BPO) expansion valve uses a ball and slotted seat arrangement - the slotted seat keeps the valve from closing completely, allowing a small amount of refrigerant to flow into the evaporator, thus providing additional refrigerant and oil to the compressor for lubrication and cooling when the system is not operating at capacity - upper illustration shows location of principal components of assembly at evaporator, lower cutaway shows operation of the valve

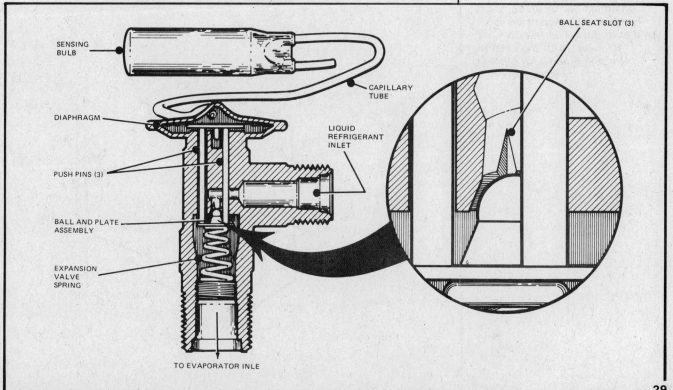

SENSING BULB

CAPILLARY TUBE

DIAPHRAGM

LIQUID REFRIGERANT INLET

PUSH PINS (3)

BALL AND PLATE ASSEMBLY

EXPANSION VALVE SPRING

TO EVAPORATOR INLE

BALL SEAT SLOT (3)

29

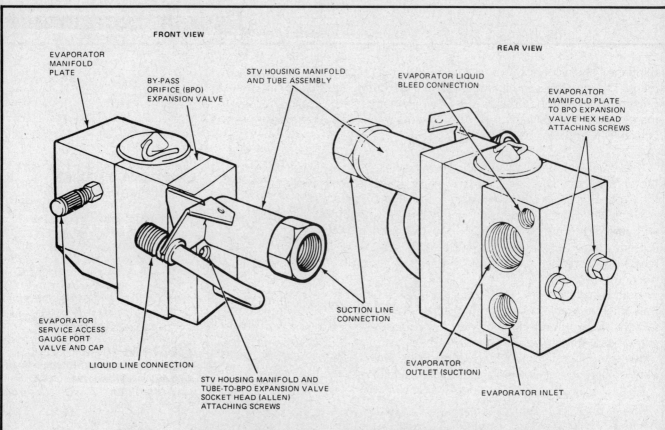

FRONT VIEW

REAR VIEW

EVAPORATOR MANIFOLD PLATE

BY-PASS ORIFICE (BPO) EXPANSION VALVE

STV HOUSING MANIFOLD AND TUBE ASSEMBLY

EVAPORATOR LIQUID BLEED CONNECTION

EVAPORATOR MANIFOLD PLATE TO BPO EXPANSION VALVE HEX HEAD ATTACHING SCREWS

EVAPORATOR SERVICE ACCESS GAUGE PORT VALVE AND CAP

LIQUID LINE CONNECTION

STV HOUSING MANIFOLD AND TUBE-TO-BPO EXPANSION VALVE SOCKET HEAD (ALLEN) ATTACHING SCREWS

SUCTION LINE CONNECTION

EVAPORATOR OUTLET (SUCTION)

EVAPORATOR INLET

Ford Motor Company's By-pass Orifice (BPO) combination valve also uses the ball and slotted seat arrangement (upper illustration shows principal features of valve, lower cutaway shows operation of the valve)

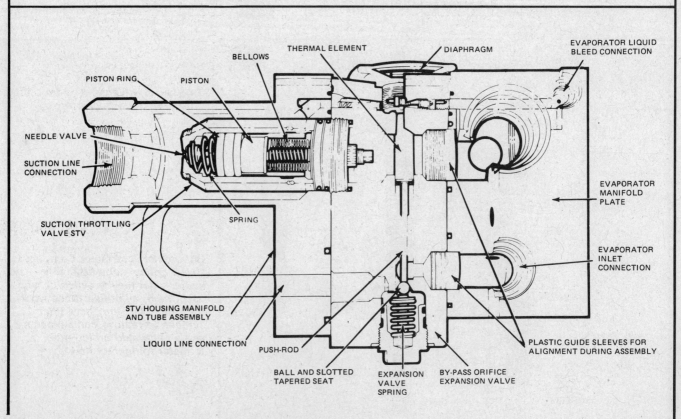

PISTON RING

PISTON

BELLOWS

THERMAL ELEMENT

DIAPHRAGM

EVAPORATOR LIQUID BLEED CONNECTION

NEEDLE VALVE

SUCTION LINE CONNECTION

EVAPORATOR MANIFOLD PLATE

SUCTION THROTTLING VALVE STV

SPRING

EVAPORATOR INLET CONNECTION

STV HOUSING MANIFOLD AND TUBE ASSEMBLY

LIQUID LINE CONNECTION

PUSH-ROD

BALL AND SLOTTED TAPERED SEAT

EXPANSION VALVE SPRING

BY-PASS ORIFICE EXPANSION VALVE

PLASTIC GUIDE SLEEVES FOR ALIGNMENT DURING ASSEMBLY

refrigerant is always allowed to flow into the evaporator with this arrangement. This provides additional refrigerant and refrigerant oil to the compressor to lubricate and cool it during minimum system cooling requirements (expansion valve closed). This type of valve is known as the By-pass Orifice (BPO) Expansion Valve.

The orifice tubes (see illustration) used on all current Ford and General Motors vehicles, and some foreign makes, perform the same function as the expansion valve but have a different configuration.

General Motors' 1975 design was a straight tube of sintered metal and was referred to as an expansion tube. The plastic orifice tubes used on current Ford FFOT systems and on 1976 and later GM CCOT systems have filter screens to remove contaminants and a calibrated orifice tube to meter refrigerant flow.

Both designs create the necessary pressure drop by metering a steady flow of refrigerant while the compressor is operating. A cycling clutch switch, either a thermostatic type or a pressure sensing type, turns the compressor on and off. The intermittent operation of the compressor controls the refrigerant flow and pressure. Like the expansion valve, the expansion and orifice tube are mounted on the inlet side of the evaporator.

Orifice tubes

General Motors' first orifice tube, in 1975, was a straight tube of sintered metal and was called an expansion tube

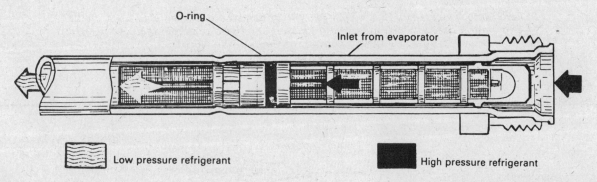

O-ring

Inlet from evaporator

Low pressure refrigerant

High pressure refrigerant

Cutaway of a typical modern orifice tube (this one's from a Volvo)

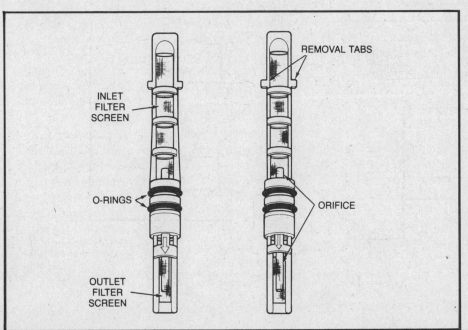

REMOVAL TABS

INLET FILTER SCREEN

O-RINGS

ORIFICE

OUTLET FILTER SCREEN

Cutaway of Ford Motor Company "fixed orifice" tube assembly — no matter what they're called or who uses them, all orifice tubes work the same way: they have filter screens to remove contaminants and a calibrated orifice tube to meter refrigerant flow

Heating and air conditioning

Evaporator

A typical evaporator (and blower motor) assembly (Pontiac Fiero shown) — the evaporator, which is simply a refrigerant coil surrounded by a lot of small, thin cooling fins, receives cool, low pressure, atomized liquid refrigerant from the orifice tube or expansion valve and transfers the heat from the passenger compartment air passing through the coils and cooling fins into the refrigerant, which changes to a low pressure vapor as it absorbs the heat

Like the heater core and condenser, the evaporator **(see illustration)** consists of a refrigerant coil packed in a dense arrangement of thin cooling fins. Because it must be located under the dash, it provides a maximum amount of heat transfer in a minimum amount of space. The evaporator is usually installed in a housing under the dash panel or cowl. When the air conditioning system is turned on, warm air from the passenger compartment is blown through the coils and fins of the evaporator.

The evaporator receives refrigerant from the thermostatic expansion valve or orifice tube as a low pressure, cold atomized liquid. As the cold refrigerant passes through the evaporator coils, heat moves from the warm air into the cooler refrigerant.

When the liquid refrigerant receives enough heat, a change of state — from a low pressure liquid into a low pressure vapor — takes place.

The thermostatic expansion valve or orifice tube continually meters the precise amount of refrigerant necessary to maintain optimum heat transfer, which ensures that all of the liquid refrigerant will have changed to a vapor by the time it reaches the evaporator outlet. The vaporous refrigerant then continues on to the inlet (suction) side of the compressor.

If too much refrigerant is allowed to enter, the evaporator floods. This results in poor cooling due to the higher pressure (and temperature) of the refrigerant. The refrigerant can neither boil away rapidly nor vaporize. On the other hand, if too little refrigerant is metered, the evaporator starves. Again, poor cooling is the result because the refrigerant boils away or vaporizes too quickly before passing through the evaporator.

The temperature of the refrigerant vapor at the evaporator outlet will be approximately 4 to 16°F higher than the temperature of the liquid refrigerant at the evaporator inlet. This temperature differential is the "superheat," described earlier, which ensures that the vapor will not contain any droplets of liquid refrigerant that would be harmful to the compressor.

The warm air blown across the evaporator usually contains some moisture (humidity). The moisture in the air will normally condense on the evaporator coils and be drained off as water. A drain tube in the bottom of the evaporator housing directs the water outside the vehicle. That's why a puddle often forms when the vehicle is parked after the air conditioner has been running.

This dehumidification of the air is an added feature of the air conditioning system that adds to passenger comfort. It can also be used as a means of controlling fogging of the windows.

Under certain conditions, however, too much moisture may accumulate on the evaporator coils. For example, when humidity is extremely high and the maximum cooling mode is selected, the evaporator temperature might become so low that moisture would freeze on the evaporator coils before it can drain off.

System components

Blower fan and motor

An important component in the cooling action of the evaporator is the blower motor/fan (usually the same one that blows air through the heater core), also located in the evaporator housing. The blower **(see illustration)** draws warm air from the passenger compartment over the evaporator and blows the "cooled" air out into the passenger area. The blower motor is controlled by a fan switch with settings from Low to High.

High blower speed will provide the greatest volume of circulated air. A reduction in speed will decrease the air volume. But the slower speed of the circulated air will allow the air to remain in contact with the fins and coils of the evaporator for a longer period of time. The result is more heat transfer to the cooler refrigerant. Therefore, the coldest air temperature from the evaporator is obtained when the blower is operated at its slowest speed. The next chapter examines various typical controls and describes how they make air conditioning more efficient.

The components discussed in the first half of this chapter are the basic hardware found in every automotive air conditioning system. But although they are necessary to make it work, they're not sufficient to make it work *efficiently*. That's why every air conditioning system used in an automobile must also have certain control devices which constantly monitor its operation and ensure optimum efficiency. A number of different means are employed

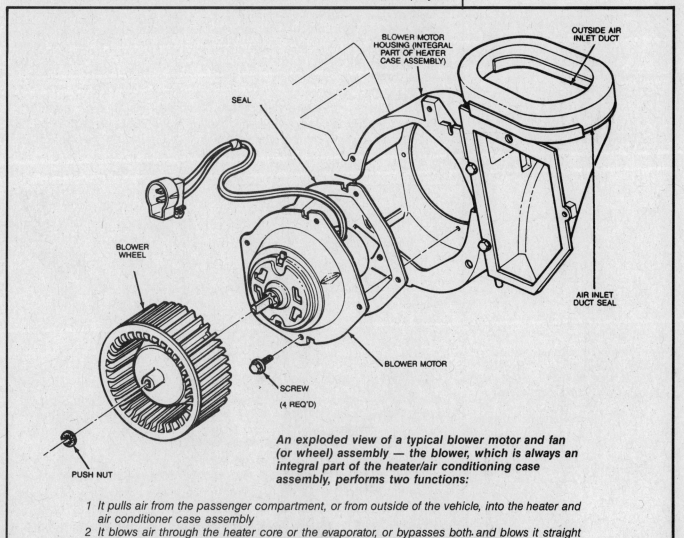

An exploded view of a typical blower motor and fan (or wheel) assembly — the blower, which is always an integral part of the heater/air conditioning case assembly, performs two functions:

1 *It pulls air from the passenger compartment, or from outside of the vehicle, into the heater and air conditioner case assembly*
2 *It blows air through the heater core or the evaporator, or bypasses both and blows it straight out the dash vents depending on the position of the doors in the heater case*

Heating and air conditioning

Controls

to help air conditioning systems operate efficiently. When we discuss the various "types" of air conditioning systems in the next chapter, we will really be referring to the means by which they are controlled. It would be difficult to truly understand air conditioning systems without first understanding the principal control components of each system. Therefore, the remainder of this chapter is devoted to a discussion of control devices.

Actually, because they are common to every automotive air conditioning system, two control devices — the compressor clutch and the thermostatic expansion valve/orifice tube — have already been covered in the first half of this chapter. These two devices regulate the flow of refrigerant (and, therefore, the transfer, and eventual removal, of heat) through the air conditioning system.

But moving refrigerant through the system does not guarantee optimal cooling efficiency. Numerous other controls are necessary to improve efficiency, protect various system components and maintain acceptable driveability of the vehicle while the air conditioning system is operating. These ancillary control devices influence the operation of the compressor, the evaporator, the condenser and the electric fan for the cooling system.

Compressor controls

Numerous control devices are employed to switch the compressor on and off, as necessary, to prevent damage to system components, to avoid excessive cooling and to protect against inordinately high, or low, system pressure. The following components are some of the most widely used devices in modern vehicles.

Ambient temperature switch

The ambient temperature switch **(see illustration)** is an outside air temperature sensing device. It's usually located in the confines of the engine compartment, usually right in front of the grille, where it can quickly and ac-

A typical ambient (outside) temperature switch like this one is usually located right in front of the radiator and condenser where it can react instantly to temperature changes

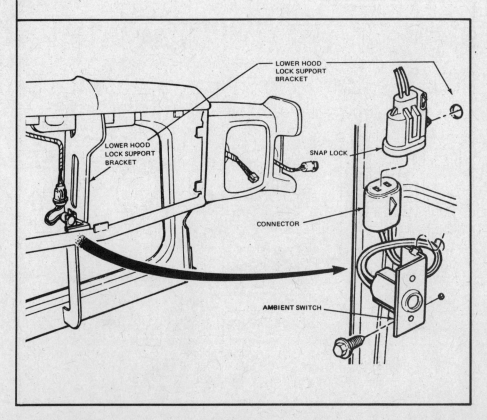

curately sense outside air temperatures. The ambient temperature switch delays compressor operation when low outside air temperatures are sensed. Operation of the compressor during extreme cold spells can cause poor oil circulation, damaging compressor seals, gaskets or reed valves.

The ambient temperature switch is really nothing more than a temperature sensor wired to a simple electrical on-off switch. When the temperature drops below the range determined by the manufacturer to be suitable for compressor operation, the switch opens. Current to the compressor clutch cannot pass through the switch and the compressor ceases to operate (we'll get to why the compressor doesn't operate without electrical current in a minute).

When the ambient air temperature once again reaches or surpasses the predetermined minimum operating temperature (usually somewhere between 32 and 50 degrees, depending on the application), the switch contacts close, electrical current can pass through the switch once more and the compressor resumes operation.

The compressor control valve (see illustration) is a device that regulates crankcase pressure in the V5 compressor used on General Motors vehicles. It's similar in operation to the pilot operated absolute (POA) type suction throttling valve found on some General Motors and Ford evaporators. A pressure-sensitive bellows is exposed to suction side pressure and acts on a ball-and-pin valve exposed to high side pressure. The bellows also controls a bleed port that is exposed to suction side pressure. Just like the POA valve in a conventional system, the compressor control valve modulates continually. In mild weather, compressor displacement is somewhere in the middle; in cool climes, it's near the minimum; on hot days, it's near the maximum.

Compressor control valve

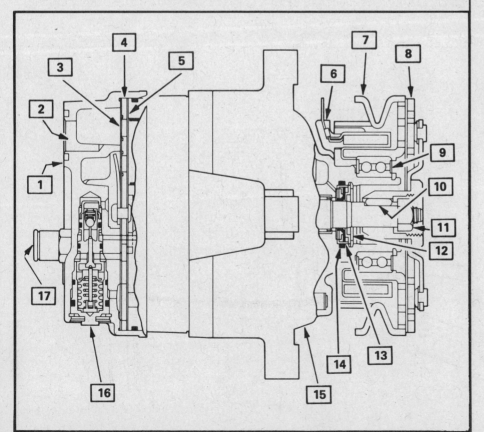

The compressor control valve (number 16 in this illustration) regulates crankcase pressure on General Motors vehicles — a pressure sensitive bellows is exposed to suction side pressure and acts on a ball and pin valve exposed to high side pressure

1 Rear head
2 Suction port
3 Rear head gasket
4 Valve plate
5 Suction reed plate
6 Clutch coil
7 Pulley
8 Drive plate
9 Pulley bearing
10 Shaft key
11 Shaft nut
12 Front seal retainer
13 Front seal
14 Front seal "O"
15 Front head
16 Compressor control valve
17 High pressure relief valve

Heating and air conditioning

Cycling clutch switch

The cycling clutch switch **(see illustration)**, located on the refrigerant plumbing sealing plate, adjacent to the "H" valve, is a device developed by Chrysler Corporation for use on its vehicles. The switch is electrically connected in series with the compressor clutch coil. It switches the compressor on or off, depending upon the temperature sensed by a refrigerant-charged capillary tube inserted into a well in the suction line. The well is filled with a special grease that is necessary for accurate sensing.

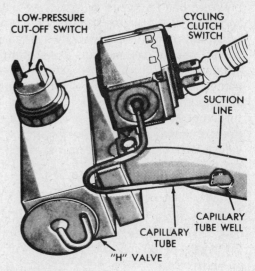

Chrysler Corporation's cycling clutch switch, located on the refrigerant plumbing seal plate, next to the "H" valve, is electrically connected in series with the compressor clutch coil — it switches the compressor on or off depending on the temperature sensed by a refrigerant-charged capillary tube inserted into a well in the suction line (typical assembly — top; exploded view — bottom)

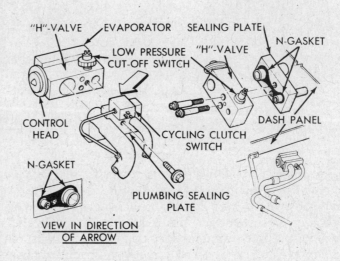

High pressure cut-out switch

The high pressure cut-out switch **(see illustration)** is used on some 1975 and later Chrysler Corporation vehicles (particularly fleet vehicles) and on some 1980 and later General Motors models. It's usually located on the service fitting of the discharge muffler or mounted in the rear of the compressor.

The high pressure cut-out switch, used on some 1975 and later Chryslers and on some 1980 and later GM vehicles, is usually located on the service fitting of the discharge muffler or mounted in the rear of the compressor — when refrigerant pressure exceeds certain levels, the switch opens and the compressor is disengaged

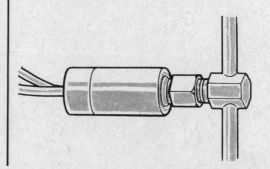

The switch is wired in series with the compressor clutch. If and when compressor discharge pressures reach a predetermined level (375 psi [Chrysler]/400 psi [GM]), the switch opens and stops compressor clutch engagement. When the pressure drops back (to 250 psi [Chrysler]/290 psi [GM]), the switch closes.

The high pressure relief valve **(see illustration)**, which is utilized in many systems, is located either on the receiver-drier (Chrysler vehicles only), the compressor or somewhere on the high side of the system. The high pressure relief valve protects the air conditioning system by bleeding off excessive pressure when it occurs. What causes high pressures? A condenser blocked by debris or a refrigerant overcharge are common causes.

On late model Chrysler vehicles, the valve, which is mounted on the receiver-drier, is calibrated to bleed off refrigerant when pressure reaches 450 to 550 psi. The valve reseats itself once sufficient refrigerant has been vented to lower the pressure to an acceptable level.

On some General Motors models, the compressor-mounted valve will open when refrigerant pressure on the high (discharge) side exceeds 440 psi. If this occurs, refrigerant and refrigerant oil should be replaced as necessary.

High pressure relief valve

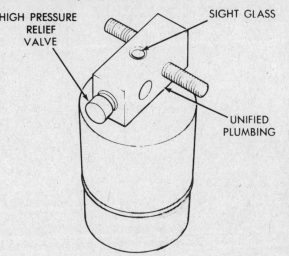

HIGH PRESSURE RELIEF VALVE

SIGHT GLASS

UNIFIED PLUMBING

The high pressure relief valve — this one's a Chrysler unit on the receiver-drier, but it could be located on the compressor or somewhere on the high side of the system on other vehicles — protects the air conditioning system by bleeding off excessive pressure when it occurs

Low pressure cut-off switch

On some late model American Motors and General Motors vehicles, the compressor is protected by a low-pressure cut-off switch **(see illustration)**, which opens in the event of a low charge condition. Also known as the compressor discharge pressure switch, this device is used on General Motors accumulator-type (CCOT) systems that don't have a pressure sensing switch and on some 1980 and later AMC models with four-cylinder engines. On American Motors vehicles, the low pressure cut-off switch is located on the receiver-drier (Alliance and Encore) or in the evaporator inlet (high side) line (Eagle). On General Motors vehicles, it's installed in the rear head of the compressor. If the switch senses an inordinately low refrigerant pressure, it opens the compressor circuit, shutting down compressor operation. Because the pressure of the switch varies directly with ambient temperature, the switch also functions effectively as an ambient temperature switch. It will not permit compressor operation at very low temperatures.

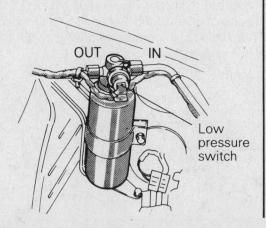

OUT   IN

Low pressure switch

The low pressure cut-off switch, which is used on some American Motors and GM vehicles, protects the compressor in the event of a low-charge condition (this device is sometimes called a compressor discharge pressure switch)

Heating and air conditioning

Low pressure cut-out switch

The low pressure cut-out switch, found on some Chrysler models, is located either on the receiver-drier through 1978, or on the "H" type expansion valve assembly after that — when a preset low charge level is sensed, the switch halts compressor operation to protect it from damage caused by insufficient refrigerant oil

The low pressure cut-out switch **(see illustration)**, which is used on some Chrysler models, is located in the high side of the system. On vehicles manufactured through 1978, the switch is found on the receiver-drier. From 1979 on, it's installed on the "H" type expansion valve assembly.

The switch is connected in series with the compressor clutch electrical circuit. When a predetermined low charge is sensed, the switch halts compressor operation. This protects the compressor from damage caused by insufficient refrigerant oil (if the system's low charge is caused by a leak, oil is often lost).

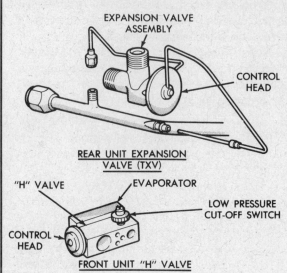

EXPANSION VALVE ASSEMBLY

CONTROL HEAD

REAR UNIT EXPANSION VALVE (TXV)

"H" VALVE

EVAPORATOR

LOW PRESSURE CUT-OFF SWITCH

CONTROL HEAD

FRONT UNIT "H" VALVE

Low pressure switch

On some Cadillac and Oldsmobile Toronado models, a low pressure switch, located on the accumulator, provides a ground signal to the body control module (BCM) when refrigerant pressure drops below 2 to 8 psi. The BCM takes corrective action to protect the compressor.

Pressure sensing (cycling) switch

The pressure cycling or sensing switch, which is used on accumulator type (orifice tube) systems, senses the low side pressure as an indicator of evaporator temperature and senses refrigerant pressure on the suction side of the system to protect the system from freeze-up

The pressure sensing (cycling) switch **(see illustration)** is used on accumulator-type (orifice tube) systems. The cycling of the compressor is controlled by the switch, which senses the low-side pressure as an indicator of evaporator temperature. The pressure cycling switch is the freeze protec-

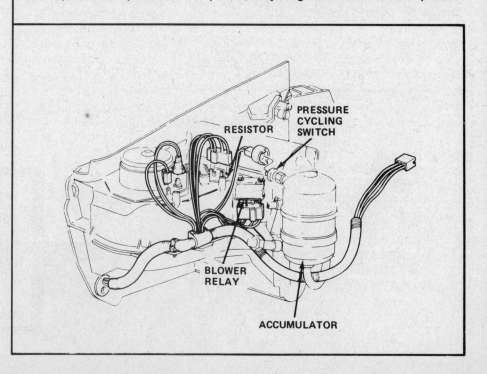

RESISTOR

PRESSURE CYCLING SWITCH

BLOWER RELAY

ACCUMULATOR

tion device in the system and it senses refrigerant pressure on the suction side. The switch also provides compressor cut-off during cold weather and low pressure conditions.

The switch is located on a fitting on the low-pressure side. On some models, the switch is screwed onto a Schrader valve fitting, which makes it possible to replace the switch without discharging the system. On models without this Schrader valve fitting, it's impossible to remove and replace the switch without first discharging the system. Always wear eye protection when replacing the switch.

Thermal limiter and superheat switch

The thermal limiter and superheat switch **(see illustration)** is a low refrigerant protection system used on General Motors systems with Valves in Receiver (VIR) or Evaporator Equalized Valves in Receiver (EEVIR). It stops compressor operation when the charge is too low.

Earlier superheat switches (manufactured prior to 1977), which are located in the rear compressor head, activate the system when they sense low pressure and/or temperature. The thermal limiter is a specially designed fuse that melts when it receives a signal from the superheat switch. This breaks the electrical connection to the compressor clutch, thus protecting the compressor from potential damage caused by lack of lubrication.

SERVICE TIP: *If you ever have to correct a low refrigerant charge condition that has blown the thermal limiter, don't replace the limiter until the system has been repaired and is functioning normally.*

Thermal limiters manufactured since 1975 have been designed to melt down at a higher temperature in order to prevent accidental blowing of the limiter when a momentary pressure fluctuation occurs. Such fluctuations, which sometimes occur during extreme operating conditions, are not system malfunctions.

In 1978, the superheat switch was redesigned so it could be activated only by pressure. Both types of switches are similar in appearance but they cannot be used interchangeably. The earlier unit is equipped with a sensing tube that is not used on later models.

The thermal limiter (top) is a specially designed fuse that melts down when it receives a signal from the superheat switch (bottom), interrupting power to the compressor clutch, protecting it from damage caused by a low lubricant level on General Motors VIR and EEVIR type systems with a low refrigerant charge

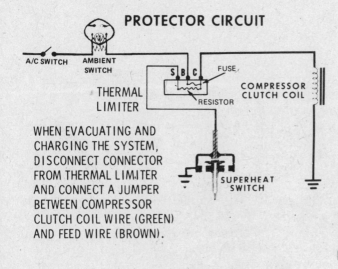

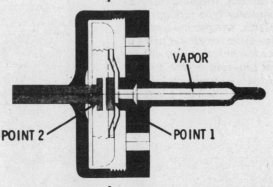

39

Heating and air conditioning

Condenser cooling system fan controls

Most vehicles now use electric cooling fan systems to ensure an adequate flow of air through the condenser and the radiator. Most fans are connected to the air conditioning system and operate when it's turned on. This helps to prevent excessive system pressure.

Although such fan systems do not have a direct effect on the operation of the air conditioner, keep them in mind when troubleshooting a system with an electric cooling fan. The three most important components of such a system are the cooling system fan temperature switch, the system high pressure fan switch and the A/C "on" switch.

Cooling fan temperature switch

Electric cooling fans are usually operated by an engine coolant switch. When coolant temperature exceeds a preset level, the fan is turned on.

SERVICE TIP: *Since most electric cooling fans will run even when the ignition is off, always be sure to unplug the fan wire harness connector before doing any service work near the fan on an engine that has just been turned off.*

System high pressure fan switch

Some imported vehicles are equipped with fan systems which are actuated by a high pressure switch. On these vehicles, the cooling fan is switched on shortly after the compressor starts to operate. When the air conditioning system is not in use, the high pressure switch relinquishes control of the fan to the coolant temperature switch.

A/C "on" fan switch

Many new vehicles are equipped with an A/C "on" fan switch that actuates the fan whenever the air conditioning system is on (ensuring that there is always adequate air flow through the condenser). The down side of this design is that the fan is turned on more than it would be in a vehicle without an A/C "on" switch. The switch is usually wired directly to the A/C control panel switch.

Evaporator controls

Sometimes, under certain operating conditions, the condensation that forms on the condenser may freeze. The evaporator coils become blocked with ice, preventing air flow through the evaporator core and diminishing system cooling ability. Evaporator controls help to prevent freeze-up and protect the evaporator.

Suction throttle valve (STV)

The suction throttle valve, or STV **(see illustration),** is a pressure sensing valve located on the low side of the system on the evaporator outlet pipe. It opens or closes in response to refrigerant pressure to control the flow of refrigerant leaving the evaporator.

The STV was first used on General Motors vehicles in 1962. This early design utilized a vacuum or cable-controlled assist which was attached directly to the A/C control panel levers. The position of the control levers regulated the operation of the valve.

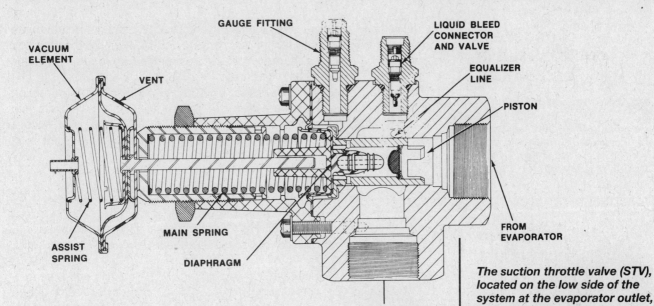

GAUGE FITTING

LIQUID BLEED CONNECTOR AND VALVE

VACUUM ELEMENT

VENT

EQUALIZER LINE

PISTON

MAIN SPRING

DIAPHRAGM

ASSIST SPRING

FROM EVAPORATOR

TO COMPRESSOR

The suction throttle valve (STV), located on the low side of the system at the evaporator outlet, opens or closes in response to refrigerant pressure to control the flow of refrigerant leaving the evaporator

The typical suction throttling valve is designed to keep the evaporator pressure in the 29 to 30 psi range. This maintains the evaporator temperature at a level which ensures proper operation of the air conditioning system without allowing the evaporator coils to freeze up.

In 1965, a newer type of suction throttling valve, the pilot operated absolute, or POA, suction throttling valve **(see illustrations on following pages)** was introduced. Used on some General Motors and Ford air conditioning systems, the POA STV performs the same task as the first generation STV: it senses and maintains evaporator pressure by opening and closing in response to pressure. But it does so without an adjustable element, fabric diaphragm or repairable components.

The POA valve can be identified by its flow-through design. It is really nothing more than a spring-loaded valve controlled by an evacuated bellows and needle valve assembly inside a housing. The valve operates independently of atmospheric pressure and is not affected by altitude changes.

By providing an opposing force to evaporator pressure, the POA valve can maintain evaporator pressure within a one psi range. The POA valve is equipped with a test port for the low side manifold gauge set to connect two fittings for the oil bleed line and external equalizer line.

As long as evaporator pressure is higher than approximately 28 to 29 psi, the POA valve remains open to allow free refrigerant flow out of the evaporator. When the pressure drops below this figure, the valve closes and refrigerant flow from the evaporator is restricted.

The pressure within the evaporator then increases, which raises the temperature and prevents possible freezing on the evaporator coils. The opening and closing cycle continues as long as the compressor is in operation.

The POA STV units pictured here are typical. POA STVs have various configurations, depending on the application, but they all share the same design elements as the models shown.

Pilot operated absolute (POA)

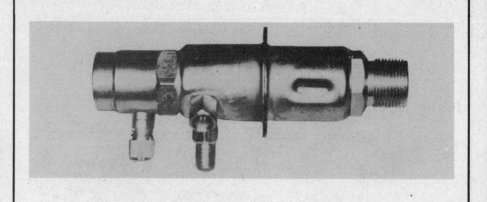

The pilot operated absolute suction throttling valve (POA STV) senses and maintains evaporator pressure by providing an opposing force to evaporator pressure

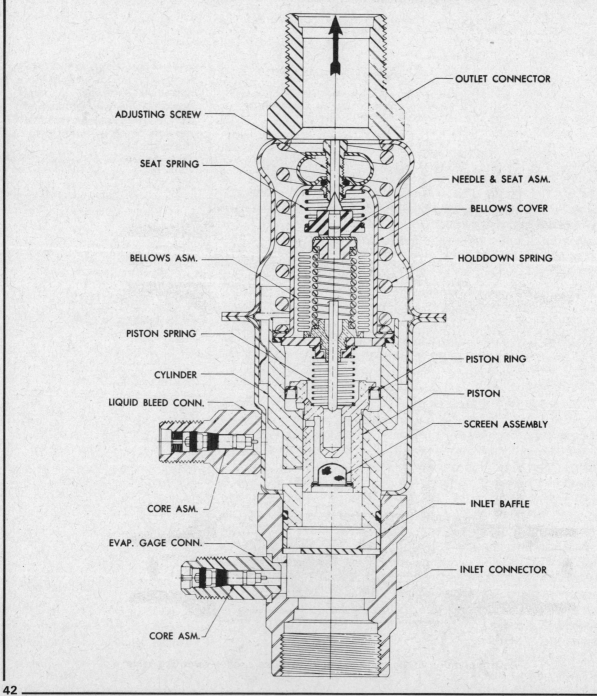

OUTLET CONNECTOR

ADJUSTING SCREW

SEAT SPRING

NEEDLE & SEAT ASM.

BELLOWS COVER

BELLOWS ASM.

HOLDDOWN SPRING

PISTON SPRING

PISTON RING

CYLINDER

PISTON

LIQUID BLEED CONN.

SCREEN ASSEMBLY

CORE ASM.

INLET BAFFLE

EVAP. GAGE CONN.

INLET CONNECTOR

CORE ASM.

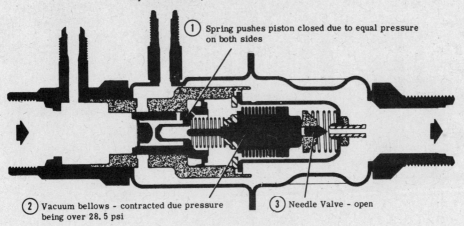

1ST STAGE EXISTING CONDITIONS

System is off, pressure equal on both inlet and outlet & pressure is approx. 70 psi (normal day of 70 - 80° F)

(1) Spring pushes piston closed due to equal pressure on both sides

(2) Vacuum bellows - contracted due pressure being over 28.5 psi

(3) Needle Valve - open

2ND STAGE EXISTING CONDITIONS
- PISTON OPENS -

System is on, compressor is pulling down pressure, therefore outlet side (compressor side) has lower pressure than inlet side.

(1) Vacuum Bellows is contracted because outlet pressure is still over 28.5 psi.

(2) Needle Valve - open allowing compressor to pull pressure down in area surrounding bellows.

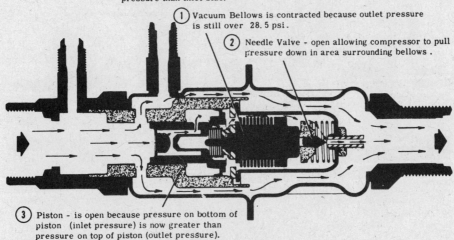

(3) Piston - is open because pressure on bottom of piston (inlet pressure) is now greater than pressure on top of piston (outlet pressure).

3RD STAGE EXISTING CONDITIONS
- BELLOWS CLOSES -

Compressor has pulled outlet pressure down to 28.5 PSI therefore:

(1) Vacuum Bellows - expands pushing needle valve closed, causing —

(2) Pressure on top of Piston to begin to increase over 28.5 psi.

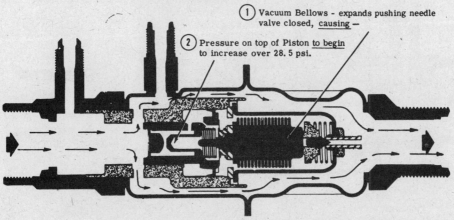

Basic operation of the pilot operated absolute suction throttling valve

4TH STAGE EXISTING CONDITIONS
- PISTON CLOSES -

The pressure surrounding bellows and on top of piston has now increased sufficiently over 28.5 psi to become nearly equal (within 1.3 psi) of inlet pressure.   Since —

① Pressures on both sides of piston nearly equal - spring takes over and pushes piston closed.

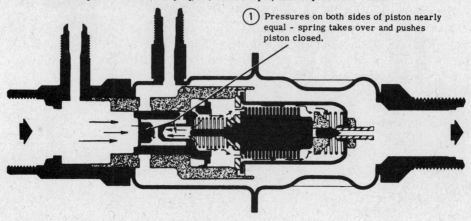

5TH STAGE EXISTING CONDITIONS
- BELLOWS OPENS -

The pressure surrounding bellows and on top of piston is now sufficiently over 28.5 psi -   The result is that —

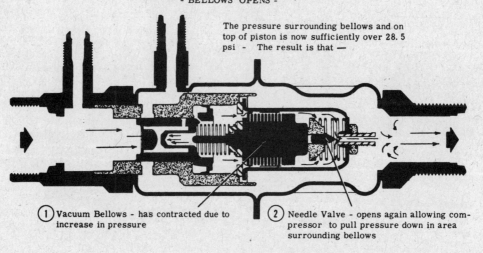

① Vacuum Bellows - has contracted due to increase in pressure

② Needle Valve - opens again allowing compressor to pull pressure down in area surrounding bellows

6TH STAGE EXISTING CONDITIONS
- PISTON OPENS -

An unequal pressure occurs because compressor is in the process of pulling outlet pressure down

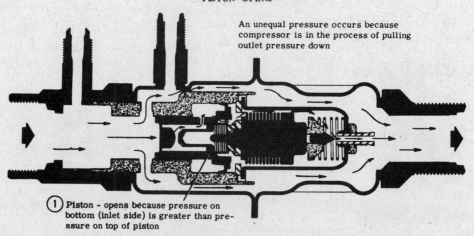

① Piston - opens because pressure on bottom (inlet side) is greater than pressure on top of piston

Basic operation of the pilot operated absolute suction throttling valve

Valves-in-receiver (VIR)

The valves-in-receiver (VIR) assembly **(see illustration)** is a combination of the thermostatic expansion valve, the Pilot Operated Absolute (POA) valve, the filter-drier and a sight glass in one integrated unit. It's usually mounted near the evaporator. The VIR design eliminates the need for an external equalizer line between the expansion valve and the POA valve. The equalizer function is accomplished instead by a hole drilled in the wall between the POA and the expansion valve housing.

The thermo-bulb and capillary line for the expansion valve are also eliminated because the diaphragm end of the expansion valve is now direct-

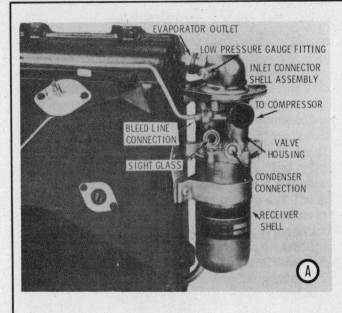

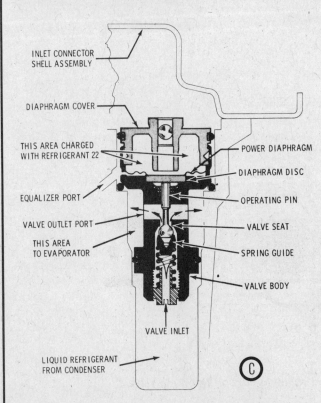

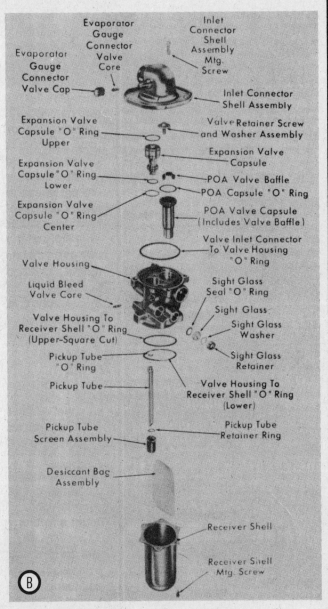

The valves-in-receiver (VIR) system:

A) *Typical VIR assembly*
B) *VIR exploded view*
C) *VIR expansion valve operation*

ly exposed to the refrigerant vapor entering the VIR assembly from the evaporator outlet. The sight glass is in the valve housing at the expansion valve inlet.

SERVICE TIP: *The filter-drier desiccant is replaceable. Simply remove the filter shell and replace the bag of desiccant. The expansion valve and POA valve capsules are also replaceable (remove the inlet connector shell assembly at the top of the valve housing).*

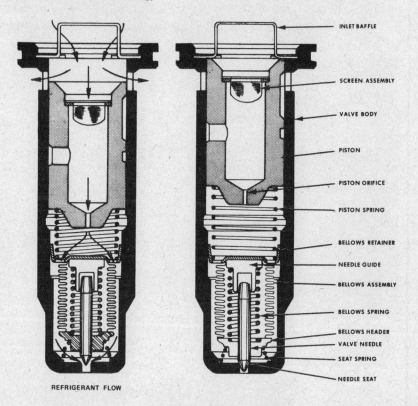

INLET BAFFLE
SCREEN ASSEMBLY
VALVE BODY
PISTON
PISTON ORIFICE
PISTON SPRING
BELLOWS RETAINER
NEEDLE GUIDE
BELLOWS ASSEMBLY
BELLOWS SPRING
BELLOWS HEADER
VALVE NEEDLE
SEAT SPRING
NEEDLE SEAT

REFRIGERANT FLOW

VIR POA valve operation

Evaporator equalized valve-in-receiver (EEVIR)

In 1975, certain General Motors air conditioning systems were equipped with a redesigned VIR assembly known as an evaporator equalized VIR, or EEVIR **(see illustration)**. This newer design helps to eliminate temperature fluctuations during some A/C modes. The result is smoother power usage and better fuel consumption during A/C operation.

The difference between the older VIR and the new EEVIR designs is centered in the expansion valve. The equalizer port, formerly between the wall of the POA and the expansion valve, was relocated to the expansion valve body. The top O-rings were removed and a new color code is used to identify the new valve. With the port on the expansion valve, evaporator outlet pressure can be directly sensed by the expansion valve and produce faster reactions to the pressure changes. The newer expansion valve is gold in color. A red label is affixed to the receiver shell to identify it as an EEVIR unit. An EEVIR expansion valve is not interchangeable with the older type.

The newer design also allows the expansion valve to remain slightly open instead of closing completely, permitting a constant partial flow of refrigerant into the evaporator. This feature has two benefits. First, the constant flow of refrigerant helps prevent freezing at the expansion valve (which clogs the system and stops operation). Second, the superheat

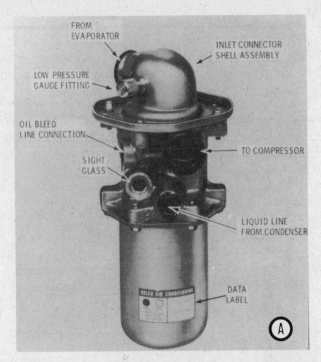

FROM EVAPORATOR

LOW PRESSURE GAUGE FITTING

OIL BLEED LINE CONNECTION

SIGHT GLASS

INLET CONNECTOR SHELL ASSEMBLY

TO COMPRESSOR

LIQUID LINE FROM CONDENSER

DATA LABEL

DELCO AIR CONDITIONING

Ⓐ

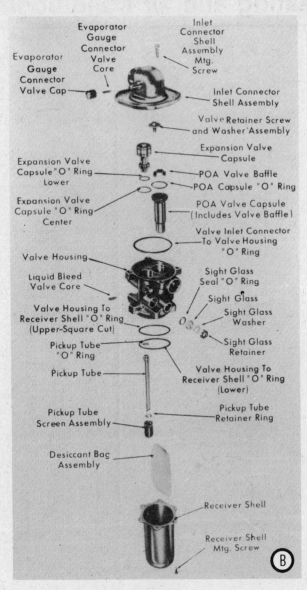

Evaporator Gauge Connector Valve Cap

Evaporator Gauge Connector Valve Core

Inlet Connector Shell Assembly Mtg. Screw

Inlet Connector Shell Assembly

Valve Retainer Screw and Washer Assembly

Expansion Valve Capsule

Expansion Valve Capsule "O" Ring Lower

POA Valve Baffle

POA Capsule "O" Ring

Expansion Valve Capsule "O" Ring Center

POA Valve Capsule (Includes Valve Baffle)

Valve Inlet Connector To Valve Housing "O" Ring

Valve Housing

Liquid Bleed Valve Core

Sight Glass Seal "O" Ring

Sight Glass

Valve Housing To Receiver Shell "O" Ring (Upper-Square Cut)

Sight Glass Washer

Sight Glass Retainer

Pickup Tube "O" Ring

Pickup Tube

Valve Housing To Receiver Shell "O" Ring (Lower)

Pickup Tube Screen Assembly

Pickup Tube Retainer Ring

Desiccant Bag Assembly

Receiver Shell

Receiver Shell Mtg. Screw

Ⓑ

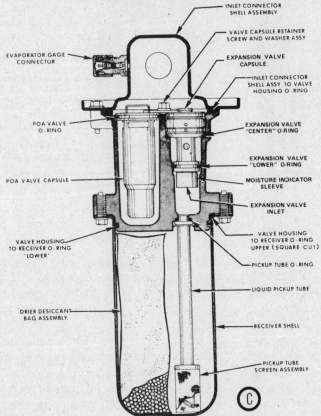

INLET CONNECTOR SHELL ASSEMBLY

VALVE CAPSULE RETAINER SCREW AND WASHER ASSY

EXPANSION VALVE CAPSULE

INLET CONNECTOR SHELL ASSY. TO VALVE HOUSING O-RING

EVAPORATOR GAGE CONNECTOR

EXPANSION VALVE "CENTER" O-RING

POA VALVE O-RING

EXPANSION VALVE "LOWER" O-RING

POA VALVE CAPSULE

MOISTURE INDICATOR SLEEVE

EXPANSION VALVE INLET

VALVE HOUSING TO RECEIVER O-RING "LOWER"

VALVE HOUSING TO RECEIVER O-RING UPPER (SQUARE CUT)

PICKUP TUBE O-RING

LIQUID PICKUP TUBE

DRIER DESICCANT BAG ASSEMBLY

RECEIVER SHELL

PICKUP TUBE SCREEN ASSEMBLY

Ⓒ

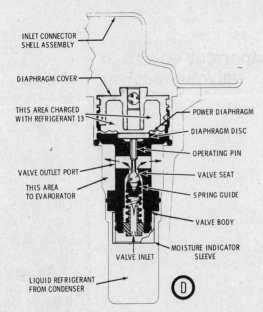

INLET CONNECTOR SHELL ASSEMBLY

DIAPHRAGM COVER

THIS AREA CHARGED WITH REFRIGERANT 13

POWER DIAPHRAGM

DIAPHRAGM DISC

OPERATING PIN

VALVE OUTLET PORT

VALVE SEAT

THIS AREA TO EVAPORATOR

SPRING GUIDE

VALVE BODY

VALVE INLET

MOISTURE INDICATOR SLEEVE

LIQUID REFRIGERANT FROM CONDENSER

Ⓓ

The evaporator equalized valves-in-receiver (EEVIR) system:

A) *Typical EEVIR assembly*
B) *EEVIR cross-sectional view*
C) *EEVIR exploded view*
D) *EEVIR expansion valve operation*

switch is not subject to a low drop in refrigerant pressure during expansion valve closed operation.

In 1976, some EEVIR expansion valves also featured a "moisture indicator sleeve," which was really nothing more than a piece of litmus paper visible through the sight glass. The moisture indicator is blue during normal system operation but turns pink if moisture is present in the system.

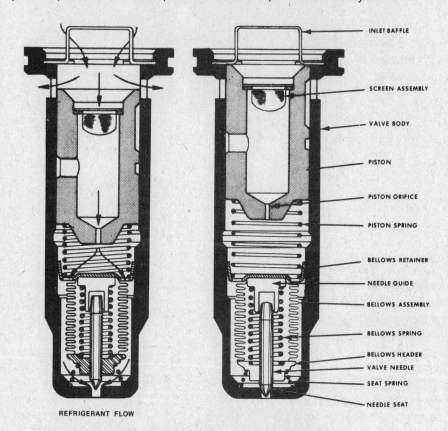

EEVIR POA valve operation

Evaporator pressure regulator (EPR) valve

The evaporator pressure regulator (EPR) valve, which is installed in the suction passage in the compressor, maintains correct evaporation outlet pressure — the EPR valve is similar in operation to the suction throttling valve

The evaporator pressure regulator, or EPR, valve **(see illustration)** is installed in the compressor suction passage. It's accessible once the suction line fitting is detached from the compressor. The EPR valve regulates evaporation outlet pressure to maintain operating pressure between 22 and 31 psi. Functionally, it is similar in operation to the suction throttling valve previously described. The operating pressure of the EPR valve is measured on the low side of the manifold gauge set connected to the suction fitting. Pressure downstream from the valve is measured with an auxiliary low side gauge hooked to the compressor head fitting. The valve is not adjustable and, if it malfunctions, must be replaced.

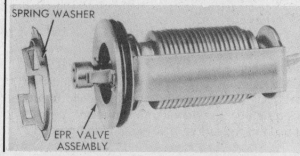

Chrysler Corporation has used three basic types of EPR valves over the years. They include the internal (bellows) type, the pilot-operated type and the evaporator temperature regulator (ETR) type.

Internal (bellows) EPR valve

The internal, or bellows, EPR valve was used on 1961 through 1969 Chrysler vehicles with manual air conditioning. The valve piston in this design is controlled by a gas-filled bellows. Incoming refrigerant pressure acts on the gas-filled bellows, causing it to expand or contract to control the flow of refrigerant into the compressor inlet.

Pilot-operated EPR valve

The pilot-operated EPR valve was used on some 1970 through 1972 models with manual air conditioning systems. It's easily identified by the protrusion on one end of the housing and the nut and stem on the other end.

The pilot-operated EPR valve has a built-in pilot device that "triggers" the main throttling valve portion, allowing it to open and close more precisely and quickly than the former type. A system using this valve is able to operate at lower pressures and temperatures without evaporator freeze-up.

Evaporator temperature regulator (ETR) valve

The evaporator temperature regulator, or ETR, valve was used on vehicles equipped with automatic air conditioning systems between 1967 and 1974. The ETR valve employs a solenoid that is normally open, but closes when actuated by the ETR switch, or control unit, mounted on the evaporator case. The switch senses changes in evaporator temperature and signals the ETR valve to increase or decrease refrigerant flow to the compressor accordingly. The ETR switch is not unlike the thermostatic switch used with some cycling clutch type systems.

EPR II valve

The EPR II valve was first used on some 1972 Chrysler vehicles. In 1974, the bullet-shaped EPR II valve replaced both EPR and ETR valves. In operation, it works exactly like early EPR valves, except it allows continuous compressor operation while the A/C selector is on. In 1978, the valve's appearance was changed slightly again, but it's still interchangeable with earlier types.

Driveability controls

Because of the trend over the last decade toward more fuel efficient vehicles, smaller engines have proliferated. Since a compressor siphons off a considerable amount of horsepower from an engine, the effect of compressor operation, in conjunction with other demands on the engine, can impose loads that detract significantly from vehicle performance.

Compressor controls relieve the load during situations when driveability might suffer. The controls do not usually affect the cooling performance of the air conditioning system but they may need to be checked if compressor problems are encountered.

Time delay relay

The time delay relay is used on some later General Motors vehicles with cycling clutch type systems and smaller engines. It prevents compressor engagement for a few seconds after engine start-up and selection of A/C operation. Upon air conditioning start-up on automatic transmission equipped vehicles, current is also supplied to the idle stop solenoid to increase idle speed.

The delay, which is normally 10 to 25 seconds, allows the engine sufficient time to purge the fuel evaporation canister. The delay also prevents compressor clutch chatter, which sometimes accompanies cold engine starts.

Wide open throttle (WOT) cut-out switch

The wide open throttle (WOT) cut-out switch is used on many smaller vehicles. The WOT switch is located on the accelerator pedal, the pedal linkage or the carburetor. When the throttle is wide open, the switch activates a relay which interrupts the compressor clutch circuit, reducing the engine load and improving acceleration.

On some vehicles, a pressure sensitive switch in the transmission overrides the cut-out switch if full throttle acceleration occurs while the transmission is in high gear.

Low vacuum switch

Low vacuum switches are used on certain vehicles to interrupt clutch operation when engine loads are heavy and vacuum is low. Several such devices are also available through the aftermarket. Because the switches halt compressor operation much more often than the OEM units, they can improve fuel economy. However, they also cycle the compressor clutch more often than stock units, reduce cooling effectiveness and are usually not recommended by the OEMs.

Power steering pressure switch

Some small engines are equipped with power steering systems. Under normal driving conditions, this makes little difference to a small powerplant. During parking maneuvers, however, a power steering system imposes its heaviest loads on the engine. Because engine speed and power output are low under these conditions, compressor operation is still another unwanted load on the engine. Some manufacturers, General Motors and Ford, for example, have equipped some of their smaller four-cylinder vehicles with a power steering pressure switch.

The switch prevents rough idling and stalling when the vehicle is being parked by disengaging the compressor whenever the power steering pressure exceeds a predetermined level.

GM uses a more sophisticated version of the device on some models. Instead of simply cutting off the compressor, it sends a signal to the electronic control module, which adjusts the engine control systems to compensate for the higher steering loads.

Power brake time relay

Some Ford Motor Company front wheel drive models with automatic transmissions and power brakes have a delay relay which interrupts compressor clutch operation for 3 to 5 seconds after the brakes are applied to prevent compressor drag from stalling the engine.

Engine coolant high temperature switch

The air conditioning system removes heat from the passenger compartment and transfers it to the air passing through the condenser. After it moves through the condenser, this heated air must also carry away the heat being transferred to the radiator by the engine's cooling system. When the outside air temperature is high, this already heated air is sometimes unable to carry away enough of the engine heat pouring off the cooling fins of the radiator. When the ambient temperature and cooling loads combine to exceed the engine's cooling capacity, overheating is the result. To reduce the likelihood of overheating and engine damage, some vehicles are equipped with a coolant temperature switch which disengages the compressor clutch when coolant temperature reaches an excessive level.

Electronic control module delay timer

Since 1981, all General Motors vehicles have been equipped with an electronic control module (ECM), or computer, which controls engine idle speed, fuel/air mixture and ignition timing. Since 1982, the computer has also controlled compressor clutch operation.

When the A/C switch is turned on, the computer delays clutch operation for several seconds while it increases idle speed slightly to compensate for the additional load. As soon as engine speed stabilizes, the compressor is engaged. This delay occurs only when engine speed is below 1400 rpm.

Anti-dieseling relay

Many new engines suffer from a tendency to "diesel" or "run on" after the ignition is turned off. General Motors vehicles employ the compressor to prevent dieseling. As soon as the ignition is turned off, the compressor clutch is engaged for 5 to 10 seconds. The additional load stalls the engine and prevents dieseling.

Constant run relay

Some General Motors vehicles are equipped with a "constant run" relay, which, under ECM control, maintains idle quality. The relay eliminates compressor cycling during periods of engine idle for a predetermined period of time after normal highway operation. If the idle period continues for an extended time, the air condtioning system returns to a conventional Cycling Clutch Orifice Tube (CCOT) mode for a short time to prevent system freeze-up.

R-134a system components

The compressor, condenser and evaporator on R-134a systems - though similar in appearance and function - are larger and more robust than their counterparts on R-12 systems. Otherwise, there's little physical difference between the components used on R-12 systems and those used on R-134a systems. However, components designed for use in one kind of system cannot be interchanged with those designed for another system. Mixing parts from two different systems could result in component failure and damage to the system.

3 Typical automotive air conditioning systems

Now that you're familiar with the basic components and controls of automotive air conditioning systems, let's look at how they work together in typical modern systems. We will also look at some older systems too. Though it's doubtful many of them are still in use nowadays, a brief description of their operation should provide you with a better perspective on the operation of contemporary systems.

A typical heating system:

1 Radiator
2 Cooling fan
3 Expansion tank with pressure cap
4 Thermostat
5 Engine coolant temperature switch
6 Water pump
7 Heater blower motor
8 Impeller (blower fan)
9 Heater core
10 Thermostat controlled valve
11 Thermostat switch (radiator fan)
12 Radiator drain
13 Engine drain
14 Bleeder valve (not used on all vehicles)
15 Air valve (cold air regulation — not used on all vehicles)

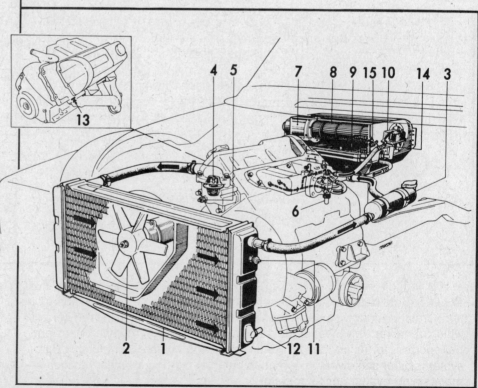

Typical air conditioning systems

Before we look at the individual components of an automotive air conditioning system, it's important to keep in mind that all air conditioning systems have a "high" and a "low" side **(see illustration)**. The dividing line for the two sides always occurs at the same point in the system.

The high side is the portion of the system in which high pressure, and high temperature, exists. The high side stretches from the outlet or discharge side of the compressor, through the condenser and, if equipped, the receiver-drier, to the expansion valve or orifice tube.

The compressor raises the pressure (and the temperature) so the refrigerant can condense and release heat as it moves through the condenser. A "pressure differential" is created at the expansion valve or orifice tube - the dividing point on the front side of the system. We will explain the expansion valve and orifice tube in detail later in this chapter.

The low side is the other half of the system. On this side, from the expansion valve, through the evaporator and accumulator (if equipped) to the inlet (suction) side of the compressor, the refrigerant is in a low pressure, low temperature state. This allows heat to be transferred from inside the vehicle to the "colder" refrigerant, which then carries it away.

Keeping these two concepts in mind, let's consider the hardware in a typical air conditioning system.

High and low sides of the air conditioning system

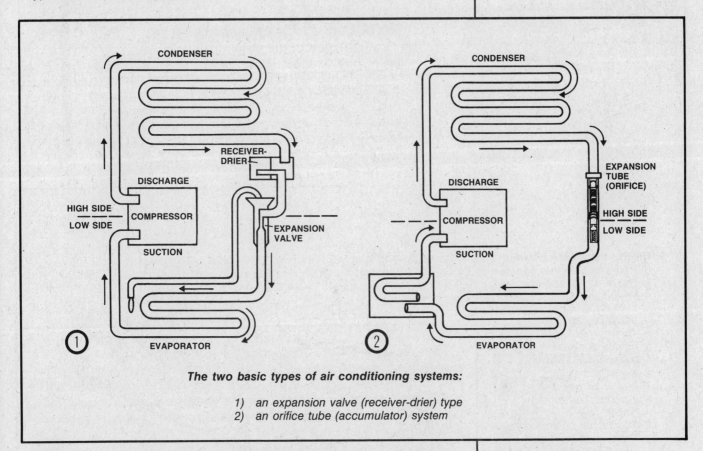

The two basic types of air conditioning systems:

1) an expansion valve (receiver-drier) type
2) an orifice tube (accumulator) system

Manually-controlled air conditioning systems

The various manually controlled systems in use today differ in detail, but all of them are designed to accomplish the same thing — control evaporator temperature. Air flowing over the evaporator gives up heat to the refrigerant, which removes this heat from the vehicle passenger compartment and transports it to the condenser. Evaporator and compressor clutch control systems differ somewhat in operation but they perform a similar function — maintaining evaporator temperature.

Heating and air conditioning

Thermostatic switch system

The thermostatic switch type of air conditioning system **(see illustration)** is the oldest design and most common cycling clutch type system. The compressor clutch is cycled on and off by the thermostatic switch. The thermostatic switch is located on or near the evaporator, where its sensing tube can 'feel' the temperature of the evaporator coils. The switch engages or disengages the compressor clutch to maintain the correct evaporator temperature. This process keeps the cooled air entering the vehicle at a constant temperature. This type of system was once typical of OEM air conditioning systems.

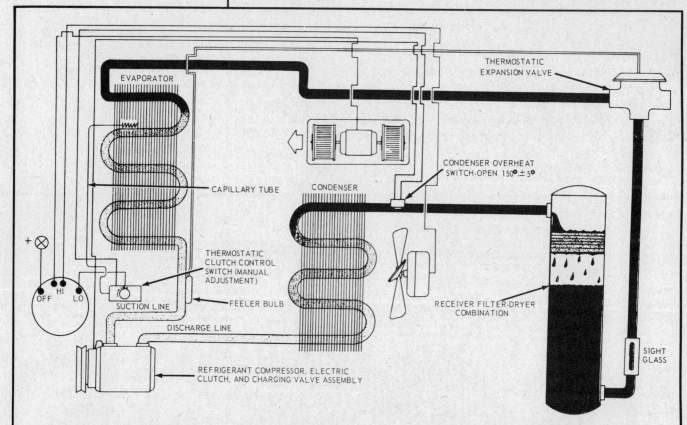

EVAPORATOR

THERMOSTATIC EXPANSION VALVE

CAPILLARY TUBE

CONDENSER

CONDENSER OVERHEAT SWITCH-OPEN 150°±5°

THERMOSTATIC CLUTCH CONTROL SWITCH (MANUAL ADJUSTMENT)

HI
OFF   LO

SUCTION LINE

FEELER BULB

RECEIVER FILTER-DRYER COMBINATION

DISCHARGE LINE

SIGHT GLASS

REFRIGERANT COMPRESSOR, ELECTRIC CLUTCH, AND CHARGING VALVE ASSEMBLY

On the thermostatic switch type air conditioning system, the compressor clutch is cycled on and off by a thermostatic switch (located on or near the evaporator) which has a sensing tube that can "feel" the temperature of the evaporator coils — the switch engages or disengages the compressor clutch to maintain the correct evaporator temperature

Accumulator system

There are three principal differences between an accumulator type system and the thermostatic type described above. First, the receiver-drier is replaced by an accumulator. Second, unlike the receiver-drier, which is located in the high side of the system at the condenser, the accumulator is located in the low side at the evaporator outlet. Third, a fixed orifice tube replaces the conventional expansion valve.

The accumulator system **(see illustrations)** is employed on all current General Motors and Ford vehicles. The GM system is known as a Cycling Clutch Orifice Tube (CCOT). Ford calls its system Ford Fixed Orifice Tube (FFOT).

Earlier accumulator systems used a standard thermostatic switch which turned the compressor off and on in accordance with evaporator temperature. Most newer systems have a pressure-sensing switch that controls compressor operation in accordance with system pressure. Measuring pressure is more

Typical air conditioning systems

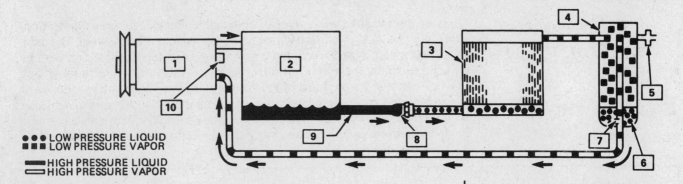

LOW PRESSURE LIQUID
LOW PRESSURE VAPOR
HIGH PRESSURE LIQUID
HIGH PRESSURE VAPOR

accurate and responsive than measuring temperature.

Small displacement engines have difficulty maintaining a stable idle when the compressor clutch is continually cycling on and off. In 1985, General Motors solved this problem with the introduction of the DA-V5 compressor, which does not cycle at all. Instead, it varies its output in accordance with system demand.

The accumulator, which serves as a reservoir for any liquid refrigerant flowing out of the evaporator, prevents liquid refrigerant from reaching the compressor. Like the receiver-drier, the accumulator stores excessive refrigerant. It also filters and removes moisture from the refrigerant.

The accompanying illustration shows the different locations of the thermo-

This schematic depicts the basic components of a typical accumulator system (General Motors shown):

1 Compressor
2 Condenser
3 Evaporator
4 Accumulator
5 Pressure cycling switch
6 Desiccant bag
7 Oil bleed hole
8 Expansion tube (orifice)
9 Liquid line
10 Pressure relief valve

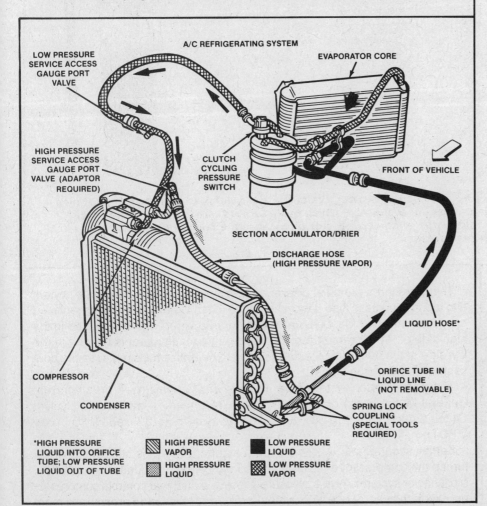

A/C REFRIGERATING SYSTEM

LOW PRESSURE SERVICE ACCESS GAUGE PORT VALVE

EVAPORATOR CORE

HIGH PRESSURE SERVICE ACCESS GAUGE PORT VALVE (ADAPTOR REQUIRED)

CLUTCH CYCLING PRESSURE SWITCH

FRONT OF VEHICLE

SECTION ACCUMULATOR/DRIER

DISCHARGE HOSE (HIGH PRESSURE VAPOR)

LIQUID HOSE*

COMPRESSOR

CONDENSER

ORIFICE TUBE IN LIQUID LINE (NOT REMOVABLE)

SPRING LOCK COUPLING (SPECIAL TOOLS REQUIRED)

*HIGH PRESSURE LIQUID INTO ORIFICE TUBE; LOW PRESSURE LIQUID OUT OF TUBE

HIGH PRESSURE VAPOR
HIGH PRESSURE LIQUID
LOW PRESSURE LIQUID
LOW PRESSURE VAPOR

Here's another look at a typical (Ford) accumulator system — note that 1) the accumulator is located in the low side of the system, at the evaporator outlet (unlike a receiver-drier, which is located in the high side of the system at the condenser) and 2) the expansion valve used on a receiver-drier type system is replaced by a fixed orifice tube

Heating and air conditioning

static switch and the pressure sensing switch. Keep in mind that they're both clutch cycling switches, but one measures temperature and the other measures pressure.

Suction throttling valve (STV) system

Some air conditioning systems use a suction throttling valve or STV **(see illustration)** as the main evaporator control. This type of system is common on older General Motors and Ford vehicles. The valves themselves differ in configuration but, functionally, they're all pretty similar. Basically, all of them maintain proper evaporator temperatures by modulating evaporator pressure. The compressor in an STV system runs continuously instead of being cycled on and off. This type of system is no longer in favor with the manufacturers because it requires too much energy (fuel) for operation.

The suction throttling valve, also known as a pilot operated absolute (POA) valve on some systems, is mounted on the outlet side of the evaporator. Because refrigerant flow from the evaporator is being regulated by the valve to maintain evaporator temperatures, this device allows the compressor to run all the time.

The POA valve also controls evaporator temperature by regulating the pressure. It does this by throttling or restricting the evaporator outlet so the pressure within the evaporator is maintained at a predetermined point. As its name implies, the POA valve contains a pilot valve. This valve has a bronze evacuated bellows. The POA is referenced to the nearly perfect vacuum in this bellows rather than to atmospheric pressure like earlier designs. The POA therefore requires no external altitude compensation device.

When the system is operating, evaporator pressure (A) **(see illustration)** is applied to the inlet fitting of the valve. This pressure passes through the piston screen and drilled holes in the piston to the area beneath the piston ring. As the evaporator pressure becomes higher, the force of the piston spring

On some systems (such as older General Motors and Ford vehicles) the main evaporator control device is the suction throttling valve (STV) — on an STV system, the suction throttling valve maintains proper evaporator temperatures by modulating evaporator pressure, so the compressor runs continuously instead of cycling on and off — unfortunately, this design results in decreased fuel efficiency so it's no longer used

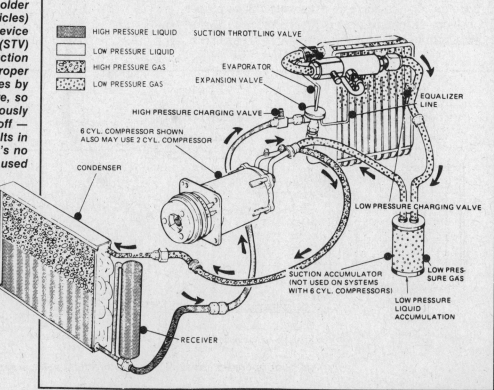

HIGH PRESSURE LIQUID
LOW PRESSURE LIQUID
HIGH PRESSURE GAS
LOW PRESSURE GAS

SUCTION THROTTLING VALVE
EVAPORATOR
EXPANSION VALVE
EQUALIZER LINE
HIGH PRESSURE CHARGING VALVE
6 CYL. COMPRESSOR SHOWN ALSO MAY USE 2 CYL. COMPRESSOR
CONDENSER
LOW PRESSURE CHARGING VALVE
SUCTION ACCUMULATOR (NOT USED ON SYSTEMS WITH 6 CYL. COMPRESSORS)
LOW PRESSURE GAS
LOW PRESSURE LIQUID ACCUMULATION
RECEIVER

will be overcome and the piston will begin to move, gradually opening the main port to refrigerant flow (B). This action is possible because the pressure in the area (C) above the piston is less than evaporator pressure.

However, as the valve is being forced open, evaporator pressure is slowly flowing through the piston bleed hole into the area (C) above the piston. As the pressure in area (C) approaches evaporator pressure (A), the spring will begin to force the piston toward the closed position. When the pressure is equal on both sides of the piston, the main port would normally be closed and the valve would be inoperative. Here is where the bellows and pilot valve come into the picture. The area (D) surrounding the bellows and needle valve is connected by a hole to the area (C) above the piston. Therefore, pressures in area (C) and area (D) will be equal. As pressure builds up in area (C), allowing the piston spring to move the piston toward its closed position, it also builds up in area (D) surrounding the evacuated bellows. The higher pressure will begin to collapse the bellows, pulling the pilot needle off the needle seat. The pressure in area (D) will be reduced through the resulting orifice to the point where the bellows will expand to close the pilot needle. When the pressure is reduced in area (D), it will also be reduced in area (C), allowing evaporator pressure to overcome the force of the piston spring and move the piston to open the main port.

Of course, in operation the various valve components balance out to hold the piston in the proper position to maintain the predetermined control pressure and the desired evaporator temperature.

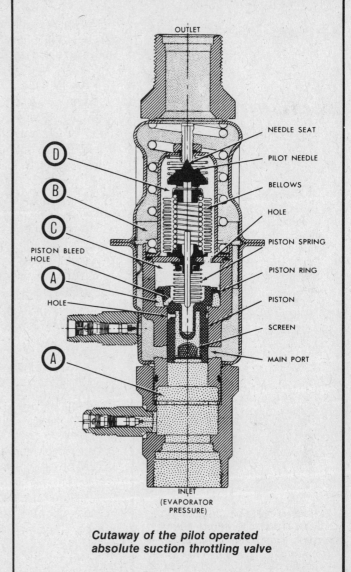

Cutaway of the pilot operated absolute suction throttling valve

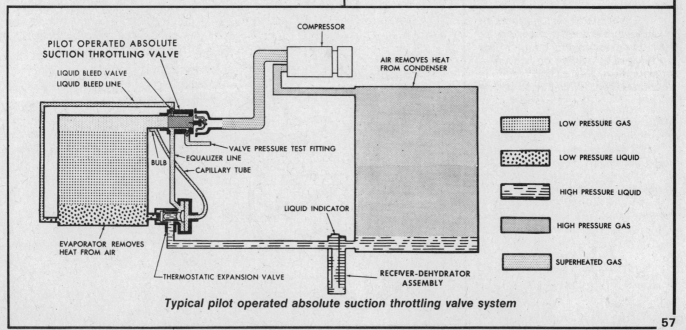

Typical pilot operated absolute suction throttling valve system

Heating and air conditioning

Valves-in-receiver system

Another variation of the STV system is GM's valves-in-receiver (VIR) system — like the STV system, the VIR system controls refrigerant flow to the evaporator and requires continuous compressor operation — but the controls — the expansion valve and pilot operated absolute suction throttling valve — are located inside the receiver

The valves-in-receiver type system (see illustration) is a General Motors design. The controls — expansion valve and pilot operated absolute suction throttling valve — are located in the same housing as the receiver-drier. This unit is mounted in the high pressure side between the condenser and the evaporator inlet.

Like the standard suction throttling valve type system, the valves-in-receiver (VIR) system requires continuous compressor operation whenever cooling is required. The VIR unit controls refrigerant flow to the evaporator and to the compressor.

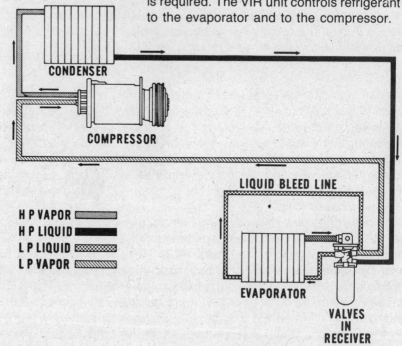

H P VAPOR
H P LIQUID
L P LIQUID
L P VAPOR

Evaporator pressure regulator (EPR) system

A third version of the STV system is Chrysler's evaporator pressure regulator (EPR) system, which is used only on Chrysler vehicles with a twin-cylinder compressor — the principal difference between an EPR system and an STV or VIR system is the location of the evaporator control device: an evaporator pressure regulator (EPR) or evaporator temperature regulator (ETR) is located inside the low pressure side of the compressor

The evaporator pressure regulator type system (see illustration) is used only on Chrysler Corporation vehicles with the twin-cylinder compressor. Unlike the suction throttling valve (STV) and valves-in-receiver (VIR) units, which are mounted in-line, but outside the compressor, the evaporator control valve is located within the low pressure side of the compressor. The EPR or evaporator temperature regulator (ETR) valve senses the pressure of the incoming refrigerant and opens or closes to regulate the flow of refrigerant through the compressor, thus controlling the evaporator temperature. This system also uses an expansion valve located at the inlet side of the evaporator (the configuration of this valve varies in newer applications). To clean or inspect the EPR valve, simply remove the inlet connection from the compressor.

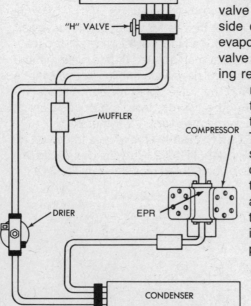

Typical air conditioning systems

Automatic air conditioning systems have the same components as manual systems, but they also have additional components which enable them to maintain a preset level of cooling, or heating, selected by the driver.

Vacuum or electronic control devices allow automatic systems to sense the in-vehicle air temperature. The system then adjusts the level of heating and/or cooling as necessary to maintain the vehicle temperature within the preset range.

Automatic systems achieve this equilibrium by opening and closing various doors within the system. When more heat is needed, the 'blend' door is opened to allow more heat to enter. If more cooling is required, the door moves to allow less warm air and more cool air to enter.

Systems using R-134a are similar in appearance and function to systems using R-12. Although they use physically larger, heavier-duty compressors, condensers and evaporators, the other components - accumulators, cycling clutch, orifice tubes, pressure switches, receiver-driers, etc. - are virtually identical to the parts used on R-12 systems. *But they're not interchangeable!* Installing a component designed for an R-12 system in a system built to use R-134a - or vise versa - may cause component failure and could damage the system.

If you're working on a l992 or newer vehicle, always determine whether it uses R-12 or R-134a before servicing or troubleshooting it. How do you know whether the system in your vehicle uses R-12 or R-134a? *Look for special identification decals or labels on the major components.* For instance, some 1992 and later Ford Taurus models with a 3.0L engine use an R-134a system. Ford distinguishes these models with a special yellow tag that says "R-134a NON-CFC" on it. These models also have a gold-colored compressor, and green-colored O-rings are used throughout the system. Other manufacturers use similar means of identifying R-134a systems.

What else should you look for? The high-side and low-side service fittings on an R-134a system are completely different from those used on an R-12 system. On an R-12 system, the high-side service fitting is a 3/8-inch 24 for screw-on couplers; the low-side fitting is a 7/16-inch 20 (also known as a 1/4-inch flare fitting). On an R-134a system, the high-side and low-side service fittings are special 1/2-inch Acme-type fittings with no external threads. They have internal threads, but they're for the specially-designed caps unique to R-134a fittings. The R-134a high-side service valve uses a special high-side service connector that's unique to R-134a systems; the low-side service valve uses a special quick-release service coupler that's also unique to R-134a systems. And the valve cores on both fittings are also unique to R-134a systems. In other words, there's no possibility of confusing these fittings with those used on earlier R-12 systems!

In 1991, Saab introduced a 1992 model as the first vehicle to use an air conditioning system designed for R-134a. In 1992, Chrysler, Ford, GM, Infiniti, Mercedes, Nissan, Saab and Volvo debuted models using R-134a.

Automatic systems

R-134a systems

4 Service and diagnostic tools

Manifold gauge set (test gauges)

The manifold gauge set **(see illustrations)** is unquestionably the most important tool used in air conditioning system servicing. Nearly all service work performed on automotive air conditioning systems requires the use of test gauges. Test gauges enable a technician to determine the system's high (head) pressure side and low (suction) side vacuum, determine the correct refrigerant charge, perform diagnosis procedures and help determine whether the system is operating efficiently.

Because pressures must be compared in order to determine how the system is operating, the gauge set is designed to allow both the high and low sides to be read at the same time. **Note:** *Some vehicles (older model Chryslers with EPR valves or Fords with POA valves, for instance) also require the use of a third (auxiliary) gauge (see below).*

The "low side" gauge

The low side gauge, which is most easily identified by the BLUE housing and hand valve, is used to measure the low side pressure at the service ports provided on the low side of the system by the manufacturer. The low side gauge pressure scale reads from 0 to between 130 and 150 pounds per square inch (psi) in a clockwise direction. The vacuum scale reads from 0 to 30 inches of mercury in a counterclockwise direction. The low side gauge is sometimes called a compound gauge because it has a dual purpose — to indicate either *pressure* or *vacuum*.

The "high side" gauge

The high side gauge, which usually has a RED housing and hand valve, is strictly a pressure gauge. It reads from 0 to 500 psi in a clockwise direction.

Auxiliary gauge

An auxiliary gauge may be required for testing older Chrysler vehicles with Evaporator Pressure Regulator (EPR) valves or Fords with Pilot Operated Absolute (POA) valves. It can be either a separate gauge used in conjunction with a two-gauge set or an integral gauge in a three-gauge set. The 0 to 150 psi reading provided by the gauge will be within the same range as shown on a low side gauge. Therefore, the auxiliary gauge should be the same type as used for low side testing. On older model Chryslers, the gauge is attached to the additional cylinder head inlet fitting on the compressor. On Fords, it's attached to the suction fitting.

Manifold hand valves

The purpose of the manifold is to control refrigerant flow. When the manifold gauges are attached to the system, pressure is indicated on both gauges at all times during normal conditions. During testing, both the low and high side hand valves are in the closed position (turned clockwise all the way until

A typical manifold gauge set has . . .

1. A hand valve for the low side of the system
2. A gauge for the low side of the system
3. A gauge for the high side of the system
4. A hand valve for the high side of the system
5. A valve for attaching the high side service hose
6. A service valve for attaching devices such as cans of refrigerant and vacuum pumps
7. A valve for attaching the low side service hose

Also note that the gauges on this unit are glycerine-filled to keep the needles steady, a nice feature to have for accurate work

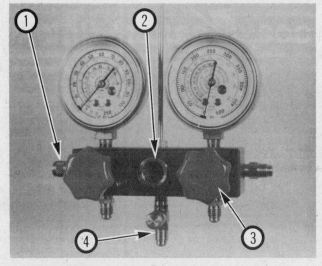

This gauge set has a few features the previous one didn't have

1. A Schrader valve allows you to purge the hoses or evacuate the system without interfering with the regular center service hose and also provides a place to hook up the low side hose — when it's not in use — to keep it clean (the valve on the other end protects the high side hose)
2. A "sight glass" in the front of the manifold allows you to visually monitor the condition of the refrigerant as it passes through the manifold (a nice feature, since a lot of newer systems don't have a sight glass anymore)
3. To reduce the likelihood of turning a valve the wrong way, the hand valves are mounted on the front of the manifold
4. A T-type center service valve allows you to access both vacuum and refrigerant at the same time

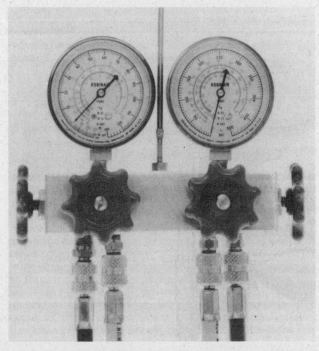

A top-of-the-line instrument like this can handle four hoses at one time, allowing you to evacuate or charge the system, or both, without unhooking the other hoses

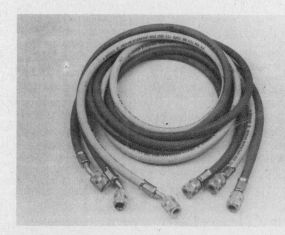

The hoses you select are just as important as the gauges you use them with - a cheaply constructed hose can burst, causing serious injury, so make sure you buy high quality hoses from a reputable manufacturer like Mac, Robinair or Snap-On (also, try to purchase hoses that are long enough and have the correct fittings for the system you intend to service). Hoses for R-134a systems have different, larger fittings, and a black stripe down each hose.

Heating and air conditioning

the valve is seated). You will note that even with the hand valves closed, the high and low side pressures are still indicated on the respective gauges. That's because the valve stems do not prevent refrigerant from reaching the gauges. They simply isolate the low and high sides from the central service hose port on the manifold.

When both hand valves are closed or when one or the other is open, the low and high side gauges will give good readings. However, when *both* valves are open, gauge readings are not accurate because high side pressure escapes into the low side of the manifold and influences the low side gauge reading.

Warning: *NEVER OPEN THE HIGH SIDE HAND VALVE WHILE THE AIR CONDITIONING SYSTEM IS IN OPERATION! High pressure refrigerant will force its way through the high side of the manifold test gauge and into the refrigerant can(s), if attached. The pressure can be high enough to rupture the can or even burst the fitting at the safety can valve, resulting in damage and physical injury.*

Manifold gauges for R-134a systems

Manifold gauges for R-134a systems work exactly the same way as R-12 gauges. But you can't use the same set of gauges for both systems. They use completely different couplers and hoses. The gauge face on manifold gauges for R-134a systems have an identification plate that says "for R-134a use only" or something similar. And that's exactly what it means! Do NOT try to use a set of R-134a gauges on an R-12 system. And don't try to use a set of R-12 gauges on an R-134a system, either. The fittings are totally different, so each type of gauge is totally incompatible with the fittings and hoses used on the other system.

Hoses

R-12 hoses are always solid blue (low-side), solid red (high-side) and solid yellow (utility hose); R-134a hoses are also blue, red and yellow but have a black stripe running the length of each hose. R-134a hoses also have different, larger service fittings than those on R-12 hoses. Don't try to adapt old R-12 hoses by installing the newer R-134a fittings - R-134a hoses look the same as the reinforced rubber or thermoplastic R-12 hoses, but they're lined with a special nylon barrier that prevents the newer refrigerant from leaking through the walls of the hose.

Measuring pressure

Pressure, which is measured when checking and diagnosing the air conditioning system, is usually expressed in pounds per square inch (psi). The reading on the manifold gauges is known as "pounds per square inch gauge," or simply "psig," because it's affected by atmospheric pressure changes, such as changes in altitude. A pressure reading which is not affected by atmospheric pressure is known as "pounds per square inch absolute," or "psia."

Atmospheric pressure

Atmospheric pressure, which is expressed and measured in pounds per square inch, is the pressure exerted on the earth's surface at any given point. Atmospheric pressure is 14.7 psia at sea level, but this figure varies with altitude. It's approximately 1/2-pound less for each 1000 feet of elevation. Pressure, and gauge readings, also vary slightly due to the weather, because changes in the weather mean changes in the barometric (atmospheric) pressure.

Pounds per square inch absolute (psia)

Pounds per square inch absolute, or psia, is sort of an "ideal" measure of pressure which is unaffected by barometric (atmospheric) conditions or by altitude. It begins with a zero psi reading in a perfect vacuum. Aside from

62

providing a handy reference point when referring to changes in atmospheric pressures at various altitudes, absolute pressures are seldom used in air conditioning work.

Pounds per square inch gauge (psig)

Pounds per square inch gauge, or psig, are the units of measurement displayed on a typical manifold gauge set. This type of gauge is referred to as a "Bourdon-tube" gauge. A Bourdon-tube gauge consists of a semicircular, or coiled, flexible metal tube attached to a gauge that records the degree to which the tube is straightened by the pressure of the gas or liquid inside.

A Bourdon-tube gauge is calibrated to read zero at sea level on a "typical" day (with atmospheric pressure at 14.7 psi). At higher elevations, of course, where the atmospheric pressure is lower, the gauge reading will be lower.

Correcting the gauge pressure reading for altitude

Atmospheric pressure is lower at high elevations. The corrected gauge pressure within a closed system can be computed by adding the gauge altitude correction factor to the reading. Don't forget to do this when checking the system's low side pressures.

Altitude pressure variations

Altitude (feet above sea level)	Absolute pressure of atmosphere (psi)	Gauge altitude correction (psi)*
0	14.7	0
1000	14.2	0.5
2000	13.7	1.0
3000	13.2	1.5
4000	12.7	2.0
5000	12.2	2.5
6000	11.7	3.0
7000	11.3	3.4
8000	10.9	3.8
9000	10.5	4.2
10000	10.1	4.6

Etc.

* Add the indicated correction to the gauge readings

The higher the elevation, the lower the atmospheric pressure (and the greater the necessary gauge correction)

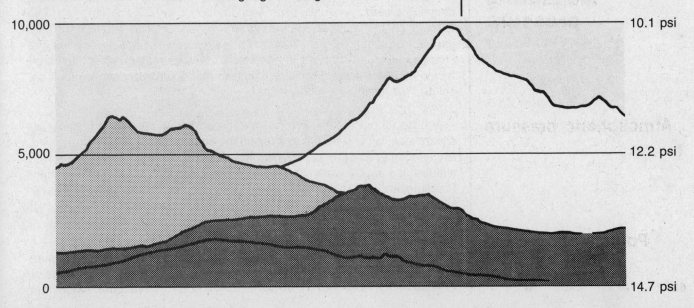

Measuring vacuum

When checking and diagnosing air conditioning systems, vacuum is customarily measured in inches of mercury, or "in-Hg." "Perfect" vacuum is defined as 29.92 in-Hg at sea level with the atmospheric pressure at 14.7 psia.

Besides its pressure readings, the compound (low pressure) gauge on the manifold set also has a vacuum section which reads in inches of mercury. The compound gauge measures vacuum accurately only at the elevation for which it is calibrated. At high altitudes, the gauge reads low. Air conditioning specifications are normally expressed in sea level terms, so at higher altitudes the gauge reading should be corrected to sea level.

Altitude vacuum variations

Altitude (feet above sea level)	Complete vacuum (in-Hg)	Gauge altitude correction (in-Hg)*
0	29.92	0
1000	28.92	+1.0
2000	27.82	+2.1
3000	26.82	+3.1
4000	25.82	+4.1
5000	24.92	+5.0
6000	23.92	+6.0
7000	23.02	+6.9
8000	22.22	+7.7
9000	21.32	+8.6
10000	20.52	+9.4
Etc.		

Add the indicated correction to the gauge reading

Attaching the manifold gauge set

Now that you know how to read the gauges and how to correct for variations in vacuum and pressure caused by different altitudes, you're ready to hook them up. Pay close attention and you'll learn how to do it right. Every time you need to diagnose a problem in the air conditioning system, you are going to have to examine the system's overall performance, particularly system pressures and refrigerant flow. These performance parameters can only be checked with the manifold gauge set.

In theory, hooking up a set of gauges, especially on R-134a systems, is simplicity itself:

1 The low side hose (usually blue on R-12 systems, blue with a black stripe on R-134a systems) is attached between the low side gauge and the low side of the system.

2 The high side hose (usually red on R-12 systems, red with a black stripe on R-134a systems) is attached between the high side gauge and the high side of the system.

3 The service hose (usually yellow, sometimes white on R-12 systems, yellow with a black stripe on R-134a systems) is attached between the service (center) fitting on the manifold and either a vacuum device or refrigerant supply, depending on what you intend to do to the system.

In reality, hooking up the test gauges on R-12 systems isn't always this simple, because the high and low side service valves differ somewhat - in size, configuration and ease of access - from system to system. So don't be surprised if you buy or borrow a gauge set only to find that it doesn't hook up as easily as you had hoped. Fortunately, there are service adapter fittings available for every conceivable purpose. Let's look at the common ones.

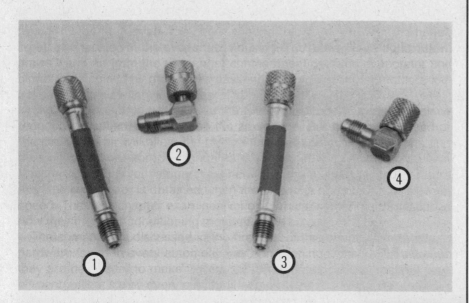

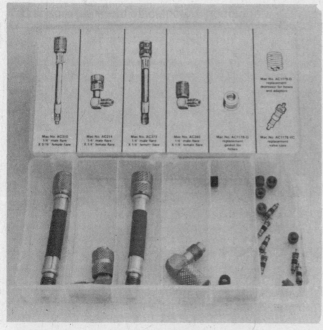

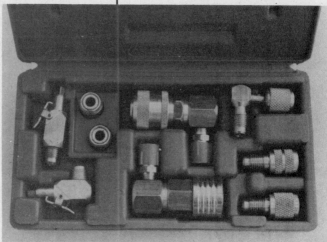

Adapter kits such as the two shown here usually include all the individual adapters shown in the previous illustration and, sometimes, lots more — but you'll pay for adapters you may not need

Like screwdrivers or wrenches or other common tools, service adapter fittings are available individually, or in sets **(see illustrations)**. Unless you know that you will be servicing all types of systems, adapter fitting sets are not the way to go. Buy adapters individually as the need arises. That way you won't end up with a bunch of useless fittings.

There are so many clever adapters that space doesn't permit an exhaustive compilation in this book. However, there are several that no mechanic should be without when servicing an air conditioning system.

First, you will probably need a high side fitting adapter, either because the service valve on the system is inaccessible, or because its outside diameter (OD) and/or thread pitch doesn't match the OD and/or thread pitch of the high side hose fitting, or because the service valve is pointing in a direction that makes a convenient hook-up difficult. While any one of these problems might seem intimidating enough in itself, you may even be looking at a combination of two or even all three of the above. Amazingly, there is a solution for every one of them!

Service adapter fittings for R-12 systems

Heating and air conditioning

For instance, there are high side adapter fittings available in straight and 90° configurations, as short flexible hose models and even as quick disconnect couplers. There are even anti blow-back refrigerant check valves which prevent refrigerant discharge when disconnecting high side service hoses.

Companies such as Mac Tools, Inc. and Snap-On Tools Corporation offer a variety of adapters in various configurations. The first step, obviously, is to obtain a Mac or Snap-On catalog, or both of them, and start studying the fittings. If you're a professional mechanic, you probably see a Mac or Snap-On dealer once a week when he stops by your shop. If you're a home mechanic, call the local dealer and ask him when he will be stopping by a shop in your neighborhood. Take the vehicle you will be servicing to make sure the fitting adapters mate properly with the service valves on the system and with the service hoses on the manifold gauges.

Service fittings for R-134a systems

The service fittings for R-134a systems are completely different in design, size and appearance from those used on R-12 systems. Instead of a 1/4-inch flare (or 7/16-inch 20) fitting, they use a 1/2-inch Acme fitting. So the threaded fittings on R-134a manifold gauges, bulk refrigerant drums, hoses, etc. look completely different from the fittings on their counterparts intended for use with R-12 systems. Practically speaking, this means that if you wish to service an R-134a system, you'll have to obtain new everything - gauges, hoses, refrigerant drum, etc.

Thermometers

Thermometers **(see illustration)** are essential for air conditioning and heating system diagnosis. Get a thermometer that reads between 25° and 125°F (a 0° to 220°F range is even better). Conventional thermometers are available in standard and dial configurations. Dial types are easier to read, tougher and more versatile than standard types.

The digital thermometer is also becoming popular, despite its high cost, because it's faster, more accurate and easier to read. Because some digital thermometers can be equipped with air, surface or immersion probes, they are much more versatile than conventional thermometers.

A variety of thermometers are currently available . . .

1 *A conventional mercury column thermometer — delicate, hard-to-read and expensive*
2 *A dial type thermometer — rugged, easy-to-read and cheap*
3 *A digital thermometer — acceptably rugged, easy-to-read, expensive, but quick responding and most accurate*

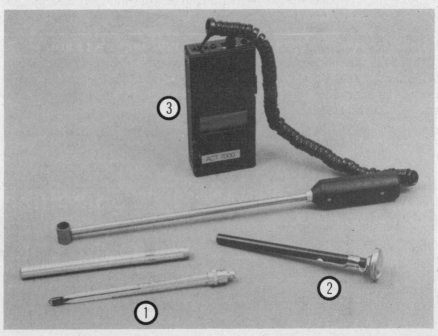

System evacuation tools

If an air conditioning system has had 1) refrigerant removed to service or repair the system, 2) refrigerant loss caused by component failure, 3) shows evidence of refrigerant contamination, or 4) is being retrofitted to operate with R-134a (see Chapter 5), it must be evacuated to get rid of all moisture and air before it can be recharged with refrigerant.

Air and moisture are extracted from the system with a vacuum pump. Pumping draws air from within the closed system to create negative pressure, or vacuum. By lowering the pressure inside the system into a vacuum condition, the boiling point of water, or moisture, is also lowered to a point at which evaporation easily occurs. This vaporized moisture is then easily drawn out by the vacuum pump.

The vacuum necessary to vaporize moisture in the system for evacuation varies with the altitude. At sea level, where the air pressure is 14.7 psi, water boils at 212°F. To evacuate a system, it is necessary to lower the boiling point of water in the system to a point that is lower than the "ambient" air temperature (the temperature of the air surrounding the vehicle). At an ambient temperature of, say, 75°F, you must draw at least 29.5 inches of vacuum (in-Hg) to bring the boiling point of water down to 72°F.

As altitude increases, the vacuum gauge reading is affected significantly. For instance, it isn't possible to obtain a vacuum reading of 29.5 inches once you're above sea level. That's because for each 1000 feet of altitude, the vacuum requirement decreases by 1 in-Hg. So the vacuum gauge must be corrected by 1 in-Hg for every 1000 feet of altitude to compensate for the change in atmospheric pressure. Thus, at 1000 feet, a gauge reading of 28.5 in-Hg will be the same as 29.5 in-Hg at sea level. The good news is that this will still accomplish the same job of lowering the boiling point enough to evacuate the moisture from the system. **Note:** *For other vacuum corrections, refer to the altitude vacuum variation chart in the manifold test gauge section of this chapter.*

Once the desired vacuum reading is obtained, regardless of the altitude, continue pumping for about 30 minutes to completely rid the system of moisture. **Note:** *A completely saturated system may require many hours of pumping to remove all the moisture, as the process of vaporizing the moisture and moving the vapor out of the coils and hoses is much slower than simply removing air alone.*

There are two kinds of vacuum pumps generally available. The cheaper of the two is the air power, or venturi type, pump **(see illustration)**. The venturi type pump is easy to use and maintenance free. It has no moving parts and requires no lubricating oil. What's the catch? Well, it requires a compressor that can

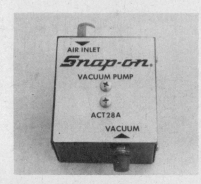

Vacuum pumps

Air power (venturi type) vacuum pumps

Venturi type vacuum pumps operate on compressed air (about 80 to 90 psi air power from a compressor) to pull down a vacuum in the system in about 1/2-hour — this type of pump is inexpensive to buy, but uses a lot of electricity (to run the compressor for 1/2-hour)

Heating and air conditioning

pump at least 80 or 90 psi. And a compressor that pumps 80 to 90 psi for half an hour is using a lot of electricity. How do you use this type of vacuum pump? Follow these steps:

1 Before using a venturi type pump, always have the system properly discharged by a dealer service department or an automotive air conditioning shop with EPA-certified recovery/recycling equipment.

2 Connect the manifold gauge set center service hose to the vacuum pump inlet labelled VACUUM.

3 Open the high and low side manifold gauge hand valves as far as possible.

4 Connect an air hose to the vacuum pump inlet labelled AIR INPUT or AIR INLET.

5 Note the reading indicated by the low side gauge and begin timing the evacuation when the gauge indicates a vacuum reading. **Note:** *If, after a couple of minutes, no vacuum is indicated on the low side gauge, inspect the system for leaks and repair it before proceeding. Check the gauge set hose connections first.*

6 After about five minutes of pumping, the required vacuum reading (which, remember, varies with altitude) should be indicated on the low side gauge. When this reading is obtained, close both the gauge valves and then disconnect the air hose. **Note:** *If the required vacuum reading is not obtained within 10 minutes, inspect the gauge set hose connections, the hand valves and the system fittings for leaks. After correcting the problem, repeat Steps 1 through 5 and continue the evacuation process.*

7 Allow several minutes for the system to stabilize and check the low side gauge to determine whether the system is maintaining vacuum.
a) If the system is holding vacuum, reconnect the air hose, open both hand valves and *continue pumping for at least 30 minutes* to complete the evacuation process.
b) If the system is losing vacuum, check to make sure the leak is not at the gauge set connections. If the leak is not at the connections, charge the system, use a leak detector to locate the source of the leak, discharge the system, repair the leak and repeat the evacuation process.

8 When the evacuation process is complete, close the gauge valves and disconnect the air hose.

9 Check the low side gauge to make sure the system maintains vacuum.

10 Disconnect the air pump at the center hose.

11 Recharge the system.

Rotary vane type vacuum pumps

The rotary vane type pump **(see illustration)**, which has a small electric motor driving the pump, is considerably more expensive than a venturi type pump. It also requires some maintenance - the pump must be routinely lubricated. But it doesn't require the use of a compressor to evacuate the system, so it uses a lot less electricity than a venturi type.

Before hooking up the pump, have the system properly discharged by a dealer service department or an automotive air conditioning shop with EPA-certified recovery/recycling equipment.

To operate a rotary vane type pump:

1 Make sure the pump is free by rotating the shaft.

2 Remove the exhaust dome and fill the pump with oil to at least the mid-point of the oil level sight glass.

3 Make sure that the vacuum breaker O-ring valve is closed tight.

4 Make sure that the electrical power matches the motor wiring (normally 115 volts, but some pumps are 220 volt models).

5 Check all hoses and connectors for leaks. Use the shortest plumbing that will work.

6 Install a shut-off valve on the end of the service hose that will connect the pump to the test gauge manifold.

7 Connect the shut-off valve to the center service port of the manifold.

8 Start the pump. You may note a gurgling sound as the residual refrigerant passes through the pump. This should be followed by a short period of almost no sound coming from within the pump. The pump will then develop a rapping sound which only occurs when it's under a deep vacuum (normally 250 microns or less).

9 After the system is pumped down to the desired vacuum level, close the shut-off valve and open the vacuum breaker valve until the pump makes a gurgling sound. Failure to break the vacuum within the pump at this time can result in damage to the pump when it restarts.

10 Turn off the motor.

The rotary vane type pump is powered by an electric motor, is much more expensive to buy than venturi type pumps but is much more economical to operate

Servicing a rotary vane type vacuum pump

1 Change the oil whenever there is a change in the performance of the pump. The oil should always be changed after pumping down a very dirty or burned out system. Always drain the pump while it's still warm. Recharge the pump with the oil specified by the manufacturer.

2 Purging the pump periodically is helpful because it often cures many ills that develop as a result of poor maintenance:

a) Rotate the pump shaft by hand to make sure it's free so the motor can operate the unit.

b) Run the pump with the intake closed until the pump is warm.

c) Shut it off, open the intake and drain the pump oil. With the drain open, the exhaust dome removed and the pump operating, slowly pour 2 ounces of the specified oil into the open intake fitting. As you hear the oil pass through the pump, cover the exhaust opening. This will cause the purging oil and any residual oil and sludge to flow rapidly out of the drain fitting. Repeat this step until all signs of contamination disappear.

Heating and air conditioning

d) When the purging is completed, close the drain fitting and, pouring through the exhaust dome hole, fill the pump with new, clean vacuum oil to the mid-point of the oil level gauge. **Note:** *It's normal for the oil level to rise somewhat as the pump warms up, but if the rise is excessive, the oil is contaminated.*

e) If the pump is going to be out of service for some time after shutdown, drain the oil, purge the pump and fill it with new, clean oil. This will prevent corrosion by any contaminants that may be present in the old pump oil. Cover the intake and exhaust openings.

R-12 system charging tools and equipment

Until recently, a do-it-yourselfer could save a bundle by charging his or her air conditioning system at home with small, inexpensive 14-ounce cans, which were available at any auto parts store. Two or three cans usually did the job.

But times change. As a result of recent Federal legislation designed to protect stratospheric ozone from further depletion, 14-ounce cans of R-12 are no longer sold to do-it-yourselfers; they're now available only to EPA-certified professional automotive air conditioning technicians. The thinking behind this decision is that do-it-yourselfers without the proper tools and

Bulk refrigerant drums

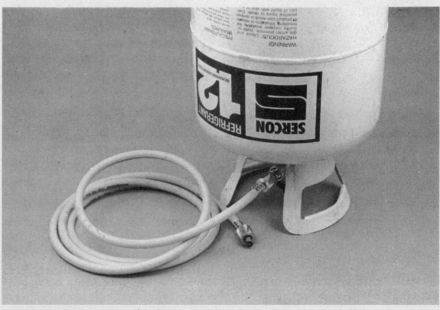

When adding refrigerant to the system from a bulk drum, invert the drum to ensure that liquid, rather than vapor, is released from the container when the valve is open

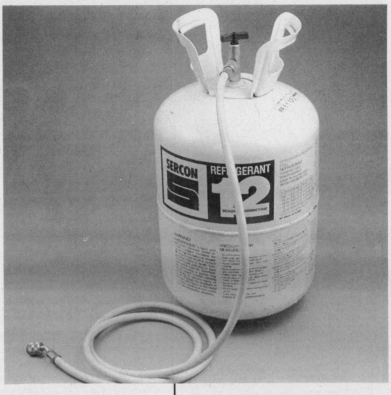

To use a bulk refrigerant drum, simply attach a service hose between the bulk can valve and the service valve on the manifold gauge set

training will simply keep adding small cans of refrigerant to a leaking system instead of first fixing the leak. As of January 1, 1993, all professional shops are required to recover and recycle all refrigerant discharged from automotive air conditioning systems. It's highly unlikely that any home mechanic will ever purchase refrigerant recovery/recycling equipment. So the government feels that the best way to discourage do-it-yourselfers from discharging their systems into the atmosphere is to make it difficult for them to obtain small cans to recharge the system.

There may be a way around this dilemma in your area, but it isn't cheap: Uncertified do-it-yourselfers can still (when this was written) legally purchase 20-pound or larger bulk refrigerant drums. However, most automotive parts stores carry only two sizes: Either the small cans (for professionals only), or 30-pound drums, which are very expensive. Basically, recharging with a 30-pound drum means you'd have to buy 10 times as much refrigerant as you'd need to charge a typical system at home. Obviously, it doesn't make much economic sense to take this route unless you own a lot of vehicles requiring air conditioning service. However, if you choose to do this, refer to the recharging information in Chapter 5 and any charging information the refrigerant manufacturer provides.

What about R-134a systems?

Finally, what about new systems using R-134a? After all, R-134a is 95 percent less destructive to the ozone layer than R-12. Can you charge an R-134a system at home? Yes, you can. At least for now. But first you'll have to invest in some new tools. Besides the R-134a itself, you will have to purchase a new service adapter hose with the new R-134a fittings. Your old can tappers, four-way dispensing valves, service hoses, etc. cannot be attached to a can of R-134a, nor can they be connected to the service valve on the low side of an R-134a system. And, to add R-134a with a set of manifold gauges, you'll have to purchase a new set of gauges and hoses designed to fit the unique service fittings on an R-134a system.

Heating and air conditioning

Don't even think about using your old R-12 charging tools on an R-134a system! Or vise versa! No adapters allowing you to use the same tools with both R-12 and R-134a systems will ever be available because mixing these two refrigerants is a recipe for disaster. They're absolutely incompatible!

There is one other obstacle you'll likely be facing in the mid 1990's. Under Federal law, R-134a must soon be captured, recycled and reused, just like R-12. The Federal government has decided to control R-134a in a manner similar to R-12 because, even though it's relatively benign with respect to ozone destruction, it's considered a "greenhouse gas," i.e., its release into the atmosphere may contribute to raising global mean temperatures.

Don't mix refrigerants!

As mentioned earlier, R-12 and R-134a are completely incompatible. DO NOT, under any circumstances, ever mix them together in one system. Do not put even the smallest amount of R-12 in an R-134a system and do not put even the smallest amount of R-134a in an R-12 system. If you do, you will damage components and maybe the whole system. Ditto for their respective lubricants: R-134a systems use a special polyalkylene glycol (PAG)-based lubricant which is incompatible with the lubricants used in R-12 systems. Nor can R-12 lubricants be used in R-134a systems. Lubricant cross-contamination can result in damage to seals and bearings in the compressor.

Leak testers

Any time more than 1/2 pound of refrigerant is required to charge the system over a period of one year, a leak is indicated. Leakage - either through loose fittings, deteriorated hoses or seals or damaged metal lines - is the usual cause for low refrigerant charge. Most leaks are caused by normal engine vibration, which loosens threaded fittings and even causes metal lines to fatigue and crack over a period of time. Snugging the fittings will usually eliminate the former; repair or replacement is necessary for the latter. But checking for, locating and repairing more subtle leaks can be time consuming.

When refrigerant was a dollar a can and plentiful and R-12 was considered a harmless substance, finding a leak was more of an annoyance than anything. Now, of course, with the discovery of the holes in the ozone layer over the Arctic and Antarctic - and the fears of scientists that we may be putting ourselves at greater risk of getting skin cancer as a result of ozone depletion - fixing leaks has become much more than an annoyance. Not only is it environmentally responsible to be sure your air conditioning system doesn't leak - it's also a good idea from a dollars-and-cents point of view. With R-12 and R-134a very expensive, you can't AFFORD leaks in your air conditioning system.

Until recently, dye-charged refrigerant cans were commercially available. These 14-ounce cans of refrigerant contained a red or fluorescent dye that made it easy to detect leaks in the system. However, dye-charged refrigerants are no longer available.

Service and diagnostic tools

This is an inexpensive way to find a leak, and a good one, especially if you've been unable to pinpoint the location of the leak using other methods. Simply apply a commercial bubble detector solution, or even a soap and water solution, to the suspected leak with a small brush. Apply the solution to all fittings and connections where leaks could occur. The leaking refrigerant will cause the detector or soapy solution to form bubbles. Tighten or repair the fittings as needed.

Bubble detector

Once a common tool in professional shops, the halide leak detector is seldom used any more, not because it isn't good at finding leaks but because of the manner in which it detects leaks. This type of detector uses a propane flame which draws the leaking refrigerant over a hot copper alloy reactor plate. A dramatic change in flame color occurs when there is refrigerant (indicating a leak) in close proximity to the flame. But, due to the fact that poisonous phosgene gas is formed when this type of leak detector comes into contact with refrigerant gas, we don't recommend the purchase or use of this type of detector. However, if you already have one, or have access to one, we have included the procedure for using it in Chapter 5. Be extremely careful and observe all the precautions included.

Halide (propane) torch leak detectors

The most sophisticated, most sensitive and easiest-to-use leak tester is the ion pump halogen leak tester **(see illustration)**. The most unique feature of this technological marvel is its pumping mechanism. The importance of a suction pump in instruments used for detecting refrigerant gas leaks has been recognized for quite some time. Up until recently, however, the use of bellows, valves and other mechanical moving parts has made suction pump-equipped leak detectors bulky, inefficient and unreliable. These problems are eliminated by the ion pump, which is small, efficient and has no moving parts.

One of the most sensitive detectors of refrigerant gases is the negative corona discharge type of ionization detector. In such a sensor, an electrical discharge is set up between a pair of electrodes inside a chamber. The negative electrode is a very sharp wire; the positive electrode is a flat or cylindrical metal plate. When the electrical discharge is set up and current is flowing, a movement of air occurs. This "electrical wind," which is the result of friction between the moving charges (ions) in the corona and the molecules of the air surrounding it, always flows from the negative electrode toward the positive electrode. The halogen leak detector utilizes this air flow to draw air and refrigerant gas into the sensor, eliminating the need

Halogen (electronic) leak testers

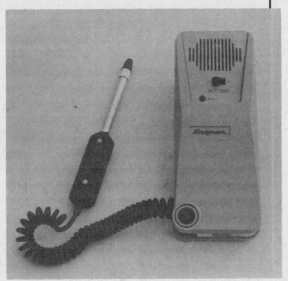

A pair of typical ion pump halogen leak testers — using them is simple, quick, convenient, accurate and safe, but they're expensive

Heating and air conditioning

for mechanical suction.

The ion pump harnesses the electrical energy generated in the sensing element to produce a precise and reliable flow of air through the sensing element chamber. The air flow rate of the ion pump is self-regulating, enabling it to detect leaks as small as 1/10 ounce per year.

Although it's expensive, the halogen leak detector is worth the money if you want a safe, simple and sensitive means of finding leaks fast. It's also less harmful to the environment than the halide, or propane, type detector.

Though newer models have digital circuits that constantly adjust the level of sensitivity to the conditions, older units have to be adjusted for the proper level of sensitivity in accordance with the magnitude of a leak. The newer models are also ready to use as soon as they are turned on; older models take about five minutes to warm up.

Electronic sight glass (non-accumulator type systems)

In recent years, a small hand-held electronic sight glass (**see illustration**) has been marketed by a few automotive tool companies. This sophisticated device, which operates on the same principle as sonar, detects the presence of bubbles in the liquid line. Although it can be used on any receiver-drier type system, the electronic sight glass should not be used on an accumulator type system because, for reasons which are explained in Chapter 5, there are always some bubbles in the liquid line on an accumulator type system. But for non-accumulator type systems, the electronic sight glass is a handy tool.

Two sensors are used — one for transmitting and one for receiving. The sensors are in the form of C-clamps for easy attachment to the outside of any metal refrigeration line. No mechanical penetration of the line is necessary for the ultrasonic waves to pass through it.

Before the electronic sight glass, there was no accurate method to determine the level of refrigerant charge in a system. Nor was there any way to accurately introduce a partial charge into newer air conditioning systems. In fact, most manufacturers stipulate that when the charge is low, it should be completely dumped and the system should be refilled with the factory specified amount of refrigerant. This practice is not only time consuming and expensive, it also unnecessarily contaminates the environment.

A typical electronic sight glass — this space age device detects the presence of bubbles in the refrigerant using a tiny sonar system

5 Heating and air conditioning system service and repair

Heating system

The heating system is so simple and (usually) troublefree that maintenance is often overlooked. However, there are two items which should be an essential part of every tune-up or inspection of the air conditioning and heating system:

1 Because the air which passes through the heater core is usually supplied from outside the vehicle through openings provided in the top or the sides of the cowl, these openings must be inspected periodically to ensure that they are kept free of leaves and other obstructions that might block the flow of air.

2 The heater hoses and the heater control valve (if equipped), must be in good working order. Some control valves are cable operated, others are vacuum operated. We will discuss how to check both kinds.

3 It is vital that the tubing of the heater core and the radiator be kept free from rust and scale accumulations. The hoses connecting the heater core to the cooling system must also be kept free of obstructions.

Note: *The following heating system checks should be a routine part of every cooling system inspection (outlined in detail in every Haynes Owner's Workshop Manual). The following recommendations are directed primarily at the cooling system itself.*

1 An inspection of the heating system should always begin with the hoses. Carefully inspect each heater hose along its entire length. Replace a hose if it's cracked, swollen or deteriorated. Cracks will show up better if the hose is squeezed.

2 Pay close attention to the hose clamps that secure the hoses at either end. Hose clamps can pinch and puncture hoses, resulting in coolant leaks.

3 Make sure that all hose connections are tight. A leak will usually show up as white or rust colored deposits on the area adjacent to the leak. If wire type clamps are used on the hoses, it's a good idea to replace them with screw type clamps.

Service and repair

Inspecting the heating system

75

Heating and air conditioning

4 Clean the front of the radiator and air conditioning condenser with compressed air or a soft brush. Remove all bugs, leaves, mud, etc. embedded in the radiator fins. Be extremely careful not to damage the cooling fins or cut your fingers on them.

5 Check the coolant level. If it has been dropping — and no leaks are detectable — have the radiator cap and cooling system pressure tested at a service station.

6 Change the coolant at least once a year to ensure that the rust inhibitors are not depleted. Once these inhibitors are worn out, rust and scale begin forming in the cooling passages of the engine block, in the radiator and in the heater core.

Obviously, changing the engine coolant once a year will go a long way toward preventing the buildup of rust or scale deposits in the heating system, but there is no way to be sure that a preventive maintenance program has been carried out on a used vehicle.

If you have recently purchased a used vehicle, or if the heating system performance is unsatisfactory, chances are that the heater core, or the heater hoses, are blocked. It's time to flush the system.

Flushing the system

Some owners seem to think that 'flushing' consists of nothing more than opening the petcock or drain valve on the bottom of the radiator and the one or two drain cocks on the engine block, sticking a garden hose into the radiator and turning on the water. Unfortunately, this kind of flush does little.

Normally, outside faucets are only connected to cold water, so sticking the hose into the radiator filler opening and running cold water through the system until the water coming out the drain cock turns clear flushes the radiator — but nothing else. Cold water won't open the thermostat, so the engine cooling passages remain closed off. Because the engine drains are open, some of the coolant in the block is drained off, but because there is no circulation, residue from old dirty coolant remains in the engine. And it is this stuff that we are primarily concerned with removing, because it eventually finds its way into the radiator, the heater hoses, the heater control valve and the heater core.

The following flushing procedure is designed to ensure that the entire cooling and heating systems are cleaned out.

1 Remove the thermostat from the engine, then replace the housing cover and hoses so the engine can be started and run without the thermostat (refer to the appropriate Haynes Automotive Repair Manual for thermostat removal instructions).

2 If the vehicle is equipped with a vacuum-operated heater control valve (used on most new vehicles with air conditioning), either remove the vacuum-operated heater control valve and reattach the hoses, or use a hand-held vacuum pump to apply vacuum to the valve so it opens. Run the engine at idle during the following flushing procedure.

3 Set the heater temperature controls to High.

4 Open the radiator drain cock and drain the coolant. Do not open the engine drain cocks. Remove the radiator cap.

5 Place a container under the heater supply fitting at the block (**see illustration**). Detach the hose from the fitting, point the hose downward and drain it into the container. Make sure that the container is big enough to catch the water that will drain from this hose when the water is turned on.

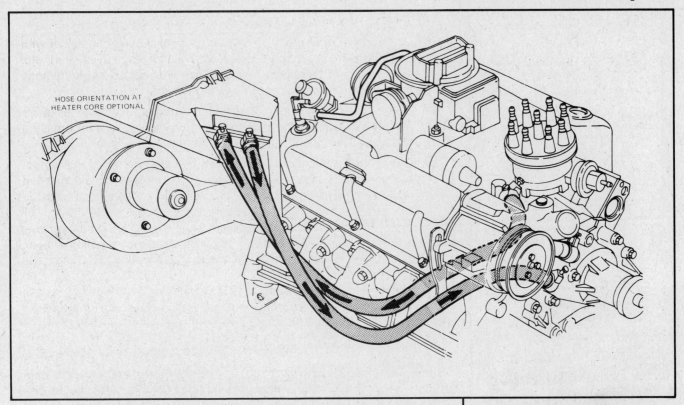

HOSE ORIENTATION AT
HEATER CORE OPTIONAL

6 Connect the water supply hose to the heater hose fitting on the engine block. If you're using a piece of hose with the right diameter, simply push it onto the fitting and hose clamp it on. If you're using a garden hose, you'll have to hold the nozzle against the fitting.

7 Turn on the water and flush for 3 to 5 minutes without the engine running (unless you have a vacuum-actuated heater control valve). Sometimes, it helps to squeeze the outlet or upper radiator hose during the last minute of flushing to remove any trapped liquid.

8 Turn off the water and close the radiator petcock. The radiator and the engine cooling passageways should be clean.

9 Now remove both heater hoses **(see illustration on next page)** and, if equipped, the heater control valve. Make sure that the hose between the valve and the engine, and the return hose, are both free of obstructions.

10 Carefully inspect the control valve for any signs of leakage or corrosion. On older vehicles which have not received annual coolant changes, severely corroded control valves are quite common. To check the control valve for proper function, attach a hand-held vacuum pump, apply vacuum and squirt water into one pipe with the garden hose. If the valve is functioning properly, the water will come out the other pipe. If the water squirts all over you instead of coming out the other pipe, replace the valve. Now, release the vacuum. The valve should not allow any water through. If it does, replace it.

11 Finally, with the heater control valve (if equipped) removed, squirt water through either heater hose and through the heater core. If the water coming out the other hose is discolored, continue flushing until it's clean.

12 Install the heater control valve and hook up the heater hoses.

13 Add the specified amount of a 50/50 solution of water and antifreeze

The easiest way to find the heater hoses is to locate them where they come out of the firewall, then trace them forward and detach them from the water pump and intake manifold (or black) — as a rule of thumb, you should force clean water through the heater hoses and the heater core in the direction opposite normal flow (the hose attached to the water pump carries coolant back to the engine, so that's the one you want to use)

	O-RINGS	SPACER	COMPLETE ASSEMBLY
⅝ IN TO ⅝ IN QUICK CONNECT	390422-S	390420-S	- 18D535 -
¾ IN TO ¾ IN QUICK CONNECT	390423-S	390421-S	- 18D535 -

COMPLETE QUICK CONNECT
ASSEMBLY CONTAINS THE FOLLOWING:

2 - O-RINGS (SILICONE FLUID)
1 - SPACER
1 - COUPLING RETAINER
1 - HOUSING

SILICONE FLUID
ESF-M99B112-A

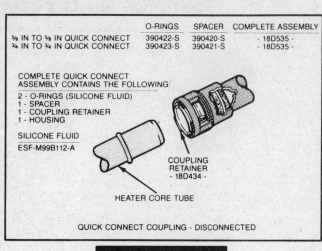

COUPLING
RETAINER
- 18D434 -

HEATER CORE TUBE

QUICK CONNECT COUPLING - DISCONNECTED

TO CONNECT COUPLING

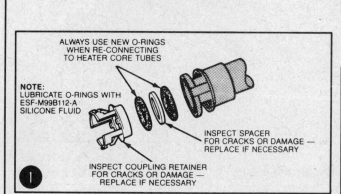

ALWAYS USE NEW O-RINGS
WHEN RE-CONNECTING
TO HEATER CORE TUBES

NOTE:
LUBRICATE O-RINGS WITH
ESF-M99B112-A
SILICONE FLUID

INSPECT SPACER
FOR CRACKS OR DAMAGE —
REPLACE IF NECESSARY

INSPECT COUPLING RETAINER
FOR CRACKS OR DAMAGE —
REPLACE IF NECESSARY

①

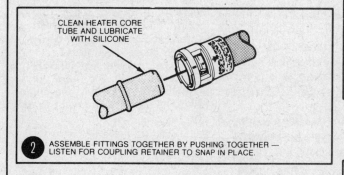

CLEAN HEATER CORE
TUBE AND LUBRICATE
WITH SILICONE

② ASSEMBLE FITTINGS TOGETHER BY PUSHING TOGETHER —
LISTEN FOR COUPLING RETAINER TO SNAP IN PLACE.

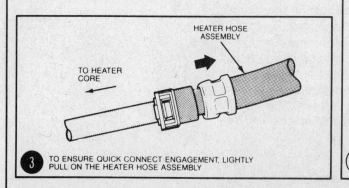

HEATER HOSE
ASSEMBLY

TO HEATER
CORE

③ TO ENSURE QUICK CONNECT ENGAGEMENT, LIGHTLY
PULL ON THE HEATER HOSE ASSEMBLY

TO DISCONNECT COUPLING

CAUTION — ENGINE SHOULD BE OFF BEFORE DISCONNECTING COUPLING

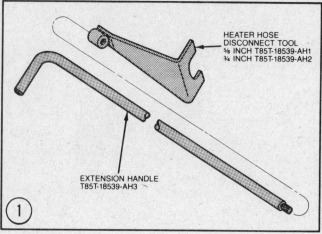

HEATER HOSE
DISCONNECT TOOL
⅝ INCH T85T-18539-AH1
¾ INCH T85T-18539-AH2

EXTENSION HANDLE
T85T-18539-AH3

①

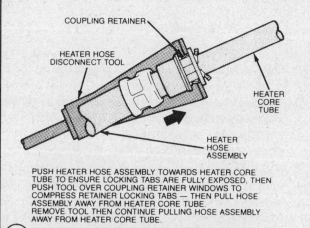

COUPLING RETAINER

HEATER HOSE
DISCONNECT TOOL

HEATER
CORE
TUBE

HEATER
HOSE
ASSEMBLY

PUSH HEATER HOSE ASSEMBLY TOWARDS HEATER CORE
TUBE TO ENSURE LOCKING TABS ARE FULLY EXPOSED, THEN
PUSH TOOL OVER COUPLING RETAINER WINDOWS TO
COMPRESS RETAINER LOCKING TABS — THEN PULL HOSE
ASSEMBLY AWAY FROM HEATER CORE TUBE.
REMOVE TOOL THEN CONTINUE PULLING HOSE ASSEMBLY
AWAY FROM HEATER CORE TUBE.

② NOTE: WHEN COMPRESSING WHITE COUPLING RETAINER,
THE TOOL MUST BE PERPENDICULAR AND ON THE HIGHEST
POINT OF THE COUPLING RETAINER AS SHOWN ABOVE.

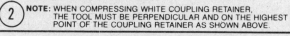

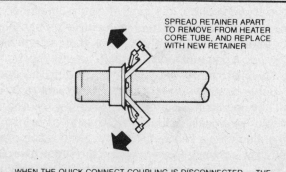

SPREAD RETAINER APART
TO REMOVE FROM HEATER
CORE TUBE, AND REPLACE
WITH NEW RETAINER

③ WHEN THE QUICK CONNECT COUPLING IS DISCONNECTED — THE
WHITE COUPLING RETAINER WILL REMAIN ON THE HEATER CORE TUBE.
INSTALL NEW COUPLING RETAINER, SPACER & NEW LUBRICATED
O-RINGS INTO QUICK CONNECT ASSEMBLY HOUSING BEFORE
RE-INSTALLING HEATER HOSE ASSEMBLY TO HEATER CORE TUBES.

Most heater hose couplings aren't this tricky — these special fittings are found on late model Ford vehicles

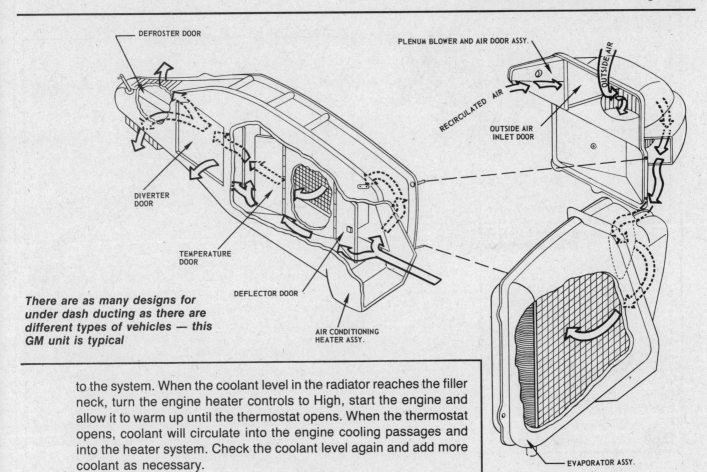

DEFROSTER DOOR

PLENUM BLOWER AND AIR DOOR ASSY.

OUTSIDE AIR

RECIRCULATED AIR

OUTSIDE AIR
INLET DOOR

DIVERTER
DOOR

TEMPERATURE
DOOR

DEFLECTOR DOOR

AIR CONDITIONING
HEATER ASSY.

EVAPORATOR ASSY.

There are as many designs for under dash ducting as there are different types of vehicles — this GM unit is typical

to the system. When the coolant level in the radiator reaches the filler neck, turn the engine heater controls to High, start the engine and allow it to warm up until the thermostat opens. When the thermostat opens, coolant will circulate into the engine cooling passages and into the heater system. Check the coolant level again and add more coolant as necessary.

Heater cables

The elaborate system of ducting under the dashboard of your vehicle is designed to put heated or air conditioned air right where you want it. Most vehicles have ducts that allow the driver to direct the heated or cooled air toward the floor, the front seat occupants or the inside of the windshield for defrosting, or a combination of the above. Air is forced through various vents in the dash via a series of cable or vacuum operated doors. Usually, the more expensive the vehicle, the more elaborate the duct system.

The cable system is virtually foolproof. Cables rarely have to be replaced during the service life of the vehicle. The first tipoff that something is wrong with a cable usually occurs when it becomes difficult to move the control lever on the control head for the heater and air conditioner. If this happens, the door at the other end of the cable is probably jammed. Don't try to force the lever or you'll probably break the cable. Instead, refer to the Haynes Owners Workshop Manual which covers your vehicle, remove the dash or under dash trim plates and try to free up the door.

Some heating and air conditioning systems utilize vacuum lines instead of, or in addition to, cables for actuating the doors. And the latest designs employ electrically actuated doors, or a combination of electrical and vacuum operated doors. These systems are highly complex and their diagnosis and repair is sometimes even beyond the scope of professional mechanics! Service on such systems is best left to an air conditioning technician.

Because this book is intended as a general guide, it would be virtually impossible to explain how to replace every heater control cable employed in every modern vehicle. This information would fill a book by itself. Most Haynes Owners Workshop Manuals include a detailed removal and installation procedure for replacing heater cables (unless the procedure is too complex for the home mechanic).

Air conditioning system

Note: *The same safety precautions apply to both R-12 and R-134a systems.*

1 Never strike a section of copper or aluminum tubing or a heat exchanger in a charged refrigeration system. A blow from a heavy tool could easily cause the relatively soft material to rupture.

2 If you have to apply force to a pressurized refrigerant threaded fitting, always use a back-up wrench to avoid the direct transfer of excessive torque to a section of refrigerant tubing. Whenever possible, use wrenches specially designed for '1/4-inch flare nut' fittings (R-12 systems) or for 1/2-inch 'Acme' fittings (R-134a systems).

3 Wear gloves when connecting or disconnecting service gauge hoses.

4 Always wear eye protection when working around refrigerant and air conditioning systems. Since the system's high side is under high pressure, severe injury to the eyes could result if a hose were to burst. Refrigerant also evaporates rapidly when exposed to the atmosphere, causing it to freeze anything it contacts. That's why it's a good idea to protect skin and clothing with a shop coat. And a bad idea to wear loose clothing or things like ties or jewelry that could get caught in the drivebelts.

5 Because refrigerant is heavier than oxygen, high concentrations of refrigerant can displace oxygen in a confined area and act as an anethesia. This is particularly important when leak-testing or soldering because toxic gas is formed when refrigerant comes in contact with a flame.

6 Never operate an air conditioning system without first verifying that test gauges are backseated, if equipped, and that all fittings throughout the system are snug.

7 Never apply heat of any kind to a refrigerant line or storage vessel.

8 Always store refrigerant containers in a cool place. Never allow them to sit out in the sun or near a heat source. And never expose them to an open flame.

9 Never store refrigerant drums around corrosives like battery acid. Drums may corrode and then burst.

10 Always wear goggles when working on an air conditioning system. And keep a bottle of sterile mineral oil and a quantity of weak boric acid solution nearby for emergencies (refrigerant is readily absorbed by this oil). If refrigerant contacts your eyes, immediately use a few drops of mineral oil to wash them out, then wash them clean with the weak boric acid solution.

11 Frostbite from refrigerant should be treated by first gradually warming the area with cool water and then gently applying petroleum jelly. A physician should be consulted.

12 Always keep refrigerant drum fittings capped when not in use. Avoid sudden shock to the drum which might occur from dropping it or from banging a heavy tool against it. Never carry a drum in the passenger compartment of a vehicle.

13 Always have the system discharged before painting a vehicle, if the paint must be baked on, and before welding anywhere near refrigerant lines.

Preliminary system inspection

Before performing any of the service procedures outlined in this chapter, you must correct any conditions that might have an adverse effect on the operation of the system. First, be sure that you have read and understand the safety precautions outlined above. Then make sure that the following items have been checked before you proceed to service the system:

1 Check the cooling system. Inspect the water pump and all cooling hoses for leaks.

2 Check the compressor and engine drivebelts. They must be in good condition and properly adjusted.

3 Check the fan clutch. Make sure it's operating properly.

4 If the vehicle is equipped with a heavy-duty fan, make sure it's operating properly.

5 Check the condenser fins. They must not be bent, damaged or clogged with bugs, leaves or mud. If the fins are in need of some work, special fin 'combs,' available at auto parts stores, can be used to clean and straighten them.

6 The operation of most modern air conditioning systems is heavily dependent on vacuum. Check all vacuum lines and connections for leaks.

7 Look for mechanical failures. Sometimes a malfunction can be traced to something as simple as a defective motor, heater air ducts or doors malfunctioning, or even a heater valve malfunction.

8 Inspect the compressor front seal and pressure relief valve for leaks.

The sight glass (non-accumulator systems)

Many older and some newer non-accumulator systems are equipped with a built-in sight glass that allows you to quickly check the condition of the refrigerant while the system is in operation **(see illustration)**. The sight glass is usually on the receiver-drier assembly; another, less common, location is the liquid line between the condenser and the expansion valve. For reasons that are explained later, most accumulator systems do not have a sight glass. On valves-in-receiver (VIR) units, the sight glass, if there is one, is in the VIR housing.

If the system in your vehicle is a non-accumulator type but doesn't have a sight glass, you can install an aftermarket in-line sight glass between the condenser and the thermostatic expansion valve. However, even though the sight glass affords a view of the refrigerant when the system is in operation, it's no substitute for a manifold test gauge set. Sight glass symptoms are not necessarily positive identification of a problem — they should be considered an adjunct to other system symptoms.

The sight glass (arrow) is a handy way to quickly check the condition of the refrigerant while the system is operating — sight glasses, if equipped, are usually on top of the receiver-drier like this one, or, less frequently, in the liquid line between the condenser and the expansion valve

Heating and air conditioning

Using the sight glass

1 Start the engine, turn on the air conditioning system, put the controls at the maximum cooling and blower settings and allow it to run for 5 minutes to stabilize (this term is explained later in the chapter).

2 If the sight glass has a cap, remove it (make sure you replace it when you're done — the cap keeps the window clean).

3 Note the condition of the refrigerant in the sight glass. There are several conditions that you should watch for **(see illustration)**:

a) **Clear sight glass** — A clear sight glass can be good or bad. It indicates one of three possibilities:
   1) The system has the correct refrigerant charge.
   2) The system has no refrigerant in it. You will know if this is the case because there will be absolutely no cool air coming out of the heater/air conditioner vents.
   3) The system is overcharged (has too much refrigerant). This condition can only be verified with test gauges.

b) **Occasional bubbles or foam in sight glass** — An occasionally bubbly or foamy sight glass indicates the system is slightly low on refrigerant and air has probably entered the system. But if the bubbles are sporadic, or infrequent (usually during clutch cycling or system start-up), their presence may not indicate a problem.

c) **Oil streaks in sight glass** — Oil streaks indicate that the system's compressor oil is circulating through the system, which, in turn, may mean that the system refrigerant charge is extremely low.

d) **Heavy stream of bubbles** — A heavy stream of bubbles indicates a serious shortage of refrigerant in the system.

e) **Dark or cloudy sight glass** — A dark or cloudy sight glass indicates that the desiccant in the receiver-drier has deteriorated and is being circulated through the system. It also indicates that contaminants are present.

As noted previously, accumulator systems do not have a sight glass. Why? Because, even with a full charge, bubbles are always present in the liquid line. In a non-accumulator system, the liquid and gaseous refrigerant

These are the five most common conditions indicated by the sight glass

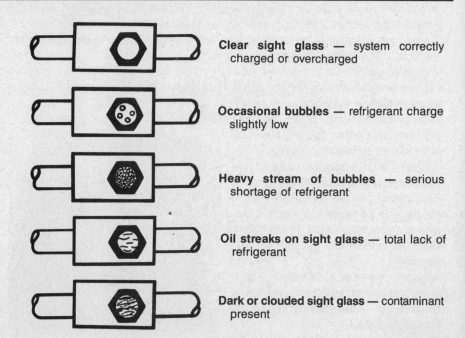

Clear sight glass — system correctly charged or overcharged

Occasional bubbles — refrigerant charge slightly low

Heavy stream of bubbles — serious shortage of refrigerant

Oil streaks on sight glass — total lack of refrigerant

Dark or clouded sight glass — contaminant present

goes straight into the receiver-drier as it comes out of the condenser. The liquid settles to the bottom of the receiver-drier. Because the pick-up tube is located at the bottom of the receiver-drier, gaseous refrigerant remains in the receiver-drier until it's converted into a liquid. Only liquid refrigerant is released through the pickup tube. On conventional systems, therefore, all refrigerant in the liquid line is in a liquid state and should have no bubbles.

Accumulator systems don't have a receiver-drier that separates the gas from the liquid as they come out of the condenser, so the liquid line always has some bubbles in it. Because this is the refrigerant's normal condition, a sight glass would be of little value.

Electronic sight glasses (discussed in Chapter 4), which were designed to sense bubbles in the lines of non-accumulator systems without sight glasses, are also of no value when servicing or diagnosing an accumulator system. **Warning:** *If refrigerant is added to an accumulator system until there are no more bubbles, the system will be overcharged and probably damaged, which could cause serious physical injury.*

In Chapter 4, we looked at the manifold test gauges, how to hook them up and how to read them. But there is one more topic that must be addressed before servicing the system - how to attach the service hoses to the valves.

Before getting started hooking up your gauges, keep in mind as you read through the following procedures that discharging either side of the system, accidentally or otherwise, is environmentally and fiscally irresponsible. R-12 is now a scarce - and rapidly dwindling - substance whose price the rest of this decade will be determined by how much is available and how many people want to buy it. No more R-12 will be produced in the future - ever. The only R-12 available from now on must come from what can be recovered and recycled. So every time someone discharges R-12 into the atmosphere, they contribute to ozone depletion, shrink the available supply of remaining R-12 and raise its price a little more. The less that leaks out of the R-12 systems still in use, the longer it will last and the less it will cost. And the less harm it will do to the environment.

System service valves are the 'eyes' into an air conditioning system through which the manifold gauges are able to monitor system performance. Without them, you would be unable to do anything to the system. All checking, troubleshooting, discharging, evacuation and recharging procedures are performed through the service valves.

At first, system service valves never seem to be located at the same place on any two vehicles. Even the number of valves differs from one system to another. Some systems have only one service valve on the high side and one on the low side. Others use more than one valve on the high and/or low side so that system operation can be checked at different locations.

One thing all service valves have in common is a protective cap **(see illustration)** which keeps the core clean and prevents accidental discharge. The cap must be removed before the manifold gauges can be attached.

Two types of service valves are in common use on air conditioning systems today — the stem type and the Schrader type.

Connecting the gauge set

R-12 Service valves

The protective cap on service valves performs two functions — it keeps the core clean so no contaminants get into the system when the service valve is open and it prevents accidental discharge of the system if the core fails

Heating and air conditioning

Stem type R-12 service valves

The stem type service valve features a unique three-connector design and an adjustable stem under a protective cap. When connecting a test gauge to this type of service valve or reading system pressures on the gauges after connection, you must manually position the valve stem. A special wrench should be used to protect it from damage. The stem type service valve has three operating positions (see illustration):

1) Back-seated (open) position
2) Mid (test) position
3) Front-seated (closed) position

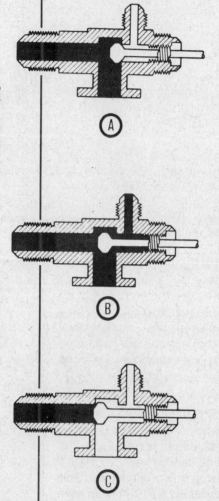

The three positions of the mechanical stem type valve:

A Back-seated (stem turned all the way out) — normal operating position, valve blocks passage to service gauge port

B Mid-position (stem turned 1-1/2 to 2 turns in) — valve permits refrigerant to flow through system and allows it to flow through service port to the test gauges

C Front-seated (stem turned all the way in) — valve blocks refrigerant flow through the system

Back-seated (open) position

The back-seated position of the stem type valve (stem turned out all the way) is the normal operating position. This position blocks the passageway to the service gauge port, preventing R-12 from flowing to the manifold test gauges, refrigerant can, vacuum pump, etc. It's the position the valve must be in when connecting or disconnecting the manifold gauge set or any other air conditioning service equipment.

Mid (test) position

After the service gauge set has been installed with the valve stem in the back-seated position, turn the valve stem 1-1/2 to 2 turns in. In this position, the valve stem still permits refrigerant to flow through the system but it also allows R-12 to flow through the service port and to the test gauges.

Front-seated (closed) position

With the service valve stem turned in as far as possible, the valve blocks refrigerant flow through the system. If the valve is installed on the compressor (it usually is), the flow of R-12 to or from the compressor is blocked. **Caution:** If the air conditioning system is operated with the service valve(s) in the front-seated position, the compressor will be damaged.

Schrader type R-12 valves

The Schrader type service valve is basically the same in design and operation as a tire valve. It has a spring-loaded mechanism that's normally (when no gauges are attached) in a closed position, preventing the escape of refrigerant from the system (see illustration). When a test gauge hose fitting (with an integral valve core depressor) is connected to the Schrader valve, the stem is pushed to the open position and the pressurized refrigerant flows through the valve to the test gauge.

Schrader type valves have pretty much displaced stem type service valves on most air conditioning systems now in use. They are convenient, safe and environmentally superior to stem types. However, a few words to the wise are in order here: Always try to use a test hose with a built-in core depressor when working with Schrader type service valves. If a hose does not have

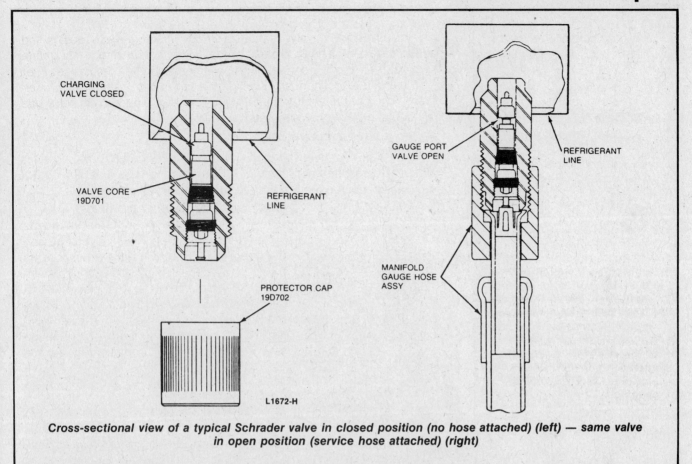

CHARGING VALVE CLOSED

VALVE CORE 19D701

REFRIGERANT LINE

GAUGE PORT VALVE OPEN

REFRIGERANT LINE

MANIFOLD GAUGE HOSE ASSY

PROTECTOR CAP 19D702

L1672-H

Cross-sectional view of a typical Schrader valve in closed position (no hose attached) (left) — same valve in open position (service hose attached) (right)

a built-in depressor, attach an adapter to the hose that does. And NEVER attach hoses or adapters to a Schrader valve before the hose has been connected to the manifold gauge set. If you fail to remember this, it could result in a total loss of the refrigerant in the system at best, and personal injury at worst. Finally, it should be noted that the Schrader valve, though basically similar in design and operation to a tire valve, cannot be replaced with a tire valve.

Recently, many manufacturers have resorted to using different size fittings for high and low side service valves. Because of the high system pressures which occur in the discharge (high) side of the system, accidentally reversing the high and low side connections must be avoided at all costs.

In 1976, General Motors introduced a high side service valve with a different thread size (3/8-24 thread) than on the low side (7/16-20 thread). This simple measure prevents the novice and the experienced technician alike from unintentionally hooking up a can of refrigerant to the high side. Special adapters are needed to make the connection (**see illustration**). The adapters can be purchased in straight fixed and flexible configurations and even in 45° and 90° angle models where necessary.

A special quick-disconnect fitting for the high side service valve is available for Ford systems. The fitting has a mechanism that immediately seals the coupling between the two fittings so no refrigerant is accidentally discharged during attachment or detachment of the high side service gauge.

Special high-side R-12 service valves

A typical high side adapter fitting like this must be used with the General Motors post-1976 type (3/8-24 thread) high side service valve before the hose can be attached

Schrader type service valves

When locating the high and low side service valves for the first time, take a few minutes to study the system before doing anything — after tracing the lines and hoses, look for the low side fitting in the line between the evaporator and the compressor (it's usually closer to the compressor)

After removing the protective cap very slowly (in case there's a leak at the service valve), attach the low side hose fitting and route the hose out of the way of all moving and hot parts

Connecting the gauge set

Warning: *Wear eye protection during this procedure.*

1 Locate the high and low side service valves **(see illustration)**. Slowly remove the protective caps (if a valve is leaking, this will prevent the cap from being blown off).

2 Check the test hoses to make sure they are equipped with a valve core depressor that matches the Schrader type valve. If they don't, install special adapters that do (see above).

3 If you have not already done so, close both manifold gauge hand valves all the way.

4 Connect the low side service hose to the low (suction) side of the compressor **(see illustration)**. Tighten it finger tight.

5 Connect the high side service hose to the high (discharge) side of the compressor **(see illustrations)**. Again, tighten it finger tight. **Note:** *If the high side service hose connector doesn't fit on the high side Schrader valve, that's because it takes a special adapter. Later model Ford and General Motors valves are smaller than earlier valves. The smaller size prevents accidental attachment of the low side service hose to the high side of the system.*

6 Connect a separate service hose to the center fitting on the gauge set.

The high side fitting is usually in the high side line between the condenser and the evaporator — if it's difficult to get at, like this one, you may need to use a 6-inch flexible extension adapter to hook up the high side hose

Note the angled metal line on this high side service hose — though not absolutely necessary, this design offers more flexibility when trying to attach it to hard to reach fittings

It's a good idea to protect the surrounding area of the engine compartment, and your eyes and skin, from refrigerant and oil with a shop rag when tightening or loosening a high side adapter fitting

Ditto for hooking up service hoses to service adapter fittings

Once the manifold gauge set is hooked up, make sure both hoses are routed away from all moving and hot components

Heating and air conditioning

Stem type service valves

Warning: *Wear eye protection during this procedure.*

1 Locate the high and low side service valves. Slowly remove the protective caps (if a valve is leaking, this will prevent the cap from being blown off).

2 If you have not already done so, close both manifold gauge hand valves all the way.

3 Connect the low side service hose to the low (suction) side of the compressor. Tighten it finger tight.

4 Connect the high side service hose to the high (discharge) side of the compressor. Again, tighten it finger tight.

5 Connect a separate service hose to the center fitting on the gauge set.

R-134a service valves

The bad news is R-134a service valves are completely different from R-12 valves. The good news is they're all the same. Both the high and the low side valves on R-134a systems:

1 Have caps unique to the high and low side fittings, respectively.

2 Have no external threads on the valves (the internal threads are for the caps only).

3 Have external shapes unique to the high and low side fittings, respectively.

4 Have valve cores unique to R-134a fittings.

The R-134 valves are different so there is no chance of confusing the service valves on an R-134a system with any of the various valves used on R-12 systems. The reason for this, of course, is that the EPA and the manufacturers don't want you to even THINK about trying to hook up a can or drum of R-12 or a set of R-12 manifold gauges to these new valves! And there's no way you can, because fitting adapters to hook up R-12 service hoses to R-134a valves will never be commercially available, so don't even try to find such fittings.

At the time of publication of this revised manual (Spring 1993), there was little information regarding the availability of service and diagnostic equipment for R-134a systems. There are gauges and service hoses for sale at this time. Be sure to follow all manufacturer's instructions for hooking everything up.

Stabilizing the system

Before actually beginning any tests, operate the system for a few minutes to stabilize the pressures and temperatures and ensure accurate gauge readings. To stabilize the system:

1 Always make sure the manifold gauge set, test hoses and other equipment are kept away from moving engine parts and hot surfaces such as rocker arm covers, exhaust manifolds, etc.

2 Start the engine and, if necessary, adjust the engine speed to a fast idle (to speed up system stabilization).

3 Position the air conditioner controls at maximum cooling. Set the blower at the highest speed.

4 Open the doors and/or windows to quickly eliminate the heat from the passenger compartment.

5 Operate the system like this for at least 5 minutes (no more than 10 minutes should be necessary). The system is now stabilized and ready for testing.

Make sure the system is fully charged

Once the system is stabilized, it's ready for testing. There is, however, one more thing you must do before starting: Make sure the system is fully charged. How do you know whether the system is fully charged?

1 Using a thermometer, measure the 'ambient' (outside) air temperature about 2 inches in front of the condenser. System pressures (particularly the high side) are directly affected by the ambient temperature. Jot down your reading and compare it to the ambient temperature column on the accompanying chart showing the relationship between pressure and temperature.

2 Insert a thermometer into the air conditioning outlet **(see illustration)** nearest the evaporator. Turn the blower switch to Low and note the indicated outlet air temperature. Again, jot down your reading and compare it to the evaporator temperature column on the accompanying chart.

3 Note the high and low side gauge readings and jot them down too. Then compare the preliminary readings to the columns for low and high side pressures, respectively, on the chart.

4 If the system is equipped with a sight glass (usually on the receiver-drier), inspect the refrigerant flowing past the window. If there are some bubbles in the window, the system refrigerant level is low or there is a small leak in the system. If the sight glass is clear or oil-streaked, the system refrigerant is excessively low or there is a major leak. Check all fittings and hoses, then have the system charged by a dealer or automotive air conditioning shop. **Note:** *If the system hasn't been checked in the last year, the loss of some refrigerant is normal. Vibration loosens the fittings, the hoses are a little porous and even the design of the system itself allows some leakage.*

The best place to check the output of the evaporator is at the dash vent nearest the evaporator (usually one of the center vents)

A rule of thumb guide to the relationship between pressure and temperature:

Low side gauge (psi)	Evaporator temp. (degrees F.)
10	2
12	6
14	10
16	14
18	18
20	20
22	22
24	24
26	27
28	29
30	32
35	36
40	42
45	48
50	53
55	58
60	62
65	66
70	70

High side Gauge (psi)	Ambient temp. (degrees F.)
130 to 160	60
140 to 170	65
150 to 180	70
160 to 190	75
170 to 210	80
180 to 220	85
190 to 230	90
205 to 250	95
220 to 270	100
240 to 290	105
260 to 310	110
285 to 335	115
310 to 370	120

Heating and air conditioning

Testing for proper refrigerant charge with an electronic sight glass

Remember, as noted in Chapter 4, that the use of this device on accumulator systems isn't really appropriate. Also, be sure to read the section entitled 'Cooling the condenser while using the electronic sight glass.'

1 Attach the manifold gauge set to the system as described earlier in this chapter.

2 Connect the C-clamps to the liquid line near the expansion valve or orifice tube **(see illustration).**
   a) The sensors must be on the condenser side of the expansion valve or orifice tube.
   b) The clamps should be tight enough to keep from moving, but not so tight that they can cause damage to the tube.
   c) The C-clamps should be about 1 to 3 inches apart (they must not touch each other).

3 Set the idle speed at 900 to 1000 rpm, turn on the air conditioning system and wait five minutes.

4 Spray the condenser with a continuous mist of water before checking or charging the system. A high volume shop fan can also be used to cool the condenser. See the comments below regarding condenser cooling.

5 What the instrument detects is the presence of bubbles in the liquid line:
   a) If there are no bubbles, the tester will beep every two seconds. No bubbles means the line is completely full of gas, completely full of liquid or completely empty. The electronic sight glass cannot distinguish between a system that is completely full or empty, so it's essential that you connect manifold gauges to the system to verify the status of the refrigerant charge. And the gauges still require regular monitoring while the system is being charged. An electronic sight glass is **not** a substitute for test gauges.
   b) The second type of signal is an erratic beep or ringing. If this signal is emitted, there are bubbles in the liquid line, which is an indication of a low refrigerant charge.

When hooking up an electronic sight glass, connect the C-clamps (arrows) to the liquid line near the expansion valve or orifice tube

a) The sensors must be on the condenser side of the expansion valve or orifice tube
b) The clamps should be tight enough to keep from moving, but not so tight that they can cause damage to the tube
c) The C-clamps should be 1 to 3 inches apart (they must not touch each other)

During testing, the vehicle is stationary. An air conditioning system does not operate efficiently when the vehicle is stationary. In a moving vehicle, the motion of the air over the condenser cools and condenses the hot gas to form a high pressure liquid. In a stationary vehicle, this air movement is absent. This situation can cause a condition known as 'flash gas' in the air conditioning system (especially on General Motors vehicles and others with an orifice tube system). The electronic sight glass senses this flash gas and emits an erratic beeping sound indicating the system is in need of charging even when the charge level is okay. To eliminate flash gas, spray the condenser with water or set up a large shop fan in front of the vehicle. This will eliminate flash gas and keep the condensing pressure at approximately 150 psi.

System performance test

Once the system charge has been brought up to the proper level, it's ready for a performance test.

1 Since the engine and air conditioning system will be running while the vehicle is stationary, place a large fan right in front of the condenser and radiator. Turn the fan motor speed selection knob, if equipped, to its highest setting.

2 Place the transmission selector lever in Neutral or Park and set the emergency brake. Block the wheels as well. Start the engine and set it at a fast idle.

3 Always note the low side gauge/evaporator temperature and high side gauge/ambient temperature readings first, as previously described, comparing the readings to the figures in the system pressure/temperature chart. If the initial readings seem to indicate an abnormality, you might want to compare the readings to the various combinations of low side/high side gauge readings in the next chapter.

4 After the system has been stabilized (normal temperatures and pressures obtained), its performance can be tested. With the engine running, the air conditioning controls in the maximum cooling position, the blower adjusted to the highest setting and the doors and windows of the vehicle closed, read both gauges. Jot down the readings and compare them to the figures in the accompanying chart showing normal system operating pressures. If they more or less match the rule of thumb figures, the system is operating satisfactorily. If they don't match, go to the next chapter and find the combination of low side and high side gauge readings that most closely approximates your readings.

5 The air blowing from the vents should be quite cold. If it isn't, go to the next chapter and study the possible causes of inadequate or non-existent cooling.

6 If the system on the vehicle is a non-accumulator type and is equipped with a sight glass, the refrigerant should be generally clear of bubbles. Most systems usually show some bubbling during system cycling, so don't rely too heavily on sight glass readings to determine whether the system is fully charged.

Leak testing

Any time more than 1/2-pound of refrigerant is required to charge the system over a period of a year, a leak is indicated. Leakage — either through loose fittings, deteriorated hoses or seals or damaged metal lines — is the usual

Cooling the condenser while using the electronic sight glass

cause for low refrigerant charge. Most leaks are caused by normal engine vibration, which loosens threaded fittings and even causes metal lines to fatigue and crack over a period of time. Snugging all the fittings usually eliminates most leaks. Repair or replacement is necessary to cure leaks caused by metal fatigue and cracks. Looking for, locating and repairing subtle leaks can be time consuming. If any of the testing procedures outlined thus far indicate a leak, find and fix it. Fortunately, there are several good leak detectors available (discussed in Chapter 4) to make the job easier.

Finding leaks with a bubble detector

This is a cheap way to find a leak, and a good one, especially if you're unable to pinpoint the location of the leak using other methods.

1 Simply apply a commercial bubble detector solution, or even a soap and water solution, to the suspected leak with a small brush. Apply the solution to all fittings and connections where the leak might be.

2 Start the engine, turn on the air conditioning system and let the pressures stabilize.

3 The leaking refrigerant will cause the detector or soapy solution to form bubbles.

4 Tighten the loose fitting or repair the leaking components.

5 Wipe off the solution and repeat the above procedure to ensure that the leak is fixed.

Finding leaks with a halide (propane) torch

Warning: *The following method is not recommended unless there is no other leak detection device available. When a refrigerant leak is detected with a propane leak tester, the normally harmless refrigerant is exposed to the leak detector's propane flame, forming poisonous phosgene gas. Never inhale vapors produced by a propane leak tester — keep the work area well ventilated.*

To use a propane torch to find a leak:

1 Open the propane can valve and light the torch. Adjust the flame just high enough to heat the reaction plate in the chimney to a cherry red (about 1/2-inch above the reaction plate).

2 Lower the flame when the plate is red and adjust the top of the flame even with (or 1/4-inch above) the reaction plate — just high enough to maintain the cherry red color. **Caution:** *If the flame burns too high, the reaction plate will be destroyed after a few uses.*

3 Holding the propane torch so the flame is visible, but away from any hazardous materials, move the pick-up hose slowly around the components of the system. Keep the hose on the underside of the components — refrigerant is heavier than air and will fall as it seeps from a leak. Be sure to check all joints, connections, seals, vacuum hoses and controls.

4 The flame color is normally a pale blue. A change in color indicates a leak:
a) A pale yellow flame indicates a very small leak.
b) A yellowish-green flame indicates the presence of a small leak.
c) A purplish-blue flame indicates a major leak.

5 Once the point of the leak is detected, repair the system as necessary.

6 Don't stop searching after finding a leak. Be sure to check the entire system. There may be other leaks.

To find a leak with an electronic tester:

1 Start the engine and turn on the air conditioning system.

2 Turn on the leak tester. Most electronic leak testers have a battery voltage indicator, usually a light emitting diode (LED). Make sure the LED is illuminated. If it isn't, replace the batteries before proceeding.

3 Search for leaks by slowly moving the sensing tip near all system components, controls, seals and fittings **(see illustration).**

4 The instrument will emit an audible alarm when the sensing tip detects the presence of refrigerant gases. Most electronic detectors have a thumbwheel to adjust the sensitivity of the alarm.

5 To increase the detection sensitivity of the sensing tip itself, you'll have to reduce the air flow rate of the pumping tip:
   a) Cover the exhaust vents at the back of the pumping tip housing by wrapping a piece of tape over them. Masking tape or cellophane tape works well.
   b) Reopen one of the vent slots by punching or slicing through the tape over the slot with a razor blade or a fingernail. The reduced air rate makes it possible for the electronic leak tester to detect leaks smaller than 1/10 ounce per year!

Sometimes leaks can be so small that they don't always show up when looking for them. And sometimes you're not really looking for a leak, because none is indicated. But whenever you discharge and evacuate the system (discussed later in this chapter), it's a good idea to perform a vacuum pump leakdown test anyway. Why? Because of the well known effects of the release of fluorocarbons into the ozone layer, most manufacturers are 'downsizing'

Finding leaks with an electronic leak tester

When using an electronic leak detector, search for leaks by slowly moving the sensing tip near all system components, controls, seals and fittings — the instrument will emit an audible alarm when the sensing tip detects the presence of refrigerant gases

Finding leaks with a vacuum pump leakdown test

93

their air conditioning systems to prepare for the anticipated stricter Federal regulations and tighter supplies of R-12. A few years ago, 4-1/2 pounds of refrigerant in a system for a full-sized vehicle was pretty typical; that same system today may have only 2 pounds of R-12. And many smaller vehicles have systems with 1-1/2 to 2 pound capacities. When systems had large refrigerant capacities, and before we knew what fluorocarbons did to the environment, the leakage of 1/4 to 1/2-pound per year was no big deal. Now, however, the same size leak has a significant effect on system cooling ability and, more importantly, has a pronounced effect on the ozone layer. So it's imperative that small leaks be eliminated.

When a vacuum pump is connected to the system and running, it's an excellent first step in leak detection. Note: The procedure for attaching and using a vacuum pump can be found later in this chapter (See 'Evacuating the system').

Obviously, if the vacuum pump is in good condition, but can't pump the system down to its normal vacuum, there is a massive leak somewhere (any of the methods discused above will locate it). But let's say the pump does pull down to its normal vacuum. Does that mean there are no leaks? Not necessarily. Close the valves on the test gauge manifold (including the shut-off valve for the pump at the center service hose), turn off the pump and wait five minutes. If the vacuum reading drops more than two inches, there is a leak somewhere that must be corrected.

Removing contaminants

Contaminated refrigerant

Eventually, contaminants such as air, moisture and dirt find their way into the air conditioning system. Sometimes they work their way in through a loose fitting, a bad compressor seal, a porous hose or some other defective component. Other times they get in during some service procedure that involves opening the system. Regardless of how they get in, foreign substances must be eliminated because they don't condense like refrigerant, obstruct the movement of refrigerant through the system and form corrosive acids when they chemically react with refrigerant.

Replacing contaminated refrigerant involves two, sometimes three, procedures:

1 The system must be **discharged** by a dealer or an automotive air conditioning shop.

2 It must then be **evacuated** or pumped down with a vacuum pump to remove all traces of air, moisture and contaminated refrigerant.

3 Sometimes, to remove foreign material from a system, it must also be **flushed**.

When is discharging necessary?

Discharging

Besides being the first step in the removal of contaminated refrigerant from the system, discharging is also necessary whenever the system must be opened for repairs or replacement of any part, with one notable exception. Compressors with stem-type service valves can be 'isolated' and removed from the system without performing a complete discharge (see "Isolating the compressor" later in this chapter). Since discharging now requires an approved recycling system, take the vehicle to an approved air conditioning shop for discharging.

Flushing removes solid contaminants — excess oil, sludge, casting flash, metal flakes from a failed compressor, etc. — that could cause poor cooling or even component failure. Flushing is essential when replacing a broken compressor. If the system isn't flushed, small particles of metal from the old compressor will remain, circulating throughout the system until they find their way back to the new compressor and destroy it. Excess oil in the system can result in poor performance — flushing removes it. Flushing is also a good preventive maintenance procedure whenever a system is disassembled for servicing.

Note: *The flushing procedure described here is for the flushing kit depicted, or one similar in design. If the instructions contained in your kit differ significantly from the following procedure, do it their way.*

1 Have the system discharged by a dealer or automotive air conditioning shop.

2 Disconnect the refrigerant lines. **Caution:** *Always remove the expansion valve and Pilot Operated Absolute/Suction Throttling Valve (POA/STV) or orifice tube assembly.* The filter screens on the valves and orifices should be cleaned by hand with a Q-tip. It's not usually necessary to remove the condenser or evaporator from the vehicle for flushing.

3 Attach one end of the flush hose to the flush gun and the other to the flushing cylinder. Attach a compressed air hose to the other end of the flushing cylinder (you'll need to install your own quick-disconnect fitting to hook up a shop air hose to the cylinder) (**see illustration**).

4 You can flush any of the components in the system or the entire system. Don't attempt to flush the compressor itself. Flushing will remove the oil and may even damage the internal parts.

Flushing to remove contaminants

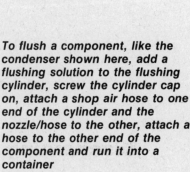

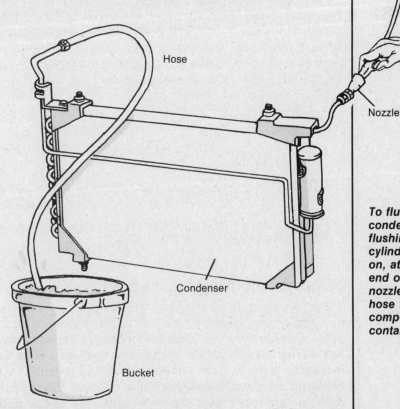

To flush a component, like the condenser shown here, add a flushing solution to the flushing cylinder, screw the cylinder cap on, attach a shop air hose to one end of the cylinder and the nozzle/hose to the other, attach a hose to the other end of the component and run it into a container

5 To flush the entire system, unscrew the cap from the flushing cylinder, pour about 20 ounces of an approved flushing solvent into the cylinder and replace the cap.

6 Use proportionally smaller amounts of solvent for flushing single components.

7 Pressurize the flushing cylinder to 90 to 125 psi with a shop compressor. **Warning:** *Do not exceed 200 psi or serious injury could result if the flushing cylinder were to burst.*

8 When flushing an evaporator or condenser, fit one end of the waste discharge hose over the component's refrigerant inlet and route the other end into a waste container. Insert the flush gun into the refrigerant outlet and press the control button on the flush gun to release the flushing solvent. Continue flushing until there is no evidence of oil or solids being dispelled from the waste hose with the flushing solvent. Note that this is a back-flushing procedure. Components can also be flushed in the other direction, but back-flushing is recommended.

9 Refrigerant lines are flushed in a similar manner, but the waste hose isn't needed since the open end of the line can be placed in the waste container.

10 After the procedure is complete, reassemble the system and replace any oil that was lost.

11 Because flushing removes oil, it's necessary to replenish the system's oil supply before returning the system to service. The correct amount of oil to be added for each component that has been flushed or replaced is as follows:

a) Condenser — 2 ounces
b) Evaporator — 2 ounces
c) Receiver-drier or suction-accumulator — 1 ounce

Caution: *Unless the unit is new and the desiccant is replaceable, do not attempt to re-use a receiver-drier or suction-accumulator once it has been opened up. Replace it with a new unit.*

12 In orifice tube systems, it's not a good idea to attempt to re-use the orifice tube assembly. Replace it with a new unit.

13 Make sure that any filter screens in expansion valves or POA/STV valves are clean and that the valves are in good condition before re-installing them.

14 When reassembling the system components, replace all O-rings in the refrigerant line fittings to prevent leaks. Pre-lube the new O-rings with refrigerant oil.

15 If the system is not going to be reassembled right away, cap the inlet and outlet fittings on all components to prevent the incursion of new contaminants. Replacement components are usually equipped with protective plastic caps which can be used for this purpose.

Repairing the system

Once the system has been completely discharged, repairs can be performed. Some of the most common repairs include fixing leaks, repairing or replacing hoses or lines, replacing expansion valve screens, overhauling valves-in-receiver accumulators, replacing receiver-drier desiccant, replacing accumulators, replacing expansion tubes, replacing STV and EPR valves, replacing compressor reed valves and checking the oil level in the compressor.

Fixing leaks

Leaks are undoubtedly the most common problem associated with automotive air conditioning systems. Normal engine vibration loosens the fittings over time and the hoses, and even steel lines, often crack as they grow old, allowing refrigerant to leak out. This is one area in which you can really do your part to help protect the environment, help save the dwindling supply of R-12 and help save yourself a lot of money. Leaking R-12 is wasted R-12. Once it leaks out of your system into the atmosphere, R-12 does nobody any good. So monitor your air conditioning system regularly for leaks and fix them as soon as you find them. Fortunately, they're one of the easiest kinds of problems to fix.

1 **Loose fittings or connections** — If a minor leak is traced to a connection, the fitting has probably loosened up from vibration. Try tightening it. After tightening a fitting or connection, always check it again for leakage to make sure the problem is solved.

2 **Deteriorated O-ring seals or gaskets** — If tightening a leaky connection doesn't stop the leak, the fitting O-ring seals or gaskets are probably deteriorated (though it's possible that the fitting itself is faulty or damaged). Discharge the system and disconnect the fittings at the leaky connection. Be sure to clean the area around the fittings before disconnecting them to prevent dirt or grit from entering the system. Use two wrenches when loosening or tightening fittings to avoid kinking the metal refrigerant lines. If the fittings appear to be in good shape, you can probably get by with replacement of the O-ring seals or gaskets. Perform a leak test to check your work when the system is reassembled.If the connection still leaks, it's either faulty or damaged. Replace the hose, or hoses, of which it is a part.

3 **Faulty, porous or worn out hoses** — If the leak is due to a defective hose, or the fittings on either end of a hose, it must be replaced (see 'Replacing hoses and lines' below).

4 **Suction Throttling Valve (STV) diaphragm leak** — If the leak is traced to the Suction Throttling Valve (STV), the problem is probably a

All systems

To leak test a compressor:

A   *Remove the compressor and attach the high and low side hoses to the corresponding fittings on the compressor (some compressors may require an adapter plate to hook up the hoses to the compressor)*

B   *Attach the center gauge hose to a can of refrigerant*

C   *Open the low and high pressure manifold gauge valves and the valve on the refrigerant can, allowing refrigerant to flow into the compressor*

D   *Check for leaks with a leak detector — if leakage is present, the compressor must be rebuilt or replaced*

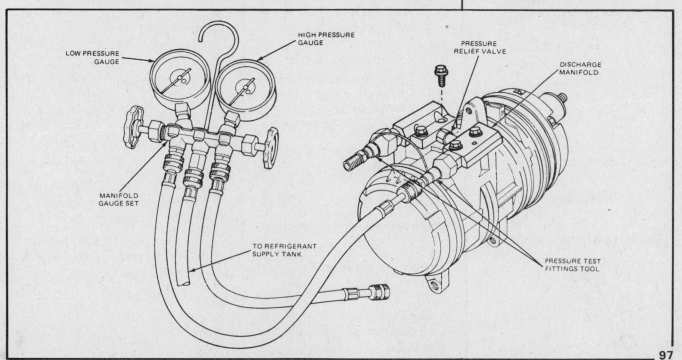

torn diaphragm. Older STV units have an adjustable, replaceable diaphragm. Later Pilot Operated Absolute (POA) type STVs don't have a replaceable diaphragm. They must be replaced with a new unit (see 'Replacing STV and EPR valves' later in this chapter).

5 Compressor seal leak — If the leak is at a compressor seal, the compressor must be rebuilt or replaced. Because of the large number of compressors in use on various systems and because of the large number of highly specialized, and different, tools necessary to rebuild each compressor, compressor overhaul is not covered in this book. We recommend that you exchange the old compressor for a new or rebuilt unit.

Repairing hoses

1 When attaching a fitting to a new hose, lubricate the hose and fitting with clean refrigerant oil. Do not use any other kind of lubricant.

2 Work the fitting into the hose end with a twisting motion. This helps to seat the locating beads or barbs in the hose. Fittings must be completely seated before use. If there's a locating bead on the fitting, push the fitting into the end of the hose until the bead is aligned with the end of the hose.

3 Install a hose clamp and tighten it securely. Some clamps have a locating tab which should be positioned against the end of the hose. Proper positioning of the hose and clamp ensures tightness.

Replacing hoses and lines

1 When disconnecting a fitting, thoroughly clean the area on both sides of the connection to prevent contaminants from entering the system.

2 Always use two wrenches (one as a back-up) when loosening a threaded fitting to prevent twisting the lines.

3 Cap off all hose ends immediately.

4 Manufacturers usually remove moisture from, then cap, all replacement hoses and lines. Do not remove the protective caps until the moment you install the part(s).

5 Replacement metal lines must be free of kinks. Inspect new lines when you buy them to ensure they are straight. Pack, stack or store them carefully to ensure that they aren't damaged between purchase and installation.

6 If the old lines are supported by brackets, make sure the new lines are attached to the same brackets. Failure to do so will most likely result in metal fatigue and cracks.

Expansion valve screen replacement

1 Discharge the system.

2 Detach the inlet line to the expansion valve from the condenser.

3 Remove the expansion valve from the evaporator.

4 The filter screen is located just inside the inlet passage. Remove and clean it thoroughly. If necessary, replace it.

5 No other service to the expansion valve is possible.

Defective fitting replacement

1 Cut off the defective fitting with a sharp knife by cutting through the hose behind the fitting clamp **(see illustration)**. Keep the hose ends square. (Discard the defective fitting and hose remnant.)

2 Inspect the shortened section of hose for adequate flexibility — it must not be so short that it will be stretched taut when the engine rolls and shakes during starting and at idle. Replace the old hose if necessary.

3 Slide the clamps onto the hose. Force the fitting into the hose with a rotating motion (you should be able to insert it rather easily by hand — don't use pliers, etc. or you could damage the fitting). Don't go past the shoulder on the fitting.

4 Position the clamps so the spacer bar is over the end of the hose. This puts clamping pressure at the proper location for a positive, leak-proof seal.

5 Tighten the clamp securely.

Defective hose replacement

1 Using a hacksaw, cut through the sleeve and the first wrap (layer) of bad hose **(see illustration)**.

2 Remove the sleeves and fittings from the hose. Discard the defective hose.

3 Cut the replacement hose to length with a sharp knife. Keep the hose ends square.

4 Assemble the original fittings to the hose with service band clamps.

5 Tighten the clamps securely.

Fitting O-rings

1 When disconnecting or connecting fittings between two metal tubes, be sure to use a backup wrench to prevent damage to the tubes.

2 After disconnecting the tubes, plug all openings immediately to prevent the entrance of dirt and moisture **(see illustration)**.

3 Discard all old O-rings.

4 Blow out all lines with refrigerant. Don't use compressed air.

5 When connecting the tubes, apply compressor oil to the portions shown **(see illustration)**. Avoid applying oil to the threaded portions.

6 Make sure the O-ring is securely butted against the raised portion of the tube.

7 Insert the tube into the fitting until the O-ring is no longer visible.

8 Tighten the nut securely.

9 After connecting the line and recharging the system, be sure to conduct a leak test and make sure the connections aren't leaking.

(A) REMOVE 1-3/4" OF HOSE WITH DEFECTIVE FITTING

(B) INSERT SERVICE FITTING

(C) ASSEMBLE WITH SERVICE CLAMP

Defective fitting replacement

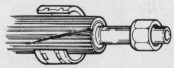

(A) SAW SLEEVE AND DEFECTIVE HOSE THROUGH FIRST WRAP

(B) REMOVE SLEEVE AND FITTING FROM HOSE

(C) REPLACE HOSE AND ASSEMBLE SAME FITTING WITH SERVICE BAND CLAMP

Defective hose replacement

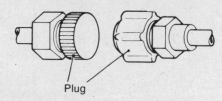

Plug

As soon as the tubes or hoses are disconnected, plug all openings to prevent dirt and moisture from contaminating them

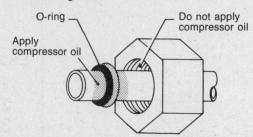

O-ring

Do not apply compressor oil

Apply compressor oil

When connecting the tubes, apply compressor oil to the shaded area and make sure that the O-ring is butted against the raised portion of the tube

Heating and air conditioning

R-134a hoses

As this revised edition went to press in Spring 1993, little information about the hoses used in R-134a systems was available. Here's what we know so far: The hoses used on R-134a systems look similar to those used in R-12 systems. Like R-12 hoses, they're made of reinforced rubber or thermoplastic. However, there is one major difference between the two: R-134a hoses are also lined with a nylon barrier that prevents HFCs from migrating through the hose wall. So don't try to use anything except R-134a hose for an R-134a system, or you'll lose refrigerant rapidly.

*ALSO SUPPLIED IN KIT E35Y-19D690-A WITH GARTER SPRINGS
† ALSO SUPPLIED IN KIT E1ZZ-19B596-A

O-RINGS — 3/8″ — 389157*†
1/2″ — 389158*†
5/8″ — 389623*
3/4″ — 390209-S

FEMALE FITTING
GARTER SPRING
MALE FITTING
CAGE

SPRING LOCK COUPLING DISCONNECTED

TO DISCONNECT COUPLING

CAUTION — DISCHARGE SYSTEM BEFORE DISCONNECTING COUPLING

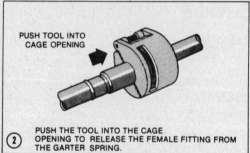

NOTE:
EACH END OF TOOL T81P-19623-G IS A DIFFERENT SIZE TO FIT 3/8 and 1/2 INCH COUPLINGS

TOOL
T81P-19623-G - 3/8 & 1/2 INCH
T81P-19623-G1 - 3/8 INCH
T81P-19623-G2 - 1/2 INCH
T83P-19623-C - 5/8 INCH
T85L-19623-A - 3/4 INCH

CAGE OPENING

① FIT TOOL TO COUPLING SO THAT TOOL CAN ENTER CAGE OPENING TO RELEASE THE GARTER SPRING.

TO CONNECT COUPLING

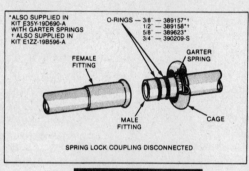

REPLACEMENT GARTER SPRINGS
3/8 INCH — E1ZZ-19E576-A*
1/2 INCH — E1ZZ-19E576-B*
5/8 INCH — E35Y-19E576-A*
3/4 INCH — E69Z-19E576-A
*ALSO AVAILABLE IN E35Y-19D690-A KIT WITH O-RINGS

GARTER SPRING

① CHECK FOR MISSING OR DAMAGED GARTER SPRING — REMOVE DAMAGED SPRING WITH SMALL HOOKED WIRE — INSTALL NEW SPRING IF DAMAGED OR MISSING.

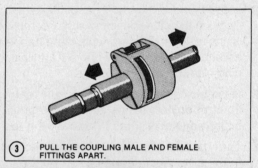

PUSH TOOL INTO CAGE OPENING

② PUSH THE TOOL INTO THE CAGE OPENING TO RELEASE THE FEMALE FITTING FROM THE GARTER SPRING.

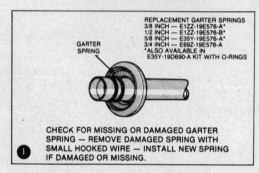

A — CLEAN FITTINGS
B — INSTALL NEW O-RINGS — USE ONLY SPECIFIED O-RINGS
C — LUBRICATE WITH CLEAN REFRIGERANT OIL
D — ASSEMBLE FITTING TOGETHER BY PUSHING WITH A SLIGHT TWISTING MOTION

②

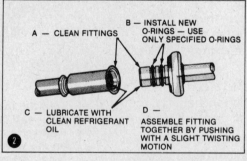

③ PULL THE COUPLING MALE AND FEMALE FITTINGS APART.

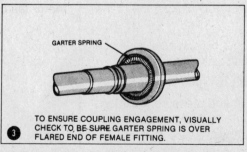

GARTER SPRING

③ TO ENSURE COUPLING ENGAGEMENT, VISUALLY CHECK TO BE SURE GARTER SPRING IS OVER FLARED END OF FEMALE FITTING.

④ REMOVE THE TOOL FROM THE DISCONNECTED SPRING LOCK COUPLING.

100   *Spring lock coupling*

Repairing Valves-In-Receiver (VIR) or evaporator equalized Valves-In-Receiver (EEVIR) units

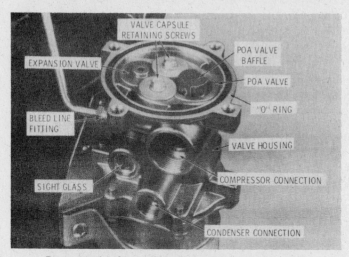

Remove the four inlet connector shell-to-valve housing screws and remove the shell from the assembly

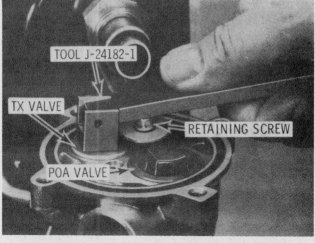

Insert the correct end of the capsule removal tool into the tapered groove projection on the expansion valve and press down on the tool to loosen the valve

Expansion valve/Pilot Operated Absolute (POA) valve replacement

1 Thoroughly clean the exterior of the VIR unit.

2 Detach all connections and mounting hardware.

3 Remove the four inlet connector shell-to-valve housing screws. Remove the shell from the assembly **(see illustration)**.

4 Clean the upper part of the valve housing. Don't scratch the sealing surface.

5 Loosen one of the valve capsule retaining screws. Remove the other retaining screw completely. If there is any residual refrigerant pressure trapped in the VIR assembly, the screw will prevent the valves from popping out and causing injury.

6 Insert the correct end of the capsule removal tool **(see illustration)** into the tapered groove projection on the expansion valve. Press down on the tool to loosen the valve.

7 Turn the tool around and insert the other end into the baffle for the POA valve. Again, press down on the tool to free the valve **(see illustration). Caution :** *Don't press down on the O-ring on top of the housing.*

8 Remove the other retaining screw and lift out both valves. Remove and discard the O-rings from the valves and valve cavities.

9 Coat the new O-rings with clean refrigerant oil. Install them.

10 Install the POA and expansion valves with thumb pressure. **Caution:** *Driving the valves into place with tools can damage them.*

11 Install the retaining screws and tighten them to 5 to 7 ft-lbs.

12 Install the inlet connector shell and the four shell-to-valve screws and tighten the screws securely.

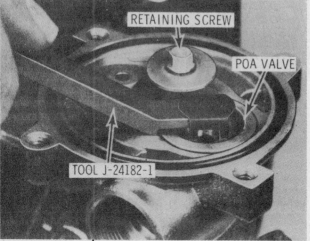

Turn the tool around and insert the other end into the baffle for the POA valve and press down again on the valve to free the valve (don't press down on the O-ring on top of the housing)

Desiccant bag replacement

1 Always replace the desiccant bag after replacing the expansion valve, POA valve and/or O-rings.

2 To get at the desiccant bag, remove the screws which attach the bottom receiver shell to the VIR housing. If the shell is stuck, bump it with your hand to free it from the housing. **Caution:** *Do not pry the receiver shell free with a tool.*

3 Lower the shell carefully to clear the pick-up tube. Remove the old desiccant bag.

4 If the receiver shell has an O-ring, remove and discard it. Drain, measure and discard any refrigerant oil present in the shell.

5 Remove the pick-up tube screen and clean the screen and the inside of the shell with solvent. Wipe it completely dry with a lint free cloth.

6 Replace the pick-up tube screen.

7 Install a new desiccant bag.

8 Replace the oil that was removed, measured and discarded with an equal amount of clean refrigerant oil, then add 1 additional ounce.

9 Place the shell back in position and attach it to the housing. Install the shell screws and tighten them to 5 to 7 foot pounds.

Receiver-drier or desiccant replacement

Unlike VIR and EEVIR type receivers, other receiver-drier units are usually sealed units and cannot be repaired. If the system becomes saturated with moisture (during, for example, a major leak), the receiver-drier must be replaced.

To quickly check a suspect receiver-drier, feel the unit and the inlet and outlet hoses or lines. Unlike Ford and General Motors accumulator type systems, the receiver-drier is located on the high side of the system, so it should feel hot to the touch when the system is operating. A cool receiver-drier or lines showing condensation indicate some sort of malfunction (a restriction, for example).

Replace the receiver-drier:

a) When a major leak (broken hose, loose connections, accident damage, etc.) allows ambient air and moisture to enter the system.

b) When the system is opened for a lengthy period of time without being capped.

c) When the sight glass turns cloudy (the desiccant has broken down and is flowing through the system).

d) When the expansion valve is replaced (expansion valve malfunctions are usually caused by moisture in the system).

e) When the Suction Throttling Valve (STV), Pilot Operated Absolute (POA), Evaporator Pressure Regulator (EPR) or expansion valve is replaced (each of these components usually malfunctions when moisture enters the system).

f) When the normally warm or hot outlet lines from the receiver-drier are cool during system operation (excessive moisture build-up near the receiver-drier causes formation of condensation on the hoses, indicating a restriction).

g) When too much refrigerant oil (more than 5-ounces) accumulates in the receiver-drier (this indicates that the oil bleed hole is clogged and it usually causes poor system performance).

Accumulator replacement

The accumulator, which is is connected to the evaporator inlet pipe on General Motors and Ford Motor Company accumulator type systems, performs the same functions as the receiver-drier. If the accumulator malfunctions, it must be replaced. It cannot be serviced. Typical accumulator malfunctions are caused by:

a) Leaks.
b) A restricted orifice tube or compressor inlet screen.
c) An internally corroded evaporator.
d) Saturated desiccant (desiccant alone can't be replaced).

The procedure for replacing the accumulator in specific vehicles is included in Haynes owners' workshop manuals. However, the following general procedure should enable you to replace the accumulator on a vehicle if you don't have the Haynes manual.

1 Detach the cable from the negative terminal of the battery.

2 Discharge the system (minimizing oil loss as much as possible) as outlined previously.

3 Disconnect the accumulator inlet and outlet lines and cap all openings to prevent contamination of the system by dirt or moisture. **Note:** *On some 1981 and later Ford Motor Company vehicles, the suction hose must be disconnected at the compressor because the line is not removable at the accumulator.*

4 If the accumulator has a pressure sensing switch, remove it and transfer it to the new accumulator.

5 Remove the accumulator mounting bracket screws and lift the accumulator from the engine compartment.

6 Pour 1-ounce of fresh, clean refrigerant oil into the new accumulator before installing it.

7 Installation is the reverse of removal.

Orifice tube (expansion tube) replacement

The accumulator type systems used in some Ford Motor Company and General Motors vehicles have a fixed orifice tube (expansion tube) instead of a standard expansion valve. The orifice tube is located in the line between the condenser and the evaporator (it's usually at the evaporator inlet; on some newer Ford vehicles, it's in the liquid line).

Because it's a relatively inexpensive part, the orifice tube assembly is normally replaced as a routine service procedure every time the system is opened for servicing. Orifice tube replacement is mandatory, however, when a clog causes a high side restriction or whenever a failed compressor is replaced. **Caution:** *NEVER clean and reinstall a used orifice tube — it could seriously damage the system.*

1 Discharge the system as previously outlined.

2 Disconnect the high side line from the evaporator. Remove and discard any O-rings, if equipped.

3 Pour a small amount of refrigerant oil into the inlet to lubricate the tube O-rings.

Heating and air conditioning

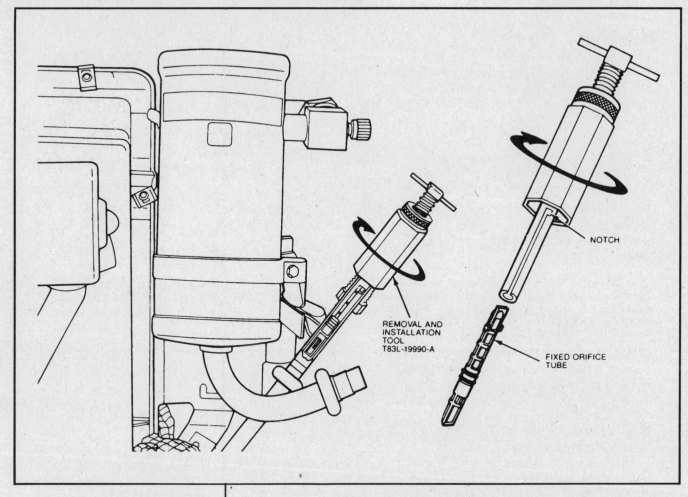

NOTCH

REMOVAL AND
INSTALLATION
TOOL
T83L-19990-A

FIXED ORIFICE
TUBE

Insert the special tool into the tube, turn the tool clockwise to engage the tangs on the tube, then turn tool nut slowly to avoid breaking the orifice tube during removal

4 Insert the special tool **(see illustration)** into the tube. Turn the tool clockwise to engage the tangs on the tube. Turn the tool nut slowly to avoid breaking the orifice tube during removal. **Note:** *If the orifice tube breaks off during removal, you'll have to obtain a special broken orifice tube tool to extract the broken section. If the special tool fails to extract the tube, a special repair kit is available for some systems.*

5 Lubricate the new O-ring(s) on the new orifice tube with clean refrigerant oil.

6 Insert the new orifice tube into the evaporator inlet pipe with the short end of the tube facing the evaporator. Push the tube in until it's seated.

7 Reconnect the high side line.

8 Recharge the system as previously outlined.

Suction Throttling Valve (STV) and Evaporator Pressure Regulator (EPR) valve replacement

Suction Throttling Valves (STVs) are found on the low side of some Ford and General Motors systems. Expansion Pressure Regulator (EPR) valves are located beneath the inlet fitting on Chrysler twin-cylinder compressors.

1 Discharge the system as previously outlined.

2 Disconnect all lines from the STV assembly. On Chrysler EPR systems, detach the inlet fitting from the compressor.

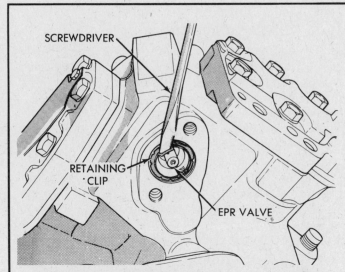

To replace an EPR valve, remove the retaining clip and pry out the valve (some valves can even be removed by simply grasping the center shaft of the valve and pulling it out — others may require a special extraction tool)

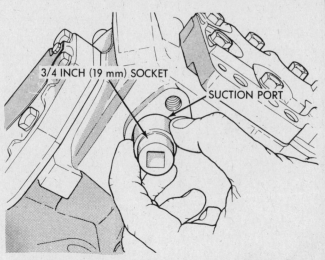

To install a new EPR valve, use a 3/4-inch or 19mm socket and carefully tap the valve into place

3 To replace an STV unit, simply unscrew it from the mount and install a new one.

4 To replace an EPR valve:

a) Remove the retaining clip.

b) Some EPR valves can be extracted by grasping the center shaft of the valve.

c) A special tool (see illustration) may be required to remove other valves from the compressor cavity.

5 Recharge the system after the STV or EPR valve is replaced.

Combination by-pass orifice (BPO) expansion valve and suction throttling valve (STV) replacement

Some Ford Motor Company systems feature a combination by-pass orifice (BPO) expansion valve and suction throttling valve (STV).

1 Discharge the system as previously outlined.

2 Disconnect the two refrigerant lines from the STV housing manifold tube assembly.

3 Remove the two mounting bolts and detach the BPO expansion valve and STV housing manifold and tube assembly from the evaporator manifold plate.

4 Remove the two socket head screws that attach the STV housing manifold to the expansion valve body.

5 Using a special wrench or a pair of curved jaw channel-lock pliers, grasp the STV body near the tapered end. Remove it by turning it counterclockwise.

6 Remove and discard the STV O-ring from the expansion valve body. Be sure to install a new one.

7 Installation is the reverse of removal.

Heating and air conditioning

Compressor reed valve replacement

If moisture has entered the system, reed valve corrosion is a common compressor problem. On the compressor models included below, reed valve replacement is a relatively straightforward procedure.

However, some common compressor units are not included here. On some Harrison (Frigidaire) compressors (the four-cylinder R-4, five-cylinder V5 and the six-cylinder A6 and DA-6), for instance, the reed valves cannot be replaced unless the compressor is overhauled. But because of the number of special tools required, and the difficulty of including accurate, up-to-date overhaul procedures for every compressor, the procedures for compressor overhaul are not included in this book. If reed valve replacement is indicated and your compressor is not included below, exchange it for a rebult unit.

Chrysler, Tecumseh and York two-cylinder and Sanden (Sankyo) five-cylinder units

1 Thoroughly clean the compressor.

2 Discharge the system.

3 Remove the head bolts and service valves (if equipped) from the compressor (note the location of any long head bolts — usually at the service valves).

4 Gently pry or tap under the tabs extending from the head plate to free it from the compressor body. Remove the head plate(s). Wrap the head(s) in a clean cloth while it's off.

5 Remove the reed valve assemblies.

6 Remove all old gasket material from the compressor body, the head and the service valve mount. Use extreme care to avoid scratching the mating surfaces.

7 Coat a new gasket with clean refrigerant oil and position it on the compressor body (use the alignment pins, if present).

8 Install the replacement reed valve assemblies. **Caution:** *Be sure the discharge valves are facing up (you can tell the two apart because the discharge valves are smaller than the suction valves).*

9 Using the alignment pins (if present), install the head(s) on the compressor.

10 If the compressor is equipped with service valves, lubricate the new valve O-rings and install the service valves and O-rings.

11 Tighten the head bolts in a criss-cross pattern and work from the inside to the outside edge of the head(s). If service valves are installed on the compressor head, tighten those bolts first.

Chrysler C-171 and Ford FS-6 6-cylinder compressors

1 Discharge the system.

2 Remove the compressor from the vehicle.

3 Remove the clutch assembly (see clutch coil replacement later in this chapter).

4 Pour the refrigerant oil in the compressor into a calibrated container and note the amount.

5 Cap the openings and thoroughly clean the compressor.

6 Mount the compressor in a vise or special holding fixture.

7 Remove the bolts and the front and/or rear head assembly, dowel pins, gaskets, plate and reed assembly.

Installation

8 Clean all parts with solvent and blow them dry with clean compressed air.

9 Lubricate all parts with clean refrigerant oil.

10 Install the dowel alignment pins, the reed assembly, the plate, the gaskets and the head(s) in the opposite order in which they were removed.

11 Using new brass washers (if originally equipped), tighten the through bolts.

12 Add fresh refrigerant oil (see 'Compressor oil check' later in this chapter).

13 Install the clutch assembly.

14 Install the compressor.

Nippondenso 10-cylinder compressor

1 Remove the magnetic clutch assembly.

2 Remove the service valve and drain the compressor oil.

3 Remove and discard the O-rings in the service valve.

4 Remove the shaft seal assembly.

5 Remove the through bolts. Discard the washers.

6 Remove the front housing by tapping on the protrusion with a hammer and punch. Be careful not to scratch the sealing surface of the rear housing.

7 Remove the front and rear O-rings from the cylinder block.

8 Clean and inspect the front and rear valve plates for scratched, bent or otherwise damaged parts. Replace any damaged parts.

9 Clean and inspect both cylinder heads and both valve plate assemblies for nicks or burrs on the sealing surfaces. Replace any damaged parts.

10 Make sure that all passages in the valve plate are unobstructed. If either the cylinder head or the valve plate is cracked, it must be replaced.

11 Install the two pins in the rear cylinder.

12 Lubricate the new rear cylinder O-ring with compressor oil and install it in the rear cylinder.

13 Install the rear suction valve over the pins on the rear cylinder (the front and rear suction valves are identical).

14 Install the rear valve plate together with the discharge valve over the pins on the rear cylinder (Note that the rear valve plate is marked with an 'R').

15 Lubricate the gasket with compressor oil and install it on the valve plate.

16 Install the rear housing on the rear cylinder.

17 Install the two pins in the front cylinder.

18 Lubricate the new rear housing O-ring with compressor oil and install it in the rear housing.

Heating and air conditioning

19 Install the front suction valve over the pins on the front cylinder.

20 Install the front valve plate and the discharge valve over the pins on the front cylinder.

21 Lubricate the new gasket with compressor oil and install it on the valve plate.

22 Install the front housing on the front cylinder and tighten the six through bolts in two or three passes to 19 ft-lbs.

23 Check the compressor shaft rotating torque. It should be 16 in-lbs.

24 Install the shaft seal assembly.

25 Fill the compressor with Denso oil 6, Suniso No. 5GS or equivalent.

26 Install the service valve with the new O-ring and tighten it to 19 ft-lbs.

27 Install the magnetic clutch assembly.

Compressor oil check

The oil level on some compressors can be checked and topped up with the compressor installed. Other units must be removed before oil can be measured or added. Unless the compressor can be isolated (in other words, is equipped with stem-type service valves), the system must be discharged first. Only those compressors which can be checked for oil level are included in this chapter. But first, here's a list of some DOs and DON'Ts pertinent to oil level checks and oil replacement:

Caution: *Do not interchange lubricating oils. R-134a systems use polyalkalyne glycol (PAG), which is incompatible with R-12 systems.*

a) **Always use new, moisture-free refrigerant oil.** This oil is highly refined and dehydrated. Its container must be kept tightly closed at all times unless you're using it. If the container is allowed to remain open even for a short time, moisture will be absorbed from the atmosphere and introduced into the system.

b) **Always run the engine and system for 10 minutes** to allow proper oil distribution through the system.

c) **If the oil level in the compressor is checked with a dipstick,** each ounce of new refrigerant oil added to the compressor will raise the dipstick reading approximately 1/4-inch.

d) **Always replace the oil plug sealing gasket or O-ring.**

e) **If you use 'charging cans' to add oil to the system,** the procedure for adding oil is identical to that for adding refrigerant. The can capacity most commonly used for adding oil this way is 4 ounces. But bear in mind that only 2 ounces of each can is oil. The other 2 ounces is refrigerant.

Rule of thumb guide for adding oil to individual components

If no major oil loss has occurred, and if only a single component must be replaced, oil can be added to the system by putting it into a specific component. Use the amounts shown below:

Condenser — 1 ounce
Receiver-drier — 1 ounce
Desiccant bag in VIR — 1 ounce plus the amount drained from the receiver-drier
Evaporator — 3 ounces

Accumulator
   a) Ford — 1 ounce plus the amount measured
   b) General Motors
      1) DA-6 — 3 ounces plus the amount measured
      2) A-6, R-4 or V5 — 2 ounces plus the amount measured

It's important to note that, since oil distributes itself throughout the system during operation, it isn't absolutely necessary to add the oil to the component being replaced. With one notable exception, as long as the amount of oil lost during the replacement procedure is added somewhere, the system will be fine. The exception? The compressor. *If the compressor is being replaced, always put the oil into the compressor and not somewhere else.*

Chrysler, Tecumseh and York two-cylinder compressors

1 Obtain a dipstick or fabricate one **(see illustration)**.

2 Discharge the system (or isolate the compressor, if equipped with stem-type service valves).

3 Remove the oil filler plug. **Caution:** *Loosen the plug very slowly — there may be residual crankcase pressure.*

4 Clean the dipstick.

5 Insert the dipstick and check the oil level. **Note:** *You may have to rotate the dipstick to be sure it clears the crankshaft.*

6 Add oil, if necessary, to bring it to the specified level.

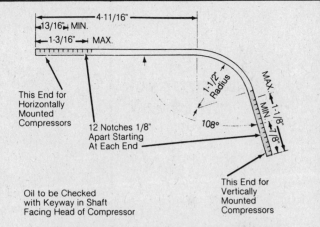

York 2-Cylinder Compressor Oil level Dipstick

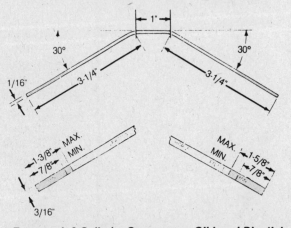

Tecumseh 2-Cylinder Compressor Oil Level Dipstick

Dipstick with Standard Sump (1968 and Earlier)

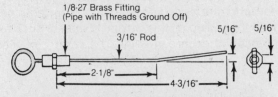

Dipstick with Stepped Sump (1968 and Later)

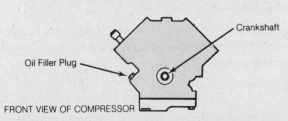

Oil Filler Plug Location on Chrysler 2-Cylinder Compressor

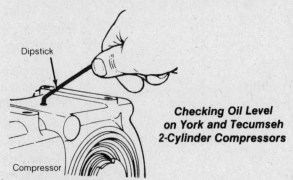

Checking Oil Level on York and Tecumseh 2-Cylinder Compressors

Heating and air conditioning

Harrison (Frigidaire) A-6 six-cylinder compressor

1 If you're replacing either the accumulator or the compressor, or find evidence of excessive oil loss, remove the accumulator and the compressor, then drain, measure and replace the oil.

   a) If the amount of oil measured from the accumulator and compressor is 6 ounces or more, add the same amount of new oil plus 2 ounces to replace the amount captured in the desiccant of the old accumulator.

   b) If the amount recovered is less than 6 ounces, add 6 ounces of new oil plus 2 ounces to replace the amount captured in the desiccant of the old accumulator.

Note: *Normally, a system will have 6 ounces of oil in the accumulator and/or compressor together. Neither unit will necessarily have 3 ounces or all 6 ounces, so both units must be measured.*

2 New compressors are normally supplied with fresh oil already inside them, but don't assume that it's the correct amount. If a new compressor is being installed, drain and measure the oil inside it before installing it. Add only the specified amount to the compressor.

3 If the old compressor is inoperable, use the following rule of thumb measurements:

   a) If the amount drained and measured is more than 1-1/2 ounces and the system shows no signs of major oil loss, add the same amount as drained to the new compressor or that amount plus an additional ounce for a new or rebuilt compressor.

   b) If the amount of oil drained is less than 1-1/2 ounces, and the system appears to have lost oil, add 6 ounces to the new or rebuilt compressor, or add 7 ounces to the old compressor after it has been overhauled.

Note: *If the oil drained from the system contains metal chips or other foreign material, remove the receiver-drier, flush the system and install a new receiver-drier or accumulator (and any other components that may have been damaged).*

Harrison (Frigidaire) R-4 four-cylinder compressor

The Harrison (Frigidaire) compressor is charged, when new, with 6 ounces of refrigeration oil. Because it doesn't have an oil sump, and retains very little oil, it doesn't normally have to be removed for oil level measurement. **Caution:** *Since this compressor has no sump, it must be well lubricated. If it runs dry, it will quickly self destruct.*

There are several conditions which warrant checking and adding oil to this compressor:

1 When replacing components (even if no oil leak is noted):

   a) If only the compressor is being replaced — remove, drain, measure and add the correct amount of new oil.

   b) If the evaporator is being replaced, add 3 ounces.

   c) If the condenser is being replaced, add 1 ounce.

2 When there is a loss of refrigerant over a period of time, (and a component is being replaced to correct the leak), add refrigerant oil to the component in accordance with the amount previously specified in the 'Rule-of-thumb guide for adding oil to individual components.'

3 When there's evidence of a major oil leak — If the system loses excessive oil, remove the accumulator, then drain and measure the oil.

a) If more than 3 ounces is measured, put in the same amount of new oil as you drained, plus an extra 2 ounces of new oil to compensate for that lost by replacing the accumulator (held by the desiccant).

b) If less than 3 ounces is measured, add 3 ounces of new oil, plus an additional 2 ounces of new oil to compensate for that lost by replacing the accumulator (held by the desiccant).

Caution: *If oil drained from the accumulator (or any other component) contains metal chips or other foreign particles, repair or replace the defective component, flush the entire system and add 6 ounces of new refrigerant oil to the compressor suction port. And be sure to replace the accumulator — if the desiccant bag has trapped any of the particles, they will circulate in the restored system, causing further damage.*

4 When the system oil level is unknown or system performance and efficiency are marginal, drain and flush the system and add a new 6 ounce charge of refrigerant oil to the system.

Harrison (Delco Air) DA-6 six-cylinder compressor

Like the Harrison (Frigidaire) described above, the Delco Air compressor has no sump, so it doesn't have to be removed for oil measurement. Check or add oil under the following conditions:

1 Components being replaced, but no evidence of excessive oil leakage

a) If the compressor is being replaced, remove it, then drain and measure the oil. Add the same amount of new oil plus an extra ounce.

b) If the evaporator is being replaced, add 3 ounces of new oil.

c) If the condenser is being replaced, add 1 ounce of new oil.

d) If the accumulator is being replaced, remove, drain and measure the old oil. Replace it with the same amount of new oil, plus 3 ounces to compensate for the oil held by the desiccant. If no oil can be drained from the old accumulator, add 2 ounces of new oil.

2 Evidence of excessive oil leakage

a) Remove the accumulator, drain the oil and measure (the DA-6 itself only holds a minimum amount of refrigeration oil because it has no sump).

b) If the amount recovered is less than 3 ounces, add 3 ounces of new oil to the system.

c) If the amount recovered is more than 3 ounces, add an amount of oil equal to that drained from the old accumulator.

Note: *If a new accumulator must be added to the DA-6 system, add an additonal 3 ounces of oil to compensate for that retained by the original accumulator desiccant.*

Harrison V5 five-cylinder compressor

1 When the compressor is removed from the vehicle for service, drain the oil from the drain plug opening to insure an accurate measurement. Measure the oil, then discard it. Add an equal amount of new oil.

2 The V5 compressor has a unique lubrication system. The crankcase suction bleed is routed through the rotating swashplate to lubricate the swashplate bearing. The rotation of the swashplate separates the oil, removing some of it from the crankcase-suction bleed and rerouting it to the crankcase where it can lubricate the compressor mechanism.

Heating and air conditioning

3 Up to 4 ounces of oil can collect in the crankcase. But new or rebuilt compressors may be shipped from the factory with up to 8 ounces of oil in the crankcase. Drain the oil from the drain plug opening, measure it and put back in an amount equal to that drained and measured from the old compressor. **Note:** *If a new accumulator is being added to the system, put an additional 2 ounces of oil into the compressor to compensate for the oil retained by the desiccant in the old accumulator.*

Sanden (Sankyo) five-cylinder compressor

1 Start the engine and run the system for 5 minutes. Make sure the compressor cycles on during this time. Turn off the system and stop the engine.

2 Clean the dipstick and allow it to cool down.

3 Remove the compressor and place it on a workbench. Position the compressor with the oil fill plug at top dead center (TDC).

4 Thoroughly clean the oil fill plug and the area around it to prevent dirt from contaminating the compressor.

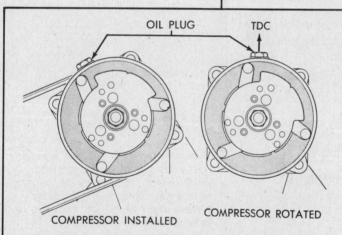

When you put the compressor on the workbench, make sure that the oil filler plug is at the top

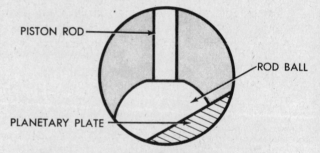

To verify that the hub plate lobe and index notch are aligned, look through the oil fill hole and verify that the ball end of the top piston rod lines up with the fill hole

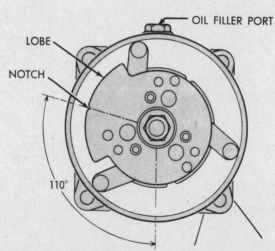

Rotate the hub plate lobe until the index notch is 110° from bottom dead center

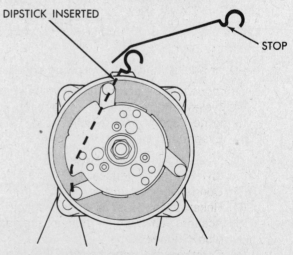

Insert the dipstick diagonally from the upper left to the lower left until the dipstick stop contacts the filler hole surface

5 Slowly loosen the fill plug to allow any residual refrigerant pressure to escape.

6 The front plate hub has a lobe which is indexed with a notch at 180° from TDC of the cam rotor. Rotate the hub plate lobe until the index notch is 110° from bottom center **(see illustration)**. Check this position by looking through the oil fill hole and noting that the ball end of the top piston rod lines up with the fill hole.

7 Looking at the front of the compressor, insert the dipstick diagonally from the upper left to the lower left until the dipstick stop contacts the filler hole surface. Remove the dipstick and note the oil level. It should be between the 4th and 6th increments on the dipstick (3 to 4 ounces). Add oil as necessary.

8 If system components are being replaced, add refrigerant oil in accordance with the amounts specified in the 'Rule of thumb guide for adding oil to individual components.'

Chrysler C-171, Ford FS-6 and Nippondenso six-cylinder compressors

1 Some of these compressors have drain plugs **(see illustration)**. After removing the oil, install the plug with a new O-ring. If there is no drain plug, discharge the system, remove the compressor, turn it upside down and drain the oil out of the suction and discharge ports.

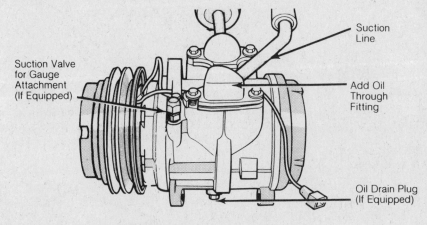

Suction Line

Suction Valve for Gauge Attachment (If Equipped)

Add Oil Through Fitting

Oil Drain Plug (If Equipped)

If the compressor on your vehicle has a drain plug, remove it and drain the oil, then reinstall the plug with a new O-ring — if it doesn't have a drain plug, you will have to remove the compressor, turn it unside down and drain the oil out of the suction and discharge ports

2 Check or add oil under the following conditions:

a) *Component replacement, no evidence of oil leakage* — Discharge the system and replace the component. Add new refrigeration oil to the new component as follows:

  1) Evaporator

    (a) Chrysler — 2 ounces
    (b) Ford — 3 ounces

  2) Condenser — 1 ounce
  3) Receiver-drier (Chrysler) — 1 ounce
  4) Accumulator (Ford) — amount drained from old accumulator plus 1 ounce
  5) Compressor — see below

b) *Component replacement, evidence of oil leakage* — Slowly discharge the system, repair or replace the faulty component, drain the oil from the compressor and remove the suction port fitting. Add

new refrigeration oil to the new component as follows:
1) Chrysler — 9 to 10 ounces
2) Ford

    (a) 1981 vehicles — 13 ounces
    (b) 1982 to 1987 vehicles — 10 ounces

c) *Compressor replacement*
1) Discharge the system.
2) Remove the compressor.
3) Drain, measure and record the amount of oil in the old compressor, then discard it.

    (a) *Replacement compressors for Chrysler vehicles* contain 9 to 10 ounces of oil. If the system has been discharged and flushed, they may be installed without an oil level check. If only the compressor is being replaced, drain the oil from the new compressor; even if more than 6 ounces are removed, pour no more than 6 ounces into the new compressor.

    (b) Drain the oil from *replacement compressors for 1981 Ford vehicles* and add new oil in proportion to the amount removed from the old compressor. If less than 3 ounces were removed from the old compressor, add 6 ounces to the new compressor. If 3 to 6 ounces were removed, pour the same amount into the new compressor. If more than 6 ounces were drained, put no more than 6 ounces into the new compressor.

    (c) *Compressors for 1982 to 1987 Ford vehicles* are charged with 10 ounces of oil. Drain 4 ounces from the new compressor before installing it.

Tecumseh HR980 4-cylinder compressor

This compressor must be charged with 8 ounces of refrigeration oil. But if a component is removed from the system, some oil will be lost. Add oil to the system as follows:

1 Compressor replacement — A new compressor is already charged with 8 ounces of refrigerant oil. Before installing the compressor, drain 4 ounces from the new compressor. This maintains the system total charge within the 8 ounce limit.

2 Component replacement

a) Evaporator — 3 ounces
b) Accumulator — Drain oil from the accumulator through the Schrader valve of the pressure sensing switch fitting. Measure the amount of oil removed and add that amount plus 1 ounce to the new accumulator.

York rotary vane compressor

1 Run the system for 10 minutes, then stop the engine.

2 Discharge the system (slowly, to prevent oil from escaping).

3 Remove the suction and discharge hoses.

4 Rotate the compressor shaft by hand in a counterclockwise direction for 10 revolutions.

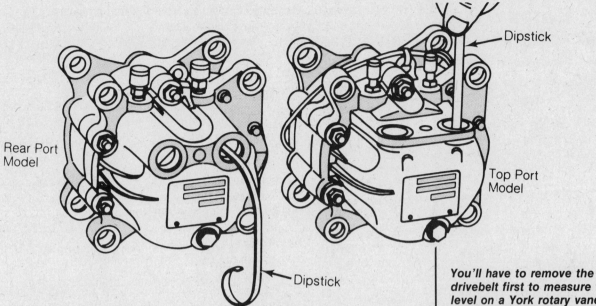

Rear Port Model

Top Port Model

Dipstick

Dipstick

You'll have to remove the drivebelt first to measure the oil level on a York rotary vane compressor installed on the vehicle

5 If the compressor is on the vehicle, remove the drivebelt and tilt the compressor until the suction and discharge ports are level. Using a dipstick **(see illustration)**, measure the oil level.

6 If the compressor is removed from the vehicle, drain the oil from the sump and from the suction and discharge ports.

a) If the oil measures less than 2 ounces, replace it with 2 ounces of fresh oil.

b) If there are more than 2 ounces, replace the oil with an equal amount of fresh oil.

7 If any system components are being replaced, add refrigerant oil to them in accordance with the 'Rule of thumb guide for adding oil to individual components.'

8 If there is any evidence that a major leak has occurred, flush the system, then add oil in the following amounts:

a) If the refrigerant charge capacity is under 2 pounds — 6 ounces.

b) If the charge is up to 3 pounds — 7 ounces.

c) If the charge is more than 3 pounds — 8 ounces.

9 Inspect the O-rings on the suction and discharge fittings and coat them with clean refrigerant oil before installing the lines.

Nippondenso 10-cylinder compressor

1 Discharge the system.

2 Remove the compressor.

3 Remove the service valve assembly.

4 Turn the compressor upside down and drain the oil.

5 Refill the compressor with 2.0 to 3.4 ounces of Denso oil 6, Suniso No. 5GS or an equivalent compressor oil **(see illustration)**.

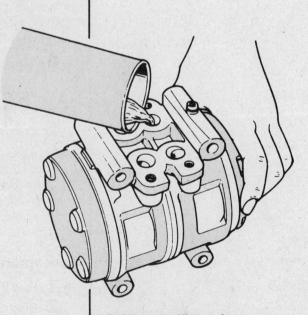

Refilling the Nippondenso 10-cylinder compressor

Heating and air conditioning

Evacuating and recharging the system

Once the system has been opened up for repairs or component replacement, or has been found to be excessively low on refrigerant, it must be completely evacuated with a vacuum pump to remove all traces of moisture before a new refrigerant charge is added.

Any amount of moisture is very harmful to air conditioning systems. Moisture reacts with refrigerant to form hydrochloric acid (HCL), which damages the system's internal components. That's why every system is equipped with either a receiver-drier or an accumulator to trap and retain the moisture that invariably infiltrates the system. You will recall from Chapter 1 that air contains moisture. So even the smallest leak will allow air and moisture into the system.

Moisture can collect and freeze in the orifice of the expansion valve, restricting the flow of refrigerant. And it can do the same thing in a system equipped with a suction throttling valve (STV) or evaporator pressure regulator (EPR) valve. In fact, it can block the flow of refrigerant through any orifice in the system. Obviously, moisture must be prevented from entering the system. Once it gets in, the desiccant in the receiver-drier or accumulator is the system's only means of removing it.

Note: *The recharging information included here is intended for R-12 systems only.*

Vacuum pumps

The basic tool for removing air and moisture from a system is the vacuum pump (see Chapter 4 for detailed descriptions of the various types of vacuum pumps). A vacuum pump simply lowers the pressure inside the system to a vacuum condition. When the system reaches a vacuum condition, the boiling point of any water in the system is also lowered, eventually to a point at which it can easily evaporate. This vaporized moisture is then sucked out of the system by the vacuum pump.

Recall from Chapter 1 that water boils at 212°F at sea level (14.7 psi). When evacuating the system, the boiling point of water in the system must be lowered to a point at which it is lower than the ambient temperature (the air temperature surrounding the vehicle). At an ambient temperature of 75°F, a vacuum pump must draw a vacuum of at least 29.5 in-Hg to lower the boiling point of water to 72°F. A vacuum of 29.5 in-Hg applied to a typical system for about 30 minutes will produce complete evacuation.

Altitude

Of course, it's impossible to obtain a vacuum reading of 29.5 in-Hg at any altitude above sea level. For each 1000 feet of altitude, the vacuum gauge must be corrected by 1 in-Hg to compensate for the change in atmospheric pressure. For example, a gauge reading of 24.5 in-Hg will have the same results at 5000 feet as 29.5 in-Hg has at sea level. (See Chapter 4 for a detailed description of the effect of altitude on vacuum.)

Caution: *Don't attempt to use the air conditioning system compressor as a vacuum pump. Refrigerant oil circulates with the refrigerant, which has a high attraction for the oil. The system compressor depends on smooth, constant oil distribution for proper operation. The compressor must not be used for evacuation because the oil cannot be properly circulated while the system is being evacuated and a low level of refrigerant oil will cause internal damage.*

Evacuating a non-accumulator type system

Note: *The following procedure DOES NOT apply to accumulator type systems such as Ford's Fixed Orifice Tube (FFOT) system or General Motors' Cycling Clutch Orifice Tube (CCOT) system. A special service procedure for these systems is discussed later in this chapter.*

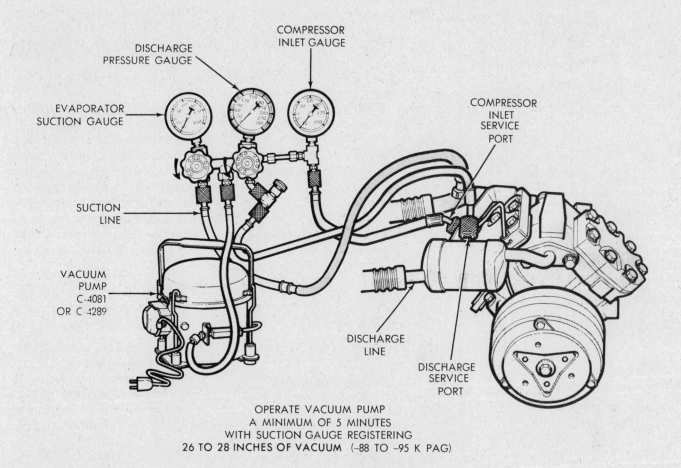

DISCHARGE
PRESSURE GAUGE

COMPRESSOR
INLET GAUGE

EVAPORATOR
SUCTION GAUGE

COMPRESSOR
INLET
SERVICE
PORT

SUCTION
LINE

VACUUM
PUMP
C-4081
OR C-4289

DISCHARGE
LINE

DISCHARGE
SERVICE
PORT

OPERATE VACUUM PUMP
A MINIMUM OF 5 MINUTES
WITH SUCTION GAUGE REGISTERING
26 TO 28 INCHES OF VACUUM (–88 TO –95 K PAG)

1 The system must be fully discharged and the test gauges must still be attached.

2 Attach the center service hose of the manifold gauge set to the inlet fitting of the vacuum pump in accordance with the pump manufacturer's instructions (see Chapter 4 for more information regarding the pump) **(see illustration)**.

3 Open the discharge valve on the vacuum pump, or remove the dust cap (if equipped) from the discharge outlet.

4 Start the vacuum pump.

5 Open the low and high side manifold hand valves all the way. Observe the low side gauge and verify that the pump draws the system down to a vacuum.

6 After about 5 minutes, note the indicated high and low side gauge readings:

    a) The low side gauge should indicate a system vacuum of 20 in-Hg or less.

    b) The high side gauge should read slightly below the zero mark on the gauge. If it doesn't, the gauge needle may be pegged against the stop. If the needle has no stop, there is a restriction in the system and evacuation cannot be continued until the restriction is located and removed.

The proper setup for evacuating the typical non-accumulator system (Chrysler shown, others similar) — note that the center service hose of the manifold gauge set is attached to the inlet fitting of the vacuum pump

Heating and air conditioning

7 After the system has been pulled down to its lowest vacuum point, close the high side valve on the manifold gauge set and turn off the vacuum pump, then note the reading on the low side gauge. Let the system stand for 5 minutes or longer and then recheck the reading on the low side gauge again.

a) If the system has lost vacuum, a leak exists. Charge the system, find the leak, repair as necessary and repeat the procedure.

b) If the reading is the same, there is no leak. Start the vacuum pump and open both hand valves. Operate the pump for 30 minutes. Then close both hand valves, turn off the vacuum pump and detach the service hose from the pump. Connect the service hose to a refrigerant supply and completely charge the system in accordance with the instructions below.

Charging (non-accumulator type systems)

Note: *The following procedure DOES NOT apply to accumulator type systems, such as Ford's Fixed Orifice Tube (FFOT) system or General Motors' Cycling Clutch Orifice Tube (CCOT) system. A special service procedure for these systems is discussed later in this chapter.*

After all indicated repairs have been made, the compressor oil level has been checked and adjusted as necessary and the system has been evacuated to remove all air and moisture, the air conditioning system should be fully charged as described below. **Note:** *If the vehicle is a General Motors model with a Low Refrigerant Protection System consisting of a thermal limiter and superheat switch, the thermal limiter must be bypassed during charging. Disconnect the thermal limiter and connect a jumper wire between terminals B and C. This will prevent the limiter from blowing because of a low refrigerant condition.*

From a bulk container

1 Purge the air from the charging hose by loosening the fitting at the manifold center connection.

2 Slowly open the refrigerant supply valve and allow refrigerant to escape through the loose connection for a few seconds, then retighten the connection and close the canister valve.

3 With the engine and air conditioning system turned off, open the high side hand valve. Note the low side gauge reading, then close the high side hand valve. If the low side gauge needle doesn't move out of the vacuum range (indicating pressure), the system is restricted. Locate and repair the restriction and evacuate the system before proceeding with the charging procedure.

4 Make sure both hand valves are closed. Start the engine and stabilize the air conditioning system. Run the engine at 1250 rpm for 5 minutes with the temperature controls set to the maximum cooling position and the blower switch on the highest setting.

5 Place the refrigerant canister on a scale, in an upright position and note its exact weight.

6 Open the valve on the bulk refrigerant container and the low side hand valve on the manifold and begin charging the system with refrigerant vapor. **Caution:** *Don't allow liquid refrigerant to enter the compressor (high) side of the system. Serious damage will result because liquid cannot be compressed.*

7 Monitor the weight change indicated on the scale. When the scale reading matches the specified amount, close the valves. **Note:** *If the capacity is not specified, add refrigerant until it just passes the sight glass, then put in an additional 4 ounces.*

8 Once the system is fully charged, close the low side hand valve and the valve on the bulk refrigerant conainer.

9 Detach the service hose between the bulk container and the manifold.

10 Run a performance test.

11 Remove the manifold gauge set and replace all protective caps.

Evacuating and charging accumulator systems

Note: *On the accumulator type systems used by Ford Motor Company and General Motors, evacuating and charging are combined into one service procedure.*

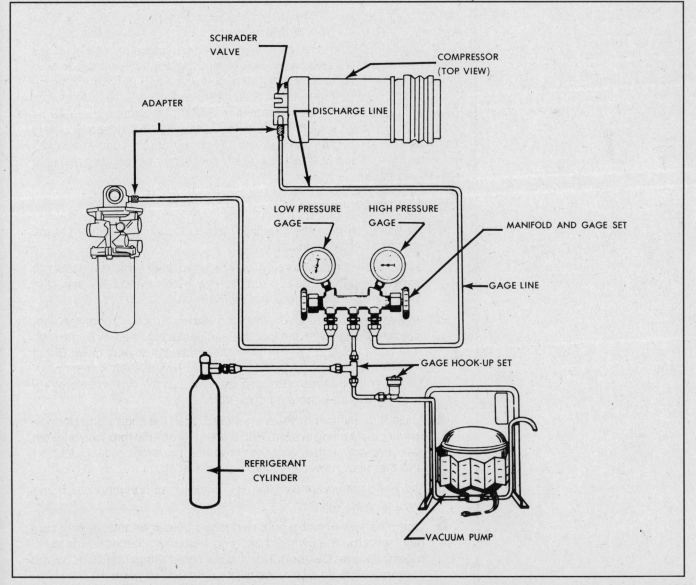

The proper setup for evacuating and charging a typical accumulator system (General Motors system shown, others similar)

Heating and air conditioning

General Motors
Cycling Clutch Orifice Tube (CCOT) system

1 If the system requires the addition of any refrigerant oil, add it now (see 'Compressor oil check').

2 Place the container on a scale, weigh it and record the total weight before starting the charging procedure. Watch the scale during the charging procedure to determine when the proper amount has been dispensed into the system.

3 Connect the low side service hose to the accumulator service fitting, the center hose to the refrigerant supply and the high side hose to the vacuum pump.

4 To start evacuation, slowly open the high side and low side manifold gauge hand valves and commence vacuum pump operation.

   a) On all vehicles except 1981 and later models, evacuate the system for at least 15-minutes AFTER the low side gauge reads 28 to 29 in-Hg of vacuum or more at sea level.

   b) On 1981 and later models, this extra 15-minutes isn't necessary.

Note: *For every 1000 feet above sea level, lower the vacuum requirement by an inch. Example: At 3000 feet, the necessary vacuum is 26.5 in-Hg (see Chapter 4).*

5 If the prescribed vacuum level cannot be reached - and maintained - close the vacuum control valve, shut off the pump and look for a leak at the hose fittings or the pump itself. When the system is completely evacuated, close the high side gauge hand valve and turn off the vacuum pump.

6 Watching the low side gauge, verify that the vacuum level holds steady for at least 5-minutes.

   a) If it does, proceed with charging **(see illustrations)**.

   b) If it doesn't, add 1/2-pound of refrigerant, leak test the system, repair the leak(s) and repeat the evacuation procedure.

7 Warm up the engine to normal operating temperature. Set the air conditioning controls to the Off position. With the refrigerant supply inverted, open the can or drum valve and the low side hand valve.

8 After 1-pound of refrigerant has been dispensed, set the air conditioning controls at their normal positions and adjust the blower selector to the highest position. When the compressor engages, it acts as a suction pump, drawing in the rest of the charge. **Note:** *This procedure can be completed more quickly by placing a large volume fan in front of the condenser. Maintaining the condenser at a temperature lower than the refrigerant will enable the refrigerant to enter the system more rapidly.*

9 Turn off the valve on the refrigerant drum. Run the engine for another 30 seconds to clear the lines and manifold. Quickly remove the low side service hose from the accumulator fitting to prevent refrigerant loss while the engine is running. Replace the cap on the fitting.

10 Leak test the system while it's operating and verify that it works properly.

Service and repair

Ford Motor Company
Ford Fixed Orifice Tube (FFOT) system

1 If refrigerant oil needs to be added, do so now (see "Compressor oil check').

2 Place the refrigerant drum on a scale, weigh it and record the total weight before charging begins. Watch the scale to determine when the system is fully charged.

3 Attach the manifold gauge set low side service hose to the accumulator low side service fitting. Attach the center hose to a vacuum pump. Using an adapter, connect the high side service hose to the high side service fitting on the compressor discharge line's condenser connection.

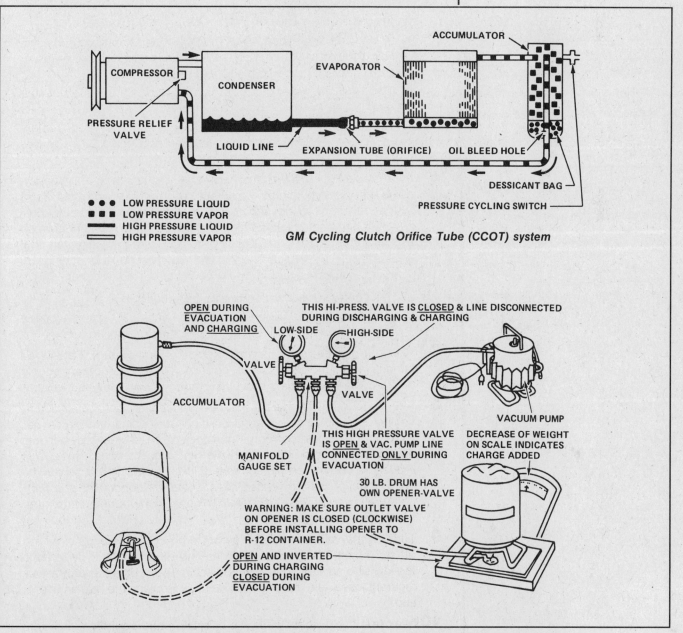

● ● ● LOW PRESSURE LIQUID
▪ ▪ ▪ LOW PRESSURE VAPOR
━━━ HIGH PRESSURE LIQUID
▭▭▭ HIGH PRESSURE VAPOR

GM Cycling Clutch Orifice Tube (CCOT) system

Once the CCOT system is discharged, verify that the vacuum level holds steady for at least 5 minutes, then charge the system in accordance with the procedure described at left

Heating and air conditioning

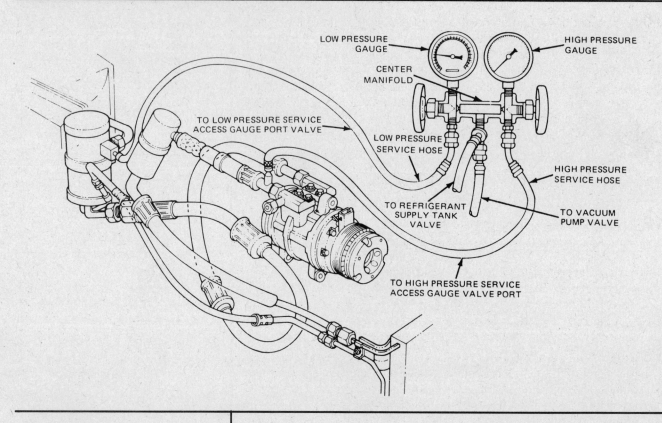

LOW PRESSURE GAUGE

HIGH PRESSURE GAUGE

CENTER MANIFOLD

TO LOW PRESSURE SERVICE ACCESS GAUGE PORT VALVE

LOW PRESSURE SERVICE HOSE

HIGH PRESSURE SERVICE HOSE

TO REFRIGERANT SUPPLY TANK VALVE

TO VACUUM PUMP VALVE

TO HIGH PRESSURE SERVICE ACCESS GAUGE VALVE PORT

This is what the gauges look like when you start the vacuum pump: both gauges read zero — and the low side gauge will continue to drop below zero into the vacuum range as the pump sucks the system dry — the reading you're looking for is at least 25 in-Hg and even 30, if you can get it

4 To begin evacuation, slowly open the high and low side **(see illustration)** manifold gauge set hand valves and start up the vacuum pump. Evacuate the system until the low side gauge reads at least 25 in-Hg and as close to 30 in-Hg as possible, then continue the evacuation an additional 15-minutes (if any components have been replaced, continue vacuum pump operation for an additional 20 to 30 minutes). **Note:** *For each 1000 feet above sea level, vacuum should be lowered by 1-inch. Example: At 4000 feet, it would have to be 25.5 in-Hg of vacuum. For other vacuum corrections, see Chapter 4.*

5 If the prescribed vacuum level cannot be reached and maintained, close the vacuum control valve, shut off the pump and look for a leak at the connections or at the pump.

6 When the system is fully evacuated, close the high side gauge valve and turn off the vacuum pump.

7 Watch the low side gauge to be sure the vacuum level holds for at least 5-minutes. If it does, proceed with charging. If it doesn't, add 1/2-pound of refrigerant and leak test the system. Repair the leak(s) and repeat the evacuation procedure.

8 With both manifold gauge set hand valves closed, detach the service hose from the vacuum pump and connect it to the refrigerant supply.

9 Loosen the center hose at the manifold gauge set and open the refrigerant drum tap. Allow a small amount of refrigerant to escape to purge the air and moisture from the center hose. Tighten the center hose connection at the manifold gauge set.

10 Disconnect the wiring harness snap-lock connector from the clutch cycling pressure switch. Attach a jumper wire across the 2 terminals of the connector. Open the manifold gauge set low side hand valve to allow refrigerant to enter the system. With the refrigerant supply inverted (to permit charging with liquid refrigerant), open the drum valve. Warning: If the low side service port isn't on the accumulator, keep the refrigerant containers in an upright position, permitting charging with refrigerant vapor only.

11 When no more refrigerant is being drawn into the system, start the engine. Move the air door lever to the vent-heat-A/C position and the blower switch to the High position. Depress the A/C On-Off pushbutton to draw the remaining refrigerant into the system.

12 Continue adding refrigerant until the specified amount is in the system. Then close the manifold gauge set low side hand valve and the refrigerant supply valve. Remove the jumper wire from the clutch cycling pressure switch connector and attach the connector to the switch. **Note:** *This charging procedure can be completed more rapidly by placing a large volume fan in front of the condenser. By keeping the condenser temperature below the temperature of the refrigerant supply, refrigerant will enter the system more rapidly.*

13 Operate the system and verify that the operating pressures are normal. Shut off the refrigerant source valve and run the engine for another 30-seconds to clear the lines and gauges. Quickly detach the low side service hose from the accumulator fitting to avoid loss of refrigerant while the engine is running. Replace the caps on all fittings.

14 Leak test the system while it's operating to ensure that it's performing properly.

After all repairs have been completed and the system has been fully charged, it should be given a final performance test to make sure that all components are functioning properly.

1 With the test gauges still hooked up, start the engine and run it at a fast idle for about 5-minutes. Close the windows and doors and lower the hood. Make sure all hoses are positioned properly so they're not pinched by the hood.

2 Place a thermometer in the far right air conditioning outlet. Put the air conditioning controls at their maximum cooling position, but adjust the blower selector to low speed.

3 Allow the system 5-minutes to stabilize. Once all components have reached normal operating temperature, note the gauge set readings and compare them to the specified pressure (see 'Normal system operating pressures').

4 If the high side reading appears too high, place a large capacity fan in front of the condenser to simulate ram air flow and assist heat transfer.

5 The thermometer in the air conditioning outlet should read 35 to 45°F at approximately 75 to 80°F ambient temperature. Note that higher temperatures and high humidity will increase the outlet temperature.

6 If the system appears to be operating normally, stop the engine, disconnect the gauge set and replace the service fitting caps. If the system is not operating within specifications or displays other abnormal conditions, refer to the next chapter.

Final performance test

Heating and air conditioning

System operating pressures

Manufacturer Year Model (or type of system)	Low side gauge (evaporator suction)	High side gauge (discharge)

Note: *The following pressure specifications are for systems in good operating condition, at sea level and (unless otherwise noted) at an ambient air temperature of 80°F.*

ACURA
1986
  Integra
  Legend . . . . 21 to 28 200

AMERICAN MOTORS
1971 through 1973 . . . . 11 . . . . 160 to 190
1974 through 1979 . . . . 15 to 30 . . . . 165 to 225
1980 through 1987 . . . . 15 to 24 . . . . 208 to 250

AUDI
1977 through 1979 Fox . . . . . . 10 to 40 . . . . 80 to 300
1978 through 1983 5000 . . . . 28 to 32 . . . . N/A
1980 through 1982 4000 . . . . 15 to 40 . . . . 100 to 300
1983 and 1984 Coupe,
  Quattro, 4000 . . . . 15 to 40 . . . . 100 to 300
1984 5000 . . . . 19 to 25 240
1985 and 1986 (all models) . . . 18.9 to 24.7 170

BMW
1977 through 1986
  Manual system (all models) . . . 24 to 34 . . . . 284 to 394
  Automatic system
    633 CSi and 635 CSi . . . . . . 15 to 30 . . . . 160 to 320

CHEVROLET IMPORTS
1985 and 1986
  Spectrum . . . . 21.3 to 28.4 . . . . 206 to 213
  Sprint . . . . 21.3 to 28.4 . . . . 206 to 213

CHRYSLER CORPORATION (DOMESTICS)
1971 and 1972 . . . . 21 to 25 . . . . 140 to 210
1973 through 1977 . . . . 22 to 29 . . . . 140 to 210
1978 and 1979
  EPR valve system . . . . 22 to 30 . . . . 140 to 240
  Thermostatic switch system . . 15 to 30 . . . . 140 to 240
1978 through 1980 . . . . 20 to 30 . . . . 140 to 240
1981 through 1983
  Front wheel drive . . . . 20 to 30 . . . . 140 to 240
  Rear wheel drive . . . . 20 to 30 . . . . 115 to 240
1984 through 1987
  Front wheel drive . . . . 16 to 30 . . . . 180 to 235
  Rear wheel drive . . . . 12 to 22 . . . . 170 to 210

CHRYSLER CORPORATION (IMPORTS)
1977 through 1983 . . . . 15 to 30 . . . . 210 to 230
1984 through 1986 . . . . 15 to 30 . . . . 170 to 200

FIAT
1977 through 1981 . . . . 7 to 42 . . . . 142 to 284

Manufacturer Year Model (or type of system)	Low side gauge (evaporator suction)	High side gauge (discharge)
FORD MOTOR COMPANY (DOMESTICS)		
1971 and 1972 (thermostatic switch)	10 to 20	180 to 225
1971 through 1973 (STV)	4 to 25*	120 to 180
1973 (thermostatic switch)	15 to 25	180 to 225
1974 through 1976 (STV)	10 to 20*	120 to 180
1977 and 1978 (STV)	5 to 20*	120 to 180
1979 (STV)	27.5 to 29.5	175 to 185
1980		
Accumulator	24 to 52	160 to 200
STV	22.5 to 30.7	175 to 195
1981 (accumulator)		
Escort and Lynx	20 to 45	130 to 230
All other models	24 to 52	160 to 250
1982 and 1983 (accumulator)		
Ford, Mercury, Lincoln, Mark VI	24 to 52	160 to 250
All other models	20 to 45	130 to 230
1984 through 1987 (accumulator)		
Ford, Mercury, Town Car	24 to 50	160 to 250
All other models	16 to 45	130 to 230
FORD MOTOR COMPANY (IMPORTS)		
1985 and 1986 Merkur XR4Ti	20	160
GENERAL MOTORS		
1971 through 1978 (STV)	28.5 to 31.5	210 to 260
1973 through 1978 (accumulator)	20 to 28	185 to 235
1979 (accumulator)	24 to 30	105 to 175
1980 and 1981 (accumulator)	24 to 35	150 to 220
1982 through 1987 (accumulator)		
Front wheel drive	22 to 29	165 to 205
Rear wheel drive	24 to 30	130 to 190
HONDA		
1977 and 1978 Accord	30	200 to 220*
1979		
Accord	30	200 to 220*
Prelude	36	213
1980 through 1982		
Accord	30	200 to 220*
Civic and Prelude	36	213**
1983 through 1985		
Accord and Civic	35	215
Prelude	37	320
1986		
Accord	35	215
Prelude	37	320
Civic and CRX	36	320

*at compressor speed of 2000 rpm
**at compressor speed of 1500 rpm

System operating pressures
(continued)

Manufacturer Year Model (or type of system)	Low side gauge (evaporator suction)	High side gauge (discharge)

Note: *The following pressure specifications are for systems in good operating condition, at sea level and (unless otherwise noted) at an ambient air temperature of 80°F.*

MERCEDES-BENZ

1977 through 1979 450SL/SLC	22	200
1977 through 1982 230, 240D	28 to 30	265
1977 (all except above)	22	205
1983 240D	15 to 30	160 to 320
1981 through 1986 (all except above)	22	265
1984 through 1986 190 Series	24 to 34	230 to 275

MITSUBISHI

1984 through 1986	15 to 30	170 to 200*

at 77 to 86°F (25 to 30°C) and 65% humidity

DATSUN/NISSAN

1977		
B210 and 280Z	27	182
200SX	23	180
710	18 to 26	220 to 260
810	16 to 24	148 to 205
Pick-up	15	205
1978		
F10, B210 and 280Z	23 to 33	152 to 185
510 and 810	16 to 24	148 to 205
200SX	23	180
Pick-up	15	205
1979		
210, 810, 200SX and Pick-up	16 to 24	148 to 205
310 and 510	26 to 34	155 to 190
280ZX	14 to 25	122 to 150
1980 and 1981		
210, 510, 200SX and Pick-up	16 to 24	148 to 205
310	26 to 34	155 to 190
280ZX	14 to 25	122 to 190
810	16 to 22	143 to 175
1982		
Maxima	15 to 19	139 to 171
Pick-up and 210	16 to 28	149 to 178
Sentra	17 to 23	175 to 189
Stanza	17 to 26	152 to 195
200SX	18 to 20	134 to 146
280ZX	13 to 22	121 to 148
310	26 to 44	154 to 188
1983		
Maxima	15 to 19	139 to 171
Pick-up	16 to 28	149 to 178
Pulsar and Sentra	18 to 30	162 to 196
Stanza	17 to 26	152 to 195
200SX	18 to 20	134 to 146
280ZX	13 to 22	121 to 148

Manufacturer Year Model (or type of system)	Low side gauge (evaporator suction)	High side gauge (discharge)
1984		
Maxima	15 to 19	139 to 171
Pick-up	11 to 28	141 to 171
Pulsar and Sentra	18 to 30	162 to 196
Stanza	17 to 26	152 to 195
200SX	6 to 17	109 to 154
300ZX	13 to 16	151 to 185
1985		
Maxima	15 to 19	139 to 171
Pick-up	11 to 28	141 to 171
Pulsar and Sentra	18 to 30	162 to 196
Stanza	17 to 26	152 to 195
200SX	6 to 17	109 to 154
300ZX	13 to 16	151 to 185
1986		
Maxima		
Manual system	7 to 17	142 to 192
Automatic system	15 to 19	139 to 171
Pick-up	11 to 28	141 to 171
Pick-up (1/2-ton)		
VG engine	17 to 26	176 to 210
Z engine	23 to 33	188 to 228
SD engine	18 to 27	182 to 220
Pulsar NX and Sentra	18 to 30	162 to 196
Stanza	17 to 26	152 to 195
200SX	6 to 17	109 to 154
300ZX	13 to 16	151 to 185
SUBARU		
1983	28	230
1984 through 1986	28	256
TOYOTA		
1977 and 1978	20 to 28	200 to 220
1979 through 1982	22 to 35	200 to 220
1983 and 1984		
Land Cruiser and pick-up	22 to 35	199 to 220
All others	21 to 28	206 to 213
1985 and 1986	21 to 28	206 to 213
1986 (automatic system)		
Celica, MR2, van	21 to 28	199 to 220
VOLKSWAGEN		
1977 through 1981 Dasher	15 to 30	175 to 250
1977 through 1984 (except		
above)	15 to 30	150 to 270
1985 and 1986	26 to 40	150 to 210
VOLVO		
1977 through 1982		
at 68°F (20°C)	24 to 28	140 to 190
at 86°F (30°C)	31 to 38	180 to 230
at 104°F (40°C)	43 to 48	260 to 310
1983 through 1986		
Diesel models	10 to 38	135 to 200
All others	20 to 37	115 to 170

Heating and air conditioning

Component replacement oil quantities

Component	Oil capacity (in ounces)
1979	
With GM compressor	
Evaporator	3.0
Condenser	1.0
Accumulator	1.0
With Air-Temp or Sankyo compressor	
Evaporator	2.0
Condenser	1.0
Receiver-drier	1.0
1980 through 1983	
Accumulator	Amount drained, plus 2 oz for GM models, Amount drained, plus 1 oz for all others
Condenser	1.0
Evaporator	
American Motors systems	1.0
Chrysler Corporation systems	1.0
All other systems	3.0
Receiver-drier	1.0
1984 and 1985	
Accumulator	On General Motors systems with DA-6 compressor, add 3 oz; on other GM and all other systems, add same amounts as above to all components
1986	
Accumulator	Same as 1984/1985
Condenser	
Ford Motor Company	
Merkur	0.5
All other models	1.0
All other manufacturers	1.0
Evaporator	
American Motors and Ford Motor Company systems	1.0
Chrysler Corporation systems	2.0
General Motors systems	
Pontiac	2.0
All other models	3.0
Receiver-drier	1.0
1987	
Accumulator	Same as 1984/1985
Condenser	1.0
Evaporator	
Chrysler Motor Corporation	2.0
Jeep	1.0
All other systems	3.0
Receiver-drier	1.0

Compressor oil level (total system capacity)

Compressor	Oil capacity (in ounces)
American Motors Corporation	
Eagle models	Fill compressor to between 4 and 6 increments on dipstick
Chrysler Corporation	
C-171 model	7.0
FWD van	
A-171 model	7.0
A-590 model	7.0
RWD van and pick-up	5.0

Compressor	Oil capacity (in ounces)
Chrysler, Ford and Nippondenso 6-cylinder	
Chrysler Corporation	9.0 to 10.0
Ford Motor Company	
1981	13.0
1982 through 1987	10.0
1988	
Eagle	4.6
All other models	7.3
1989	
FWD and RWD car and truck	
C-171 compressor	7.3
6C-17 compressor	8.7
Eagle	amount drained plus one ounce*
All other models	7.3
1990	
Laser	3.3
Monaco	7.9
All others	
C-171 compressor	7.3
6C-17 compressor	8.7
Eagle	
Premier	7.9
Talon	3.3
1991	
Eagle	
Premier	7.9
Talon	2.6
Laser	2.6
Monaco	7.9
Shadow	7.3
All other models	
C-171/A590 and 10PA17 compressors	7.3
6C-17 compressor	8.7
1992	
Eagle	
Premier	7.9
Talon	5.0
Laser	5.0
Monaco	7.9
Shadow and Sundance	7.3
All other models (FWD)	
6C-17 compressor	9.0
10PA17 compressor	7.3
Ford Motor Company	
FS-6 and 6P148 models	10.0
HR-980 model	8.0
1988 through 1992	
Aerostar	
With rear A/C	10.0
Without rear A/C	7.0
Bronco	7.0
E series vans	
With rear A/C	10.0
Without rear A/C	7.0

Heating and air conditioning

Compressor oil level
(total system capacity)
(continued)

Compressor	Oil capacity (in ounces)
Ford Motor Company (continued)	
1988 through 1992	
F series	7.0
All other models not listed but equipped with:	
6E171 compressor	13.0
FS6, 10PA17, 6P148 and 10P15A compressors	10.0
HR980, 10PA17A,	
10P15, 15C and 15F compressors	8.0
FX15 compressor	
With rear A/C	10.0
Without rear A/C	7.0
General Motors	
A-6 model	10.0
V-5 and DA-6 models	8.0
R-4 model	6.0
Harrison (Frigidaire)	
4-cylinder	5.5 to 6.5
6-cylinder	10.0 to 10.5
Delco Air DA-6 6-cylinder	8.0
V5 5-cylinder	8.0
1988 through 1992 Cars* (body codes are determined by the 4th digit of the VIN)	
A, W and Y body styles	
1988 through 1991	8.0
1992	9.0
B, D and F body styles	6.0
C, E, H. J, K and N body styles	8.0
W and Y Body styles	
1989 through 1991	8.0
1992	9.0
1988 through 1992 Trucks*	
C and K series	6.0
G series	
1988 through 1990	
With rear A/C	
A6 compressor	13.0
R4 compressor	9.0
Without rear A/C	
A6 compressor	10.0
R4 compressor	6.0
1991	
With rear A/C	9.0
Without rear A/C	6.0
1992	
With rear A/C	10.0
Without rear A/C	8.0
M series	
1988 and 1989	
With rear A/C	8.0
Without rear A/C	6.0
1990	
With rear A/C	8.0
Without rear A/C	8.0

Compressor	Oil capacity (in ounces)
General Motors (continued)	
M series	
1991 and 1992	
With rear A/C	11.0
Without rear A/C	8.0
R series and V series	
1988	
With rear A/C	
HR6 compressor	11.0
R4 compressor	9.0
Without rear A/C	
HR6 compressor	11.0
R4 compressor	6.0
1989	
With rear A/C	
HR6 compressor	11.0
R4 compressor	9.0
Without rear A/C	
HR6 compressor	8.0
R4 compressor	6.0
1990 and 1991	
With rear A/C	9.0
Without rear A/C	6.0
S series and T series	
1988	10.0
1989 and 1990	
V5 comressor	8.0
R4 compressor	11.0
1991	
V5 comressor	9.0
R4 compressor	6.0
1992	8.0
U series	8.0

For 1988 through 1992 Cars or Trucks not found above use the refrigerant oil capacity listed by compressor model listed below.

HR6, V5, 10P15 and 10PA20 compressors	8.0
R4 compressor	6.0
Jeep	
4 and 6-cylinder	Fill compressor to between 4 and 6 increments on the dipstick
8-cylinder	7.0 (fill compressor to between 7 and 10 increments on the dipstick)
1988	
York compressor	8.0
Sanden compressor	7.0
1989	
Cherokee and Wagoneer	4.0
Comanche and Wrangler	3.2
Grand Wagoneer	3.6
1990	
Grand Wagoneer	3.2
All others	3.8

Heating and air conditioning

Compressor oil level
(total system capacity)
(continued)

Compressor	Oil capacity (in ounces)
Jeep (continued)	
1991 and 1992	
Cherokee	
Two door	3.2
Four door	3.8
Comanche	3.8
Grand Wagoneer (1991)	3.2
Nippondenso 6-cylinder	
Chrysler Corporation systems	9.0 to 10.0
Ford Motor Company systems	3.0
Nippondenso 10-cylinder	5.5 to 7.5
Sanden (Sankyo) 5-cylinder	7.0 to 8.0
Tecumseh 4-cylinder	8.0
York 2-cylinder	
American Motors systems	7.0
Rotary Vane	6.0 to 8.0

Chrysler Corporation 2-cylinder compressor oil level

Application	Dipstick reading
Non-stepped sump models	
170 cu in 6-cylinder engine (1966 through 1968)	2 in
225 cu in 6-cylinder engine	
Dart and Valiant	
1966	2 in
1967 and 1968	2-3/8 to 3 in
All others	
1966	2-3/8 in
1967 and 1968	2-3/8 to 3 in
273 and 318 cu in V8	
1966	2 in
1967 and 1968	2 to 2-3/8 in
All other V8s	
1966	2-3/4 in
1967 and 1968	2-7/8 to 3-1/2 in
Vertical on bench, all models	
1966 through 1968	2-3/8 in
Stepped-sump models (identified by its unique step-shaped oil sump)	
225 cu in 6-cylinder	
1968 and 1969	
Dart and Valiant	1-5/8 to 2-1/8 in
All others	2-1/8 to 2-3/4 in
1970 (all models)	1-5/8 to 2-1/8 in
273, 318 and 340 cu in V8s	
1968 and 1969	1-9/16 to 2-3/8 in
1970	1-5/8 to 2-3/8 in
383 and 440 cu in V8s	
1968	2-3/4 to 3-5/8 in
1969	1-9/16 to 2-3/8 in
1970	1-5/8 to 2-3/8 in
Vertical on bench	
1968 and 1969	1-9/16 to 2-3/8 in
1970 through 1975	1-5/8 to 2-3/8 in
1976 through 1978	2-3/8 in
1979	3 to 3-7/16 in

Application	Dipstick reading
1966 (all models)	7/8 in
1967	
Horizontally mounted	7/8 to 1-1/8 in
Vertically mounted	7/8 to 1-1/16 in
1968	
Horizontally mounted	7/8 to 1-5/8 in
Vertically mounted	7/8 to 1-1/16 in
1969	
Horizontally and vertically mounted	7/8 to 1-5/8 in
Diagonally mounted	1-1/2 to 2 in
1970	
Horizontally mounted	13/16 to 1-3/16 in
Vertically mounted	7/8 to 1-3/8 in
1971 through 1973	
Horizontally mounted	7/8 to 1-1/8 in
Vertically mounted	7/8 to 1-1/16 in
1974 through 1988	
Horizontally mounted	7/8 to 1-5/8 in
Vertically mounted	7/8 to 1-3/8 in
American Motors	
1976 through 1981	
Horizontally mounted	13/16 to 1-3/16 in
Vertically mounted	7/8 to 1-1/8 in
Ford Motor Company	
1966 (all models)	3/4 in
1967	
Horizontally mounted	1-1/2 in
Vertically mounted	7/8 to 1-1/8 in
1968 and 1969	
Horizontally and vertically mounted	7/8 to 1-3/16 in
Diagonally mounted	1-1/2 to 2 in
1970	
Horizontally mounted	13/16 to 1-3/16 in
Vertically mounted	7/8 to 1-3/8 in
1971 through 1973	
Horizontally mounted	13/16 to 1-1/8 in
Vertically mounted	7/8 to 1-1/16 in
1974 through 1988	
Horizontally mounted	13/16 to 1-3/16 in
Vertically mounted	7/8 to 1-1/8 in

Tecumseh 2-cylinder (Ford Motor Co.)

York 2-cylinder

Compressor	Capacity (in ounces)
Chrysler	
2-cylinder	10.0 to 20.0
6-cylinder	9.0 to 10.0
Frigidaire	
4-cylinder	5.5 to 6.5
6-cylinder	10.5
Sankyo 5-cylinder	8.0
Tecumseh 2-cylinder	11.0
York 2-cylinder	10.0

Compressor oil change

Heating and air conditioning

System refrigerant oil capacity
(imported vehicles)

Year Model	Refrigerant oil capacity (in ounces) (Total system capacity unless otherwise noted)
ACURA	
1987 through 1989	
Integra	2.4 to 5.0*
Legend	2.7*
1990	
Integra	2.0 to 3.4*
Legend	2.7*
1991	
Integra	2.0 to 3.4*
Legend	3.7 to 4.7*
AUDI	
1977 Fox	10.0
1978 through 1981	
Fox, 4000	10.0
5000	11.3
1982 through 1984	
4000, Coupe and Quattro	10.0
5000	11.0
1985	
GT Coupe, 4000S and 4000S Quattro	8.0
5000S, 5000S Turbo and 5000S Turbo Diesel	10.3
1986	
GT Coupe, 4000S and 4000CS Quattro	8.0
5000S and 5000CS Quattro	10.3
5000CS Turbo	20.4
1987	
Octagon head	8.0
Square head	6.0
1988 and 1989	
80/90	2.7
100/200 and 5000	3.8
1990 and 1991	
80/90	2.7*
100/200	12.7*
BMW	
1977 through 1982	11.5
1983 and 1984	
320i, 318i and 325e	11.5
All other models	5.7
1985 and 1986	5.7
1987 through 1989	5.7
1990 and 1991	10.0
CHEVROLET IMPORTS	
1985 and 1986	
Spectrum	3.4
Sprint	2.7

Capacity for compressor only

Year Model	Refrigerant oil capacity (in ounces) (Total system capacity unless otherwise noted)

CHRYSLER CORPORATION IMPORTS

1977 through 1984 (all models)	Checked with dipstick
1985	
Colt	1.31*
Colt Vista	1.38*
Conquest	3.7
Ram 50	4.0
1986	
Colt and Colt Vista	1.38*
Conquest	3.7
Ram-50	4.0
1987	
Colt and Colt Vista	1.5
Conquest and Raider	3.7
Ram 50	4.0
1988 and 1989	
Colt, Colt Vista and Ram 50	2.7
Conquest	5.7
Raider	3.7
1990 and 1991	
Colt	5.0
Colt Vista and Ram 50	2.7*
Stealth	4.6 to 6.0*

DATSUN

1977	
6-cylinder compressor	9.1
2-cylinder compressor	9.0
1978	
F10, 510, 810 and pick-up	3.4
B210 and 280Z	9.1
200 SX	
6-cylinder compressor	9.1
2-cylinder compressor	8.0
1979	
510, 810 and pick-up	3.4
310 and 280ZX	5.1
210	8.1
200SX	
6-cylinder compressor	9.1
2-cylinder compressor	8.0
1980 and 1981	
210	8.1
280ZX	9.1
All other models	5.1
1982	
210	8.0
Diesel pick-up	6.0
All other models	5.0

Capacity for compressor only

Heating and air conditioning

Year Model	Refrigerant oil capacity (in ounces) (Total system capacity unless otherwise noted)

DATSUN/NISSAN
1983
   Diesel pick-up 6.3
   All other models 5.1

FIAT
1977 through 1982 (all models) .... Checked with dipstick

FORD MOTOR COMPANY IMPORTS
1985 and 1986 Merkur XR4Ti... 0.7*
1987 through 1989
   Festiva .... 2.1 to 3.5*
   Merkur XR4Ti (1987 and 1988)..................................... 7.0
   Tracer (1987) 10.0
   Scorpio and Tracer (1988 and 1989).................... 2.1 to 3.4*
1990
   Festiva .... 2.1 to 3.5
1991
   Festiva and Capri 10.0

GENERAL MOTORS IMPORTS
1987 (Spectrum)... 3.0
1988 and 1989
   Spectrum.. 3.4
   Lemans... 8.0
   All other models 2.7
1990
   Storm.. 7.1
   Tracker and Prizm 2.7
   Metro .... 2.0 to 3.3
   Lemans... 8.0
1991
   Metro and Tracker... 3.0
   Prizm 6.0
   Storm.. 7.1
   Lemans... 8.0

HONDA
1977 through 1981 Accord... 7.9
1979 through 1982 Civic and Prelude............................... 3.0
1982 Accord.. 8.0
1983 and 1984
   Accord and Prelude 7.9
   Civic .... 2.0 to 3.0
1985 and 1986 (all models) 7.9
1987
   Accord... 2.5
   Civic
      Keihin compressor .... 2.0 to 3.0
      Sanden compressor 6.0

Capacity for compressor only

Year Model	Refrigerant oil capacity (in ounces) (Total system capacity unless otherwise noted)

HONDA (continued)
1987
   Prelude 2.5
1988
   Accord 2.5
   Civic
      Matsushita compressor 5.0
      Sanden compressor 6.0
   Prelude 5.0
1989
   Accord 2.5
   Prelude 5.7
   Civic and CRX 4.0
1990 and 1991
   Accord .... 3.0 to 4.0
   Civic and CRX .... 4.0 to 4.4
   Prelude 4.0

HYUNDAI
1986 .... 5.1
1987 through 1989 .... 5.0
1990 and 1991 .... 8.0

INFINITI (1990 and 1991)
M30 and G20(1991) 6.8
Q45 .... 8.0

ISUZU
1984 (all models) 7.3
1985 and 1986 (all models) 5.0
1987 through 1989
   I-Mark 3.5
   Impulse, Pickup and Trooper II 5.0
1990
   Amigo and Trooper II 5.0
   Impulse 6.7
   Pickup 6.0
1991
   Amigo 6.0
   Impulse and Stylus 6.7
   Pickup
      Kiki Diesel compressor 5.0
      Harrison R4 compressor 6.0

LEXUS
ES250
   1990 .... 4.0
   1991 .... 2.6*
LS400 (1990 and 1991) 4.0*

Capacity for compressor only

Heating and air conditioning

System refrigerant oil capacity
(Imported vehicles)
(continued)

Year Model	Refrigerant oil capacity (in ounces) (Total system capacity unless otherwise noted)
MAZDA	
1986	
B2000	5.9
626	3.4
RX-7	
Sanden compressor	4.5
Nippondenso compressor	2.0 to 3.4
323	2.0 to 3.4
1987 and 1988	
B2200	4.5
B2600	4.0 to 5.9
RX7	
Nippondenso compressor	2.0 to 3.4
Sanden compressor	4.0 to 5.9
323	2.0 to 3.4
626	
1987	3.4
1988	2.1
929	3.3
1989	
B2200	4.5
B2600i	4.0 to 5.9
MPV	2.6 to 3.3
MX6 and 626	2.1*
RX7	
Nippondenso	2.1 to 3.4*
Sanden	4.0 to 5.9
323	2.1 to 3.4*
929	3.3*
1990	
B2200 and B2600i	4.5
MPV	2.6 to 3.3
MX 6 and 626	3.3 to 3.4
RX7	
Nippondenso	2.1 to 3.4*
Sanden	4.5
Protege and 323	3.8
929	5.0
1991	
B2200 and B2600i	8.2
Miata	2.7 to 3.3*
MPV	4.9 to 6.1
MX 6 and 626	2.0 to 3.3*
RX7	
Nippondenso	2.0 to 3.3*
Sanden	4.5*
Protege and 323	3.3 to 4.0*
Navajo	7.0
929	2.0 to 3.3*

* Capacity for compressor only

Year Model	Refrigerant oil capacity (in ounces) (Total system capacity unless otherwise noted)

MERCEDES-BENZ

1977 through 1981 (manual system) .... 7.5 to 9.4
1977 (automatic system)
  6.9L engine 10.1
  All others 8.1
1978 through 1980 (automatic system)
  280 Series, 300C and 300CD 8.1
  300SD and 300 Series 5.8
  450 Series and 6.9L engine 10.1
1981 (automatic system)
  380 Series 10.1
  All others .... 7.0 to 9.0
1982
  Manual system (240D) .... 7.5 to 9.5
  Automatic system
    380 Series 10.0
    All others .... 7.0 to 9.0
1983
  240D .... 6.9 to 9.6
  300 Series 5.8
  380 Series 10.1
1984
  190 Series .... 6.9 to 9.6
  300 Series 5.8
  380 and 500 Series 10.1
1985
  190D 4.1
  190E and 300 Series 5.8
  380 and 500 Series 10.1
1986
  190D 4.1
  All others 5.8
1987 through 1989 (all models) 4.1
1990 and 1991
  190E 5.0*
  All others 4.0*

MITSUBISHI

1984 .... 7.5
1985 and 1986
  Cordia and Tredia 1.3*
  Galant and Mirage 1.4*
  Montero and Starion 3.7
  Pick-up 6.8
1987
  Cordia, Tredia, Galant and Mirage 1.3
  Montero and Starion 3.7
  Pickup 4.0
  Precis 5.1
  Van/Wagon 5.0

* Capacity for compressor only

Heating and air conditioning

Year Model	Refrigerant oil capacity (in ounces) (Total system capacity unless otherwise noted)
MITSUBISHI (continued)	
1988 and 1989	
Galant	2.7*
Montero	3.7
Precis	5.1
Van/Wagon	5.0
Other models	5.7
1990	
Eclipse	2.6
Galant	5.0 to 5.7
Mirage and Wagon	5.0
Montero	
2.6L	3.7
3.0L	2.1 to 3.3
Precis	8.1
Sigma and Van	2.7
1991	
Eclipse and Montero	2.7*
Galant	5.0 to 5.7*
Mirage	5.0
Pickup	4.3 to 5.0
Precis	8.1
3000GT	4.6 to 6.0*
NISSAN/DATSUN	
1984	
Diesel Pick-up	6.3
All others	5.1
NISSAN	
1985 and 1986	
Maxima and 200SX	9.1
Pick-up (excluding 1986-1/2 Hardbody)	8.5
Pulsar, Sentra, Stanza and 300ZX	5.1
1987	
Maxima, Stanza wagon, 200SX and 300ZX	5.1
Pathfinder, Pickup, Pulsar NX, Sentra and Stanza	7.0
Van	8.5
1988	
Pathfinder, Pickup, Pulsar NX, Sentra and Stanza	7.0
Van	8.1
All other models	5.1
1989 (all models)	7.0
1990 (all models)	6.8
1991	
240SX	8.0
All other models	6.8

Capacity for compressor only

Year Model	Refrigerant oil capacity (in ounces) (Total system capacity unless otherwise noted)

SUBARU

1983 and 1984	4.1
1985 and 1986	
XT Coupe	2.1*
All others	4.1
1987 through 1989	4.1
1990 (Legacy only)	6.5
1991	
Legacy	
Kiki Diesel compressor	2.4*
Calsonic compressor	3.2*
Loyale, XT and XT6	2.4*

SUZUKI (all models)

1989	2.7*
1990	5.0

TOYOTA

1977 through 1979	
Celica	7.8
Corolla	Checked with dipstick
Cressida	9.0
Land Cruiser	10.0
Pick-up	
1977 and 1978	10.0
1979	7.6
Corona	
1977 and 1978	7.8
1979	7.6
1980 through 1982	
Celica, Corona and pick-up	7.5
Corolla	
1980	5.5
1981 and 1982	7.5
Cressida	
1980 and 1981	9.0
1982	8.0
Tercel	5.0
Land Cruiser	10.0
Starlet	9.0
Supra	6.0
1983 and 1984	
Corolla and pick-up	5.2 to 6.3
Land Cruiser	10.0
All others	2.0 to 3.4
1985 and 1986	3.4*
1987 through 1989	
Tercel	4.7
Land Cruiser, Van, Cressida and Supra	2.7*
All other models	3.4

* *Capacity for compressor only*

Heating and air conditioning

System refrigerant oil capacity (imported vehicles) (continued)

Year Model	Refrigerant oil capacity (in ounces) (Total system capacity unless otherwise noted)
TOYOTA (continued)	
1990 and 1991	
All models (except Supra)	4.7
Supra	4.1
1991	
MR2	4.1
Previa	4.7
VOLKSWAGEN	
1977 and 1978	
Dasher	10.0
All others	
R209 compressor	10.0
SC209 compressor	8.0
Sankyo compressor	6.0
1979 through 1981	
R209 compressor	10.0
SC209 compressor	8.0
Sankyo compressor	6.0
1982 through 1984	
Sankyo/Sanden SD-508 compressor	10.0
York SC-209 compressor	8.0
1985 and 1986	
Cabriolet and Scirocco	6.0
All others (except (Vanagon)	4.6
1987	
Fox	1.4
Cabriolet, Scirocco and Vanagon	6.0
Quantum and all other models	4.6
1988 and 1989	
Cabriolet and Scirocco	6.0
Fox	1.4*
Vanagon	5.0*
Quantum and all other models	4.6
1990	
Cabriolet	4.8
Fox	1.4*
Corrado,Golf and Jetta	4.5
Vanagon	5.0*
1991	
Cabriolet	6.0
Corrado, Fox, Passat, Golf and Jetta	4.5
Vanagon	7.0
VOLVO	
1977	
240	12.7
260	12.5
1978 through 1981	12.7
1982	12.5

142

* *Capacity for compressor only*

Year Model	Refrigerant oil capacity (in ounces) (Total system capacity unless otherwise noted)

VOLVO (continued)
1983 through 1986
760 GLE
Gas	5.1
Diesel	7.2

All others
Gas	10.2
Diesel	4.6
1987 through 1989 (all models)	6.8

1990
240 series	4.8

740, 760 and 940 series
Delco compressor	4.3 to 6.8
Sankyo compressor	4.5
York compressor	10.0
1991 (all models)	6.8

* *Capacity for compressor only*

Manufacturer Year Model	Refrigerant capacity (in ounces)

ACURA
1987 through 1992
Integra	33.0
Legend	33.0

AMERICAN MOTORS
1979 and 1980
AMX, Concord and Spirit	32.0
Pacer	34.0
1981 and 1982	32.0

1983
Alliance	28.0
All others	32.0

1984 and 1985
Alliance and Encore	28.0
Eagle	32.0

1986 and 1987
Alliance	29.0
Eagle	32.0
GTA	30.0

AUDI
1977 through 1984
Fox, Coupe, Quattro and 4000	34.0
5000	49.0

1985 and 1986
GT Coupe, 4000S and 4000S/CS Quattro	34.0
All others	38.0
1987	34.0
1988 through 1991	37.0

System refrigerant capacity

Heating and air conditioning

System refrigerant capacity
(continued)

Manufacturer Year Model	Refrigerant capacity (in ounces)
BMW	
1977 through 1982	35.0
1983 through 1986	
318i and 325e	42.0
320i	35.0
All others	44.0
1987 through 1989	45.0
1990 and 1991	
318, 325, 525 and 535	38.0
525i, 535, 735i and iL	69.0
CHRYSLER CORPORATION	
1979 and 1980	
Horizon and Omni	34.0
All others	42.0
1981 and 1982	
Aries, Reliant, Horizon and Omni	34.0
All others	38.0
1983	
Omni and Horizon	34.0
All other FWD models	40.0
RWD models	42.0
Dodge and Plymouth trucks	
Pick-ups and Ramcharger	42.0
Vans	
Front system only	48.0
Front and rear system	64.0
1984 and 1985	
Horizon, Omni and Rampage	33.0
All other FWD models	37.0
RWD models	42.0
Dodge and Plymouth trucks	
Pick-ups and Ramcharger	42.0
Vans	
FWD models	38.0
RWD models	
Front system only	48.0
Front and rear system	64.0
1986	
Charger, Horizon, Omni and Turismo	34.0
All other FWD models	38.0
RWD models	42.0
Dodge and Plymouth trucks	Same as 1985
1987	
Charger, Horizon, Omni and Turismo	34.0
All other FWD models	38.0
RWD models	42.0
Dodge and Plymouth trucks	
Dakota, pick-up and Ramcharger	42.0
All other models	Same as 1985

Manufacturer Year Model	Refrigerant capacity (in ounces)
CHRYSLER CORPORATION (continued)	
1988 and 1989	
FWD, except van/wagon	38.0
RWD	41.0
FWD van/wagon	
Without rear A/C	49.0
With rear A/C	65.0
1990	
Laser and Eagle Talon	33.0
All others models	38.0
1991 and 1992	
All except Monaco	33.0
Monaco	36.0
CHRYSLER CORPORATION IMPORTS	
1977 through 1984	32.0
1985 and 1986	
Colt	
1985	25.0
1986	26.0
Colt Vista and Conquest	26.0
Ram 50	32.0
1987	
Colt and Colt Vista, Conquest and Raider	26.0
Ram 50	32.0
1988 and 1989	32.0
1990 and 1991	
Colt	36.0
Colt Vista	32.0
Ram 50	30.0
Stealth	34.0
DATSUN	
1977	28.0
1978	
F10	24.0
510 and 810	35.0
B210, 200SX, 280ZX and pick-up	28.0
1979	
210, 200SX and pick-up	32.0
310	38.0
510, 810 and 280ZX	35.0
1980 and 1981	
210, 510 and 810	32.0
Pick-up	28.0
All others	37.0
1982	
200SX	35.0
All others	32.0

Heating and air conditioning

System refrigerant capacity
(continued)

Manufacturer Year Model	Refrigerant capacity (in ounces)
DATSUN/NISSAN	
1983	
Maxima	35.0
Pick-up and 200SX	32.0 to 38.0
All others	29.0 to 35.0
FIAT	
1977 and 1978	
131	45.0
X1/9	40.0
1979 through 1982	
Brava	38.0
Strada	37.0
X1/9	32.0
FORD MOTOR COMPANY	
1979	
Bobcat and Pinto	36.0
Capri, Fairmont, Mustang and Zephyr	56.0
Granada, Monarch and Versailles	64.0
All others	68.0
1980	
Bobcat and Pinto	36.0
Continental, Ford, Mercury and Mark VI	52.0
Granada, Monarch and Versailles	64.0
All others	56.0
1981	
Escort and Lynx	40.0
Ford and Mercury	52.0
Mark VI and Town Car	48.0
All others	56.0
1982	
Ford and Mercury	52.0
Mark VI and Town Car	48.0
All others	30.0
1983	
Ford and Mercury	52.0
Mark VI and Town Car	48.0
EXP and LN7	36.0
All other car models	40.0
Trucks	
F100, F350 pick-ups and Bronco	52.0
Ranger	44.0
Vans	
Front system only	56.0
Front and rear system	68.0
1984	
FWD models	41.0
Town Car	48.0
Crown Victoria and Grand Marquis	52.0
All other car models	40.0

Manufacturer Year Model	Refrigerant capacity (in ounces)
FORD MOTOR COMPANY (continued)	
1984	
Trucks	
F100, F350 pick-ups and Bronco	48.0
Bronco II and Ranger	40.0
E150 and E350 Vans	
Front system only	56.0
Front and rear system	68.0
1985	
FWD models	41.0
Town Car	52.0
Crown Victoria and Grand Marquis	48.0
All other car models	40.0
Trucks	
F100, F350 pick-ups and Bronco	48.0
Bronco II and Ranger	40.0
E150 and E350 Vans	
Front system only	52.0
Front and rear system	64.0
1986 and 1987	
FWD models	42.0
Town Car	52.0
Crown Victoria and Grand Marquis	56.0
Merkur XR4Ti	40.0
Sable and Taurus	46.0
All others	42.0
Trucks	
Aerostar	
Front system only	60.0
Front and rear system	72.0
F150, F350 pick-ups and Bronco	52.0
Bronco II and Ranger	44.0
E150 and E350 Van	
Front system only	56.0
Front and rear system	68.0
1988	
Cars	
Continental, Cougar, Mark VII, Mustang and Thunderbird	40.0
Crown Victoria, Grand Marquis	52.0
Escort	36.0
Sable and Taurus	
2.5L (Taurus) and 3.0L	44.0
3.8L	40.0
Tempo and Topaz	36.0
Town Car	48.0
Trucks	
Aerostar	56.0
Bronco and F series	52.0
Bronco II and Ranger	40.0

Heating and air conditioning

Manufacturer Year Model	Refrigerant capacity (in ounces)
FORD MOTOR COMPANY (continued)	
1988	
Trucks	
E series	
Without rear A/C	56.0
With rear A/C	68.0
1989 through 1992	
Cars	
Escort, Tempo and Topaz, Tracer	36.0
Continental, Mark VII, Mustang, Probe	40.0
Cougar and Thunderbird	42.0
LTD Crown Victoria, Marquis and Town Car	48.0
Sable and Taurus	44.0
Trucks	
Aerostar	
Without rear A/C	56.0
With rear A/C	60.0
Bronco and F series	52.0
Bronco II, Explorer and Ranger	32.0
E series	
Without rear A/C	60.0
With rear A/C	72.0
FORD MOTOR COMPANY (IMPORT)	22.0 to 27.0
GENERAL MOTORS (DOMESTIC)	
1979	
Buick	
Skyhawk	40.0
Skylark	56.0
All others	60.0
Cadillac	
Seville	56.0
All others	60.0
Chevrolet	
Camaro	52.0
Chevette	36.0
Corvette	48.0
Monza	
"S' Hatchback and Station Wagon	48.0
All others	56.0
Nova	56.0
All others	60.0
Oldsmobile	
Starfire	
A-6 compressor	48.0
R-4 compressor	40.0
Omega	56.0
All others	60.0

Manufacturer Year Model	Refrigerant capacity (in ounces)

GENERAL MOTORS (DOMESTIC) (continued)

1979
  Pontiac

Bonneville and Catalina	60.0
Firebird	52.0
Sunbird	40.0
All others	56.0

1980
  Buick

Century and Riviera	56.0
Electra and LeSabre	60.0
Skyhawk	40.0
Skylark	44.0
Cadillac	60.0

  Chevrolet

Camaro	52.0
Chevette	36.0
Citation	44.0
Corvette	48.0
Monza	56.0
All others	60.0

  Oldsmobile

Omega	44.0
Starfire	40.0
Toronado	56.0
All others	60.0

  Pontiac

Bonneville and Catalina	60.0
Firebird	52.0
Phoenix	44.0
Sunbird	40.0
All other models	56.0

1981
  Buick

Century, Regal and Riviera	52.0
Electra and LeSabre	56.0
Skylark	48.0
Cadillac	60.0

  Chevrolet

Camaro, Malibu and Monte Carlo	52.0
Caprice and Impala	52.0
Chevette	36.0
Citation	44.0
Corvette	48.0

  Oldsmobile

Omega	44.0
Cutlass and Toronado	52.0
All others	56.0

  Pontiac

Bonneville and Catalina	56.0
Firebird, Grand Prix and LeMans	52.0
Phoenix	44.0

Heating and air conditioning

System refrigerant capacity
(continued)

Manufacturer Year Model	Refrigerant capacity (in ounces)
GENERAL MOTORS (DOMESTIC) (continued)	
1982	
Buick	
Electra and LeSabre	56.0
Regal and Riviera	52.0
All others	44.0
Cadillac	
Cimarron	44.0
All others	60.0
Chevrolet	
Camaro and Corvette	48.0
Cavalier, Celebrity and Citation	44.0
Caprice and Impala	56.0
Chevette	36.0
All others	52.0
Oldsmobile	
Ciera, Firenza and Omega	44.0
88 and 98	56.0
All others	52.0
Pontiac	
Bonneville and Grand Prix	52.0
Firebird	48.0
6000	44.0
J2000	40.0
T1000	36.0
1983	
Buick	
Electra and LeSabre	56.0
Regal and Riviera	52.0
Skyhawk	40.0
All others	44.0
Cadillac	
Cimarron	44.0
All others	60.0
Chevrolet	
Camaro	48.0
Cavalier, Celebrity and Citation	44.0
Caprice and Impala	56.0
Chevette	36.0
All others	52.0
Chevrolet and GMC trucks	
Pick-ups and Blazer	58.0
"S' pick-ups and Blazer	40.0
Suburban	
Front system only	48.0
Front and rear system	80.0
Vans	
Front system only	48.0
Front and rear system	64.0
Oldsmobile	
Ciera, Firenza and Omega	44.0
88 and 98	56.0
All others	52.0

Manufacturer Year Model	Refrigerant capacity (in ounces)
GENERAL MOTORS (DOMESTIC) (continued)	
1983	
Pontiac	
Bonneville and Grand Prix	52.0
Firebird	48.0
6000	44.0
J2000	40.0
T1000	36.0
1984	
Buick	
Electra and LeSabre	56.0
Regal and Riviera	52.0
Skyhawk	40.0
All others	44.0
Cadillac	
Cimarron	44.0
All others	56.0
Chevrolet	
Camaro	48.0
Cavalier	40.0
Caprice and Impala	56.0
Celebrity, Citation II and Corvette	44.0
Chevette	36.0
All others	52.0
Chevrolet and GMC trucks	
Blazer and pick-ups	48.0
'S' Blazers and pick-ups	40.0
Suburban	
Front system only	48.0
Front and rear system	72.0
Vans	
Front system only	48.0
Front and rear system	72.0
Oldsmobile	
Ciera, Firenza and Omega	44.0
88 and 98	56.0
All others	52.0
Pontiac	
Bonneville and Grand Prix	53.0
Fiero	56.0
Firebird	48.0
Parisienne	60.0
Phoenix and 6000	44.0
1000	36.0
2000	40.0
1985	
Buick	
Electra and LeSabre	56.0
Regal and Riviera	52.0
Skyhawk	40.0
All others	44.0

Heating and air conditioning

Manufacturer Year Model	Refrigerant capacity (in ounces)
GENERAL MOTORS (DOMESTIC) (continued)	
1985	
Cadillac	
Cimarron	44.0
All others	56.0
Chevrolet	
Camaro	48.0
Cavalier	40.0
Caprice and Impala	56.0
Celebrity, Citation II and Corvette	44.0
Chevette	36.0
All others	52.0
Chevrolet and GMC trucks	
Blazer and pick-ups	48.0
"S' Blazers and pick-ups	40.0
Suburban	
Front system only	48.0
Front and rear system	84.0
Full-size vans	
Front system only	48.0
Front and rear system	72.0
Astro and Safari	
Front system only	32.0
Front and rear system	48.0
Oldsmobile	
Ciera, Firenza and Omega	44.0
88 and 98	56.0
All others	52.0
Pontiac	
Bonneville and Grand Prix	53.0
Fiero	44.0
Firebird	48.0
Parisienne	60.0
Phoenix and 6000	44.0
1000	36.0
2000	40.0
1986	
Buick	
Century	44.0
Electra	46.0
Estate Wagon	56.0
LeSabre	38.0
Regal	52.0
Riviera	44.0
Skyhawk	
1.8L	44.0
2.0L	36.0
Skylark and Somerset	36.0
Cadillac	
Cimarron	36.0
Deville and Fleetwood	46.0
Seville and Eldorado	44.0
All others	56.0

Manufacturer Year Model	Refrigerant capacity (in ounces)

GENERAL MOTORS (DOMESTIC) (continued)

1986

Chevrolet

Camaro	48.0
Cavalier	36.0
Caprice and Monte Carlo	56.0
Celebrity and Corvette	44.0
Chevette	36.0
Nova	27.0
All other models	52.0
Chevrolet and GMC trucks	Same as 1985

Oldsmobile

Calais	36.0
Cutlass	
Supreme and Coupe	48.0
Custom Cruiser	53.0
Ciera	44.0
Delta 88	
3.0L	44.0
3.8L	38.0
Firenza	36.0
Ninety-Eight	46.0
Toronado	44.0
All others	52.0

Pontiac

Bonneville and Grand Prix	53.0
Fiero	40.0
Firebird	48.0
Grand Am	44.0
Parisienne	60.0
Sunbird 2000	44.0
T1000	36.0
6000	
STE	36.0
All others	44.0

1987

Buick

Century	44.0
Electra	46.0
Estate Wagon	56.0
Lesabre	38.0
Regal	52.0
Riviera	44.0
Skyhawk	36.0
Skylark and Somerset	36.0

Cadillac

Allante	46.0
Cimarron	36.0
Deville and Fleetwood	46.0
Seville and Eldorado	44.0
All others	56.0

Heating and air conditioning

System refrigerant capacity
(continued)

Manufacturer Year Model	Refrigerant capacity (in ounces)
GENERAL MOTORS (DOMESTIC) (continued)	
1987	
Chevrolet	
Beretta	36.0
Camaro	48.0
Cavalier	36.0
Caprice and Monte Carlo	56.0
Celebrity and Corvette	44.0
Chevette	36.0
Corsica	36.0
Nova	27.0
All other models	52.0
Chevrolet and GMC trucks	Same as 1985
Oldsmobile	
Calais	36.0
Cutlass	
Supreme and Coupe	48.0
Custom Cruiser	53.0
Ciera	44.0
Delta 88	
3.0L	44.0
3.8L	38.0
Firenza	36.0
Ninety-Eight	46.0
Toronado	44.0
All others	52.0
Pontiac	
Bonneville and Grand Prix	53.0
Fiero	40.0
Firebird	48.0
Grand Am	44.0
Sunbird 2000	44.0
T1000	36.0
6000	
STE	36.0
All others	44.0
1988 through 1992 Cars (body codes are determined by the 4th digit of the Vehicle Identification Number [VIN])	
A Body	
1988 through 1991	44.0
1992	40.0
B Body	
1988 through 1990	56.0
1991 and 1992	50.0
C Body	
1988 through 1992 (except 1990 and 1991 Deville and Fleetwood)	38.0
1990 and 1991 Deville and Fleetwood	45.0
D Body	
1988	56.0
1989 through 1992	Not available

Manufacturer Year Model	Refrigerant capacity (in ounces)

GENERAL MOTORS (DOMESTIC) (continued)

1988 through 1992 Cars (body codes are determined by the 4th digit of the
Vehicle Identification Number [VIN])

E and K body
    1988 .... 44.0
    1989 .... 36.0
    1990 through 1991 .... 38.0 to 42.0
F Body
    1988 .... 36.0
    1989 through 1992 .... 52.0
G Body (1988) 56.0
H Body
    1988 .... 53.0
    1989 .... 46.0
    1990 through 1992 .... 38.0
J Body (1988 through 1992) 36.0
L Body (1988 through 1992) 44.0
N Body
    1988 through 1991 .... 36.0
    1992 .... 44.0
P Body (1988) 40.0
S Body (1988) 27.0
W Body
    1988, 1990 and 1991 .... 36.0
    1989 and 1992 .... 44.0
Y Body
    1988 and 1989 .... 44.0
    1990 through 1992 .... 36.0
1988 through 1992 Trucks
C and K series (full to size pick to ups) 40.0
G series (full to size vans)
    1988 through 1990
        With rear A/C (except 454 engine) 72.0
        With rear A/C and 454 engine 64.0
        Without rear A/C (except 454 engine) 56.0
        Without rear A/C and 454 engine 46.0
    1991 and 1992
        With rear A/C 72.0
        Without rear A/C 48.0
M series
    1988
        With rear A/C 32.0
        Without rear A/C 48.0
    1989
        With rear A/C 60.0
        Without rear A/C 36.0
    1990 through 1992 (includes L series)
        With rear A/C 60.0
        Without rear A/C 48.0

Heating and air conditioning

System refrigerant capacity

(continued)

Manufacturer Year Model	Refrigerant capacity (in ounces)
GENERAL MOTORS (DOMESTIC) (continued)	
1988 through 1992 Trucks	
R series and V series	
1988 through 1992	
With rear A/C	52.0
Without rear A/C	84.0
S series and T series	
1988	37.0
1989	56.0
1990 and 1991	61.0
1992	40.0
U series	
1990	44.0
1991	51.0
1992	
With rear A/C	67.0
Without rear A/C	51.0
GENERAL MOTORS (IMPORTS)	
Spectrum	28.0
Sprint	25.0
Lemans	35.0
Metro and Prizm (through 1991)	18.0
Storm (through 1991)	26.0
Tracker (through 1991)	21.0
HONDA	
1977 through 1982	
Accord	25.0
Civic and Prelude	23.0
1983 and 1984	
Accord	23.0
Civic	20.0
Prelude	25.0
1985 and 1986	
Accord	23.0
All others	26.0 to 30.0
1987 through 1989	
Accord and Civic	23.0 to 26.0
Prelude	34.0
1990 through 1992	
Accord and Civic	30.0
Prelude	34.0
HYUNDAI	
1986	30.0
1987 through 1989	30.0 to 35.0
1990 and later	30.0

Manufacturer Year Model	Refrigerant capacity (in ounces)

INFINITI
1990 (M30 and Q45) ....32.0 to 36.0
1991
   G20 .... 24.0 to 29.0
   M30 .... 29.0 to 32.0
   Q45 .... 38.0 to 41.0

ISUZU
1984
   Trooper.. 33.4
   All others 30.0
1985 and 1986
   Trooper II 34.0
   All others 30.0
1987 and 1988
   I Mark 30.0
   Impulse, Pickup and Trooper II 34.0
1989
   I Mark 28.0
   Impulse, Amigo, Pickup and Trooper II............... 34.0
1990
   Impulse.. 27.0
   Amigo, Pickup and Trooper II........................... 34.0

JEEP
1984 through 1987
   CJ, Scrambler and Wrangler........................... 40.0
   Comanche.. 32.0
   All others 36.0
1988 and 1989
   Wrangler (1988), Cherokee and Wagoneer...................... 40.0
   Comanche and Wrangler (1989) 32.0
   Grand Wagoneer and all others 36.0
1990
   Grand Wagoneer.. 32.0
   All others 38.0
1991 and 1992
   Cherokee
      Two to door 32.0
      Four to door 38.0
   Comanche.. 38.0
   Grand Wagoneer.. 28.0

MAZDA
1986
   B2000.. 33.0
   626 .... 32.0
   RX-7
      Sanden compressor 30.0
      Nippondenso compressor...................... 22.0 to 25.0
   323 .... 30.0

Heating and air conditioning

Manufacturer Year Model	Refrigerant capacity (in ounces)
MAZDA (continued)	
1987 and 1988	
B2200 and 1987 323	30.0
1988	
323, B2600 and 626	30.0 to 33.0
929	35.0
RX7	
Nippondenso compressor	2.02 to 25.0
Sanden compressor	30.0
1989	
B2200	30.0
B2600i	30.0 to 33.0
MPV	
Dual	49.0
Single	42.0
MX-6 and 626	34.0 to 37.0
RX7	
Nippondenso	22.0 to 25.0
Sanden	30.0
323	24.0 to 27.0
929	35.0
1990	
B2200 and B2600i	26.0
MPV	
With rear A/C	49.0
Without rear A/C	42.0
MX-6 and 626	34.0 to 37.0
RX7	26.0
Protege and 323	26.0 to 28.0
929	37.0 to 40.0
1991	
B2200 and B2600i	26.0
Miata	28.0
MPV	
With rear A/C	51.0
Without rear A/C	37.0
MX-6 and 626	32.0
RX7, Protege, 323 and 929	26.0 to 28.0
MERCEDES-BENZ	
1977	
230, 240D, 300D, 280E and 6.9L	42.0
280SE and 340 Series	35.0
1978 through 1980	
280SE and 450 Series	35.0
All others	42.0
1981	56.0
1982 and 1983	
240D	
1982	41.0
1983	42.0
All others	56.0

Manufacturer Year Model	Refrigerant capacity (in ounces)
MERCEDES-BENZ (continued)	
1984 through 1986	
190 Series	42.0
All others	56.0
1987 through 1989 (all models)	39.0
1990 and 1991	
190E	36.0
300 series	39.0
All others	46.0
MITSUBISHI	
1984	24.0
1985 and 1986	
Pick-up	25.0
All others	26.0
1987	
Cordia, Tredia, Montero, Galant and Starion	26.0
Mirage	28.0
Pickup and Precis	32.0
Van/Wagon	49.0
1988 and 1989	
Van/Wagon	51.0
Other models	32.0
1990	
Eclipse	33.0
Galant and Mirage	36.0
Montero	
2.6L	32.0
3.0L	28.0 to 30.0
Precis	28.0 to 30.0
Sigma and Van	33.0
Wagon	51.0
1991	
Eclipse, Galant, Montero and 3000GT	33.0
Mirage	36.0
Pickup and Precis	30.0
NISSAN/DATSUN	
1984	
300ZX and Maxima	35.0
Pick-up and 200SX	32.0 to 38.0
All others	29.0 to 35.0
NISSAN	
1985 and 1986	
Maxima, pick-up, 200SX and 300ZX	32.0 to 38.0
Pulsar, NX, Sentra and Stanza	29.0 to 35.0
1987	
All except Van	32.0 to 38.0
Van	46.0 to 53.0

Heating and air conditioning

System refrigerant capacity
(continued)

Manufacturer Year Model	Refrigerant capacity (in ounces)
NISSAN (continued)	
1988	
Pathfinder and Pickup	29.0 to 32.0
Pulsar NX, Sentra and Stanza	32.0 to 38.0
Van	
With ice maker	50.0 to 56.0
Without ice maker	46.0 to 53.0
All other models	32.0 to 38.0
1989	
Maxima	32.0 to 35.0
Pathfinder, Pickup and Sentra	30.0 to 33.0
300ZX, 240SX, Pulsar and Stanza	32.0 to 38.0
1990	
Axxess, Maxima and 240SX	32.0 to 36.0
Pathfinder, Pickup, Pulsar NX and Sentra	29.0 to 32.0
Stanza and 300ZX	31.0 to 34.0
1991	
Sentra and NX	23.0 to 26.0
Stanza and 300ZX	26.0 to 30.0
Maxima, 240SX, Pathfinder and Pickup	29.0 to 32.0
SUBARU	
1983 and 1984	27.0
1985 and 1986	26.0 to 28.0
1987 through 1989 (all)	26.0 to 28.0
Legacy and Kiki diesel (1990 and 1991)	29.0 to 32.0
Loyale, XT and XT6 (1991)	26.0 to 28.0
SUZUKI	
Samurai and Swift	18.0
Sidekick	21.0 to 23.0
TOYOTA	
1977	20.0
1978 through 1982	24.0
1983 and 1984	23.0 to 26.0
1985 and 1986	
MR2	27.0 to 31.0
Pick-up and 4-Runner	21.0 to 29.0
Van	
Single unit	23.0 to 27.0
Dual unit	48.0 to 51.0
All others	23.0 to 27.0
1987 and 1988	
Land Cruiser	23.0 to 27.0
Van	
Single unit	21.0 to 27.0
Dual unit	48.0 to 51.0
All other models	21.0 to 27.0

Manufacturer Year Model	Refrigerant capacity (in ounces)
TOYOTA (continued)	
1989	
Cressida	27.0 to 30.0
Land Cruiser	23.0 to 27.0
Tercel	21.0 to 27.0
Supra	22.0 to 37.0
Van	
Single unit	21.0 to 27.0
Dual unit	48.0 to 51.0
All other models	27.0 to 30.0
1990 and 1991	
Camry	21.0 to 27.0
Celica, Corolla, Pickup and 4-Runner	24.0 to 29.0
Cressida	27.0 to 30.0
Land Cruiser	29.0 to 32.0
Supra and Tercel	21.0 to 27.0
MR2	30.0 to 34.0
Previa	
Single unit	32.0 to 35.0
Dual unit	41.0 to 44.0
VOLKSWAGEN	
1977 through 1980	34.0
1981	
Rabbit pick-up	35.0
All others	34.0
1982	
Quantum	39.0
All others	34.0
1983 and 1984	
Quantum	39.0
All others	32.0 to 35,0
1985 and 1986	
Quantum	34.0
Scirocco	29.0 to 35.0
Vanagon	42.0 to 46.0
All others	38.0 to 40.0
1987	
Quantum	34.0
Scirocco	29.0 to 35.0
Vanagon	42.0 to 46.0
Cabriolet, Fox and all other models	38.0 to 40.0
1988	
Quantum	34.0
Scirocco	29.0 to 35.0
Vanagon	50.0
Cabriolet, Fox and all other models	38.0 to 40.0
1989	
Golf and Jetta	38.0 to 42.0
Vanagon	50.0
Cabriolet, Fox and all other models	38.0 to 42.0

Heating and air conditioning

System refrigerant capacity
(continued)

Manufacturer Year Model	Refrigerant capacity (in ounces)
VOLKSWAGEN (continued)	
1990	
Vanagon	50.0
All other models	38.0 to 42.0
1991	
Passat	41.0 to 44.0
Vanagon	50.0
All other models	38.0 to 42.0
VOLVO	
1977 through 1979	
240	40.0
1977 through 1979	
260	
1977	38.0
1978 and 1979	47.0
1980	
4-cylinder models	40.0
V6 and Diesel models	47.0
1981 and 1982	
4-cylinder models	40.0
V6 and Diesel models	
1981	47.0
1982	40.0
1983 through 1986	42.0
1987 and 1988	46.0
1989	38.0 to 42.0
1990 and 1991	
240 series	46.0 to 53.0 (39 in 1991)
740, 760 and 940 series	43.0

6 Troubleshooting

Heaters

Little can go wrong with a heater. If the fan motor will run at all speeds, the electrical part of the system is okay. The three basic heater problems fall into the following general categories:

1 Not enough heat
2 Heat all the time
3 No heat

If there's not enough heat, the control valve or door is stuck in a partially open position or the coolant coming from the engine isn't hot enough. If the coolant isn't hot enough, the thermostat in the engine cooling system is stuck open, allowing coolant to pass through the engine so rapidly that it doesn't heat up quickly enough. If the vehicle is equipped with a temperature gauge instead of a warning light, watch to see if the engine temperature rises to the normal operating range after driving for a reasonable distance.

If there's heat all the time, the control valve or the door is stuck wide open. If there's no heat, coolant is probably not reaching the heater core. The likely cause is a collapsed or plugged hose or a frozen heater control valve. If the heater is the type that flows coolant all the time, the cause is a stuck door or a broken or kinked control cable.

The following troubleshooting guide lists some of the more specific heating system problems that may occur.

Heater system trouble diagnosis

Cause	Correction
Insufficient, erratic or no heat	
Low engine coolant level	
Coolant leaks	Fill to proper level. Pressure test for engine cooling system and heater system leaks. Service as required.
Engine overheating	Remove bugs, leaves, etc. from radiator and/or condenser fins. Check for: Sticking thermostat, Incorrect ignition timing, Water pump impeller damaged, Clogged radiator or hoses, Slipping drivebelt, Cooling fan inoperative

Heating and air conditioning

Heater system trouble diagnosis (continued)

Cause	Correction

Insufficient, erratic or no heat (continued)

Cause	Correction
Engine fails to warm up	Check the thermostat and radiator cap. Replace if necessary. Check the coolant level.
Plugged heater core	Clean and back flush engine cooling system and heater core separately. If foreign material still obstructs flow of coolant through core, replace it.
Damaged or deteriorated hoses	Replace damaged hoses and back flush engine cooling system, then heater core, until all deposits have been removed.
Blocked air inlet	Check cowl air inlet for leaves, foreign material, etc. Remove as required.
Improperly adjusted control cables	Readjust cables.
Airflow control doors sticking or binding	Check to see if cable operated doors respond properly to movements of control levers. If hesitation in movement is noted, determine cause and service sticking or binding door as required.
Vehicle interior warms up too slowly	Incorrect operation of controls. Read the owner's manual to make sure you know how to operate the controls and vents properly. Are you using the High blower speed? Check the engine coolant level. Check control cable and blower operation.
Insufficient heat to rear seat	Check for an obstruction on the floor, such as wrinkled or torn sound deadener or insulation material between the seat and the floor. Are you using the blower to force air to the rear seat area?
Cold drafts on floor	Locate and seal any air leaks. Check the operation and adjustment of the vent cables. Are you operating the heating system controls and vents properly? Make sure the front floor mat is not blocking a vent.
Air valves do not operate	See "Vacuum system does not operate air valves." Check for proper installation and/or adjustment of air control cable. Check for proper installation and/or adjustment of air/de-ice control cable.

No high heat output

Cause	Correction
Blower switch	Check the fuse. Check for power and continuity.
Heater control valve	Check for sticking. If closed, repair or replace.
Vacuum line leak	Check vacuum lines to and from electro/vacuum control solenoid for heater doors.
Open circuit at electro/vacuum solenoid	Check for voltage at High output solenoid. Check for a good circuit to ground at solenoid.

Heater system trouble diagnosis (continued)

Cause	Correction

Blower motor operates only on high speed setting

Blower motor resistor	Check resistor for open circuit with a self-powered test light. Replace if open. Make sure wire harness connector makes good contact with resistor spade terminals. Service as necessary.
Blower motor wire harness	Check wire harness from resistor assembly to blower switch for a short to ground. Service as necessary.

Blower motor inoperative

Blown fuse	Check fuse for continuity. Replace fuse as necessary.
Thermal limiter	Check thermal limiter for an open condition.
Open circuit	Check for voltage at the blower motor. Check for a good circuit to ground at blower motor.
Blower motor	Check blower motor operation by it directly to the battery with jumper wires.
Blower switch	Perform a continuity check on the blower switch.

No defrost

Air valve doesn't open	See "Vacuum system does not operate air valves." Adjust operating linkage. Check cable operation.
Air door doesn't open	Check for proper installation and/or adjustment of air or air/de-ice control cable.
Temperature control door doesn't open	Check and adjust temperature control cable if necessary.
Obstructions in defroster outlets at windshield	Remove obstructions. Look for and fix loose instrument panel pad cover at defroster outlets.
Dinged defroster outlets	Reshape outlet flange with pliers (outlet should have a uniform opening).
Blower motor not connected	Connect wire.
Inoperative blower motor	Check heater fuse and wiring. Replace motor, if necessary.
Inoperative blower motor	Check connectors, switch and switch wiring — replace switch as necessary.

Too warm in vehicle

Temperature door improperly adjusted	Check air diaphragm and vacuum supply hose.
Incorrect operation of controls	Are you operating the heater system controls properly?
Inoperative blower switch	Replace switch, if faulty.
Shorted or open resistor	Check the resistor block.

Heating and air conditioning

Heater system trouble diagnosis (continued)

Cause	Correction

Vacuum system doesn't operate air doors (doesn't apply to all vehicles)

Cause	Correction
Little or no vacuum at door diaphragm	Check for vacuum leaks and disconnected hoses.
Leak in vacuum system	Check the vacuum hoses for leaks and obstructions. Check the heater control panel vacuum switch — replace if necessary.
Air door sticking	Check for binding and obstructions at the air door.
Air door doesn't operate	Check for a loose vacuum hose connection at the diaphragm.
Defroster door doesn't operate	Check for a loose vacuum hose connection at the diaphragm.

Miscellaneous

Cause	Correction
Blown fuses	Locate and correct the short.
Front floor mat wet under heater core	Improperly sealed windshield — reseal windshield or lead-in from antenna. Leaking heater core — repair, if possible, or replace heater core. Check for proper seal at dash. Check for leak at connection on heater core (a hose leaking into the heater core is often misdiagnosed as a leaking core).
Heater 'gurgle'	Check engine coolant level.
Objectionable engine or exhaust fumes in vehicle	Check the seals between the engine compartment and the heater/air conditioning box. Check for proper sealing between the air inlet duct assembly and the dash. Locate and seal any other leaks.

Air conditioning systems

Before troubleshooting the system

None of the information included thus far is much use unless you know when to use it. Remember that the manifold gauge set is the most important diagnostic tool available. The key to quick and accurate troubleshooting of most internal system problems is correct interpretation of the test gauges.

If the system isn't producing enough cool air, inspect it for defects and correct as necessary (see ''Preliminary system inspection'' in Chapter 5).

If cool air output is inadequate:

1 Make sure the outside air vents are closed.

2 Inspect the condenser coils and fins to make sure they're clear.

3 Check the compressor clutch for slippage.

4 Make sure there's sufficient refrigerant in the system.

5 Check the blower motor for proper operation.

6 Inspect the blower discharge passage for obstructions.

7 Check the system air intake filter for clogging.

8 Inspect the evaporator. Make sure it's not clogged. Flush it if necessary.

Note: *The remaining general checks for this condition require that the manifold test gauges be hooked up.*

9 If the high side gauge indicates normal pressure and the low side gauge indicates high pressure, the evaporator pressure regulator, hot gas by-pass valve or suction throttling valve is defective or improperly adjusted.

10 If the discharge air temperature is higher than it should be but is accompanied by normal gauge pressures, or slightly increased high side pressure and low suction pressure, the screen in the expansion valve is clogged.

11 If the low side gauge indicates a high pressure and there's excessive sweating of the evaporator and suction line, the expansion valve thermal bulb has lost its charge.

12 If the high side gauge indicates a higher than normal pressure, the low side gauge indicates a lower than normal pressure and the receiver-drier and liquid lines are cold to the touch (even frosting), the screen in the receiver-drier is clogged.

13 If the high pressure gauge indicates a higher than normal pressure, there may be excessive moisture in the system. If there are also bubbles in the sight glass, there's air in the system.

14 If the low pressure gauge indicates high pressure or the clutch cycles at too high a pressure, the thermostat is defective or incorrectly adjusted.

If the system provides intermittent cooling air:

1 Check the circuit breaker, blower switch and blower motor for a malfunction.

2 Inspect the compressor clutch coil and solenoid for an open or bad ground or for a loose connection in the compressor clutch coil or solenoid.

3 Make sure the compressor clutch isn't slipping.

4 Inspect the plenum door to make sure it's operating properly.

5 Inspect the dashboard control head vacuum lines. Make sure they're securely attached.

6 Inspect the evaporator to make sure it isn't clogged.

7 If the unit is icing up, it may be caused by excessive moisture in the system, incorrect super heat switch adjustment or low thermostat adjustment.

General system troubleshooting guidelines

Note: *The last two general checks for this condition require that the manifold test gauges be hooked up.*

8 If the low side gauge indicates low or excessively high pressure and adjustments to the thermostat don't correct the condition, the thermostat is defective.

9 If the low side gauge indicates low pressure and the high side gauge also indicates low pressure, there's moisture in the system and the it has probably clogged the hot gas bypass valve or suction throttle valve.

If the system provides no cooling air:

1 Inspect the compressor drivebelt. Make sure it's not loose or broken.

2 Check for a blown fuse.

3 Check the system wire harness for a blown fusible link (not used on all systems).

4 Inspect the wire harness for a broken or disconnected wire.

5 Inspect the wire harness for a broken or disconnected ground wire.

6 Inspect the clutch coil and solenoid. Make sure that neither is burned out or disconnected.

7 Make sure the electrical switch contacts in the thermostat are not burned excessively and that the sensing element is not defective.

8 Make sure the blower motor is not disconnected or burned out.

9 Check the ignition switch ground and relay. Make sure they're not burned out.

10 Make sure the compressor isn't partially or completely frozen.

11 Inspect the refrigerant lines for leaks.

12 Check the components for leaks.

13 Inspect the receiver-drier/accumulator or expansion valve/tube for clogged screens.

14 Inspect the compressor shaft seal for leaks.

15 If there's hot water in the heater and hot discharge air from the evaporator, the heater valve is inoperative.

Note: *The remaning general checks for this condition require that the manifold test gauges be hooked up.*

16 If there is only a slight variation in both gauge readings at any engine speed, the compressor reed valves are inoperative.

17 If the high side gauge indicates normal pressure but the low side gauge indicates high pressure, and the evaporator is flooding, the expansion valve is stuck open.

If the system is noisy:

1 Look for loose panels in the passenger compartment.

2 Inspect the compressor drivebelt. It may be loose or worn.

3 Check the compressor mounting bolts. They should be tight.

4 Listen carefully to the compressor. It may be worn out.

5 Listen to the idler pulley and bearing and the clutch. Either may be defective.

6 Inspect the wiring to the compressor clutch coil and solenoid for defects.

7 The winding in the compressor clutch coil or solenoid may be defective.

8 The compressor oil level may be low.

9 The blower motor fan bushing or the motor itself may be worn out.

10 If there is an excessive charge in the system, you'll hear a rumbling noise in the high pressure line, a thumping noise in the compressor, excessive pressure indicated on the high and low side gauges, bubbles or cloudiness in the sight glass or low pressure on the high side gauge.

11 If there's a low charge in the system, you'll hear hissing in the evaporator case at the expansion valve, bubbles or cloudiness in the sight glass or low head pressure indicated on the high side gauge.

12 If there's excessive moisture in the system, the expansion valve will be noisy and suction side pressure will be low.

13 If the high side service valve is closed, the compressor will make a knocking noise and the high pressure gauge will indicate above normal pressure.

Expansion valve system troubleshooting

1 Connect a manifold gauge set to the system and purge it (see Chapters 4 and 5).

2 The engine should be running at the normal fast idle speed.

3 Use a large fan to blow air through the condenser and radiator.

4 Run the air conditioning system for about 5 minutes to allow it to stabilize.

5 Conduct a system performance test (see Chapter 5).

6 Note the gauge readings and other symptoms indicated on the following pages. Since gauge readings can vary, and their interpretaion is often based on personal opinion and previous experience, they should be considered only as a general guide.

7 Note any indicated symptoms as listed under "Symptoms" and perform additional tests if indicated. Perform the remedial procedures indicated under "Repair."

Interpreting the gauges when troubleshooting an expansion valve system

The high and low side system pressures on the following pages are typical pressure values you can expect to see on the gauges (assuming an ambient temperature of 85°F at sea level) when any of the following malfunctions occur.

An auxiliary low side gauge, and the typical pressure reading it would indicate for a given condition, are also included where appropriate. Of course, this assumes that you will use an auxiliary gauge on systems such as Chrysler's Evaporator Pressure Regulator (EPR) system and some Ford Suction Throttling Valve (STV) systems. If you're using a two-gauge set, disregard any information about the auxiliary gauge. **Note:** *The pressures shown in the following chart are intended as a general guide. They may or may not correlate exactly with the pressure values indicated on the gauges.*

Heating and air conditioning

Pressure/temperature relationship

Low side gauge (psi)	Evap. temp (°F)	High side gauge (psi)	Ambient temp* (°F)
10	2	130 to 160	60
12	6	140 to 170	65
14	10	150 to 180	70
16	14	160 to 190	75
18	18	170 to 210	80
20	20	180 to 220	85
22	22	190 to 230	90
24	24	205 to 250	95
26	27	220 to 270	100
28	29	240 to 290	105
30	32	260 to 310	110
35	36	285 to 335	115
40	42	310 to 370	120
45	48		
50	53		
55	58		
60	62		
65	66		
70	70		

* Always try to measure ambient temperature two inches in front of the condenser

Some air and moisture in the system

Low Side NORMAL   **High Side NORMAL**   **Aux. Low Side NORMAL**

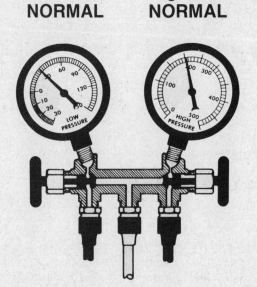 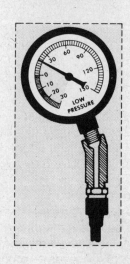

System pressure:
    The low side gauge indicates normal pressure.
    The high side gauge indicates normal pressure.
    The auxiliary gauge indicates normal pressure.

Symptoms:
    The sight glass is clear, or shows a few bubbles.
    The discharge air slightly cool.
    On a thermostatic switch system, the low side gauge doesn't fluctuate with the switch "on" and "off" cycles.

Troubleshooting

Diagnosis: There is some air and moisture in the system

Solution:

1 Leak test the system (check the compressor seal area very carefully).

2 Discharge the system.

3 Locate and repair any leaks found.

4 Replace the receiver-drier, accumulator or desiccant bag.

5 Evacuate the system for at least 30 minutes.

6 Charge the system with R-12.

7 Operate the system and check its performance.

Excessive moisture in the system

| Low Side NORMAL | High Side NORMAL | Aux. Low Side NORMAL |

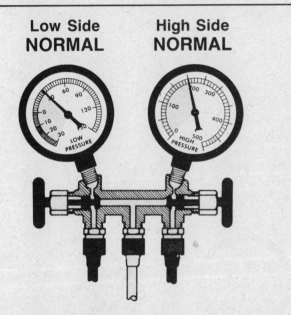 

System pressure:
The low side gauge indicates normal pressure.
The high side gauge indicates normal pressure.
The auxiliary gauge indicates normal pressure.

Symptoms:
Tiny bubbles are visible in the sight glass.
The discharge air warms when the low side cycles into vacuum.
As moisture is released by the saturated desiccant, it becomes trapped — and freezes — at the expansion valve, blocking the flow of refrigerant into the evaporator.

Diagnosis: There is excessive moisture in the system

Solution:

1 Discharge the system.

2 Replace the receiver-drier, accumulator or desiccant bag.

3 Evacuate the system with a vacuum pump.

4 Recharge the system.

5 Operate the system and check its performance.

Heating and air conditioning

Excessive air and moisture in the system

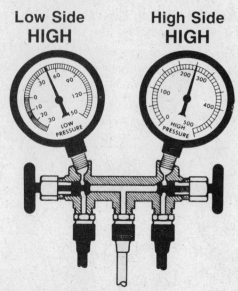
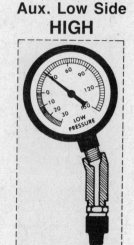

Low Side HIGH   **High Side HIGH**   **Aux. Low Side HIGH**

System pressure
The low side gauge indicates high pressure.
The high side gauge indicates high pressure.
The auxiliary gauge indicates high pressure.

Symptoms:
There are occasional bubbles visible in the sight glass.
The discharge air is slightly cool.

Diagnosis: There is an excessive amount of air and moisture in the system

Solution:

1 Discharge the system.

2 Replace the receiver-drier, desiccant or accumulator.

3 Evacuate the system.

4 Charge the system.

5 Operate the system and check its performance.

Defective thermostatic switch

System pressure:
The low side gauge indicates normal pressure.
The high side gauge indicates normal pressure.

Symptoms:
The compressor cycles on and off too quickly.
The low side gauge doesn't indicate sufficient range.

Diagnosis: The thermostatic switch is defective

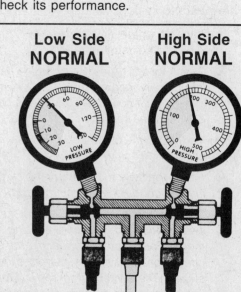

Low Side NORMAL   **High Side NORMAL**

Solution:

1 Remove and discard the old thermostatic switch.

2 Install a new switch. **Caution:** *Make sure the capillary tube is installed in the same position and to the same depth in the evaporator core as the old switch tube. Don't kink or bend the capillary tube sharply - it's gas-filled.*

3 Operate the system and check its performance.

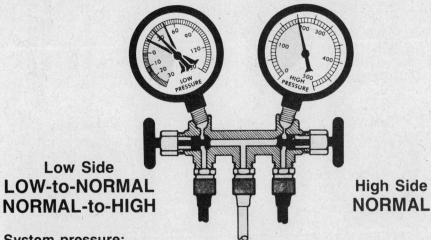

Low Side
LOW-to-NORMAL
NORMAL-to-HIGH

High Side
NORMAL

System pressure:
The low side gauge indicates low-to-normal pressure.
The high side gauge indicates normal pressure.

Symptoms:
The compressor cycles at the wrong temperature or pressure.
The evaporator freezes and restricts airflow if the switch allows the compressor to remain in operation too long

Diagnosis: The thermostatic switch is misadjusted, or the pressure sensing switch (if equipped) is defective

Solution:
Thermostatic switch

1 Remove whatever components necessary to gain access to the thermostatic adjustment screw.

2 Check for the presence of the adjusting screw or thermostatic switch (it's usually located under the cover on the end of the switch housing). **Note:** *If no adjusting screw is present, the switch is non-adjustable and must be replaced.*

3 Verify that the electrical wiring is routed so that a short circuit cannot occur.

4 Adjust the switch. **Note:** *The battery must be hooked up so the engine and air conditioning system can be operated during the adjustment.*

5 Operate the system and check its performance. Pressure sensing switch **Note:** *The pressure sensing switch, which is used on some late model Ford Motor Company and General Motors vehicles with accumulator type systems, performs the same function as the thermostatic switch. The switch is non-adjustable and is mounted on a Schrader valve fitting. No system discharge, therefore, is required.*

Misadjusted thermostatic switch or defective pressure sensing switch

Heating and air conditioning

Solution:
Pressure sensing switch

1 Detach the electrical connector from the pressure sensing switch at the accumulator.

2 Remove the pressure sensing switch.

3 Install a new switch.

4 Operate the system and check its performance.

Low R-12 charge

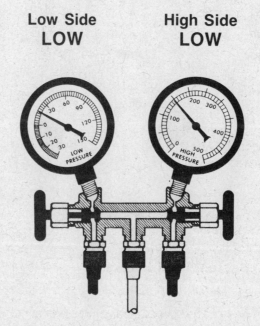 

Low Side **LOW** High Side **LOW** Aux. Low Side **LOW**

System pressure:
The low side gauge indicates normal pressure.
The high side gauge indicates low pressure.
The auxiliary gauge indicates low pressure.

Symptoms:
The discharge air is slightly cool.
Some bubbles are visible in the sight glass.

Diagnosis: The system is slightly low on refrigerant

Solution:

1 Leak test the system.

2 Discharge the system, if necessary.

3 Repair any leaks found, or replace leaking components.

4 Check the compressor oil level. The system may have lost oil due to leakage.

5 Evacuate the system.

6 Charge the system.

7 Operate the system and check its performance.

**Low Side
LOW** **High Side
LOW** **Aux. Low Side
LOW**

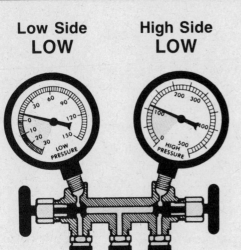 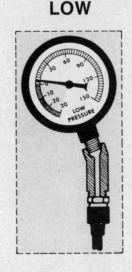

Very low R-12 charge

System pressure:
  The low side gauge indicates low pressure.
  The high side gauge indicates low pressure.
  The auxiliary gauge indicates low pressure.

Symptoms:
  The discharge air is warm.
  Clear, or oil, streaks are visible in the sight glass.
  The compressor has ceased operation (will occur on a system equipped
    with a refrigerant pressure sensing device).

Diagnosis: The system refrigerant level is very low

Solution:

1 If compressor operation has ceased because of a pressure sensing
  device, bypass the device with a jumper wire until testing and repairs
  are completed.

2 Add a partial charge to the system (at least half of the system capacity).

3 Perform a leak test.

4 Discharge the system.

5 Check the compressor oil level. The system may have lost oil due to
  leakage.

6 Evacuate the system.

7 Charge the system.

8 Operate the system and check its performance.

System pressure:
  The low side gauge indicates low pressure.
  The high side gauge indicates low pressure.
  The auxiliary gauge indicates low pressure.

Symptoms:
  The discharge air is slightly cool.
  The expansion valve is sweating or there is frost build-up.

Expansion valve stuck

Heating and air conditioning

Expansion valve stuck
(continued)

Low Side
LOW

High Side
LOW

Aux. Low Side
LOW

Diagnosis: The expansion valve is stuck closed, the screen is plugged or the sensing bulb is malfunctioning

Solution:

1 If the expansion valve inlet is cool to the touch:
   a) Turn on the air conditioner and set it to its maximum cooling mode.
   b) Spray liquid refrigerant onto the head of the valve or the caillary tube. Note the low side gauge reading. The low side gauge should drop into a vacuum. **Note:** *This test may not be possible on some vehicles if the expansion valve or the capillary tube is not accessible.*
   c) If a low side vacuum reading is obtained, warm the expansion valve diaphragm chamber with your hand, then repeat the step above.
   d) If the expansion valve test indicates that valve operation is satisfactory, clean the contact surface of the evaporator outlet pipe and the temperature sensing bulb. Make sure that the bulb is in snug contact with the pipe. Proceed to step 3.
   e) If the expansion valve test indicates that the valve is defective, discharge the system, replace the valve and proceed to step 3.

2 If the expansion valve inlet shows sweating or frost:

   a) Discharge the system.
   b) Detach the inlet line from the expansion valve.
   c) Clean and replace the screen and reconnect the inlet line.
   d) Proceed to the next step.

3 Evacuate the system.
4 Charge the system.
5 Operate the system and check its performance.

Low Side
LOW

High Side
LOW

Aux. Low Side
LOW

Restriction in high side

System pressure:

The low side gauge indicates low pressure.

The high side gauge indicates low pressure (may be normal to high if a restriction is located right after the service valve).

The auxiliary gauge indicates low pressure.

Symptoms:

The discharge air is slightly cool.

The high side lines are cool and show sweating or frost (which will appear immediately after the point at which the line is restricted).

Diagnosis: There is a restriction in the high side

Solution:

1 Discharge the system.

2 Remove and replace the receiver-drier, liquid lines or other faulty components.

3 Evacuate the system with a vacuum pump.

4 Charge the system.

5 Operate the system and check its performance.

Note: *The following two conditions apply only to Chrysler Corporation vehicles equipped with an Evaporator Pressure Regulator (EPR) valve*

System pressure:

The low side gauge indicates high pressure.

The high side gauge indicates normal-to-low pressure.

The auxiliary gauge indicates low pressure.

Symptoms:

The evaporator outlet pipe is warm.

The discharge air is warm.

The difference in pressure between the low side gauge and the auxiliary gauge is excessive (it shouldn't exceed 6 psi).

Evaporator pressure regulator (EPR) valve stuck closed

Heating and air conditioning

EPR valve stuck closed
(continued)

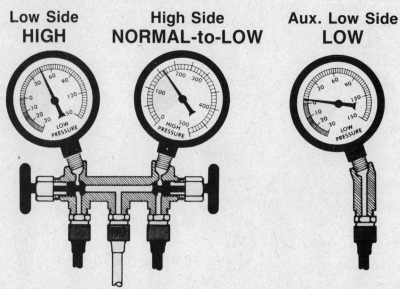

**Low Side
HIGH**

**High Side
NORMAL-to-LOW**

**Aux. Low Side
LOW**

Diagnosis: The Evaporator Pressure Regulator (EPR) valve is stuck closed

Solution:

1 Discharge the system.

2 To gain access to the valve, which is located in the suction passage, remove the fasteners from the suction line fitting on the rear of the compressor and detach the fitting.

3 To remove the valve:

a) Remove the retaining snap-ring (if installed) from the EPR valve cavity.

b) Rotate the valve counterclockwise and remove it. **Note:** *On earlier valves, a special Chrysler tool (C-3822 or C3822A) is needed to engage the valve; on later valves, a protrusion on the valve can be grasped with needle-nose pliers.*

4 Lubricate the new O-ring with refrigerant oil and install it on the new valve.

5 Install the new valve (with the special tool, if necessary).

6 Clean the suction screen (if equipped).

7 Reposition the screen, spring and fitting. Tighten the fasteners to about 8 to 14 ft-lbs.

8 Evacuate the system.

9 Charge the system.

10 Operate the system and check its performance.

EPR valve stuck open

System pressure:
The low side gauge indicates low pressure.
The high side gauge indicates normal-to-high pressure.
The auxiliary gauge indicates low pressure.

Symptoms:
The evaporator outlet pipe is very cold.
The low side gauge indicates vacuum when the blower is disconnected.
The drop in pressure between the low side gauge and the auxiliary gauge is excessive (it should not exceed 6 psi).

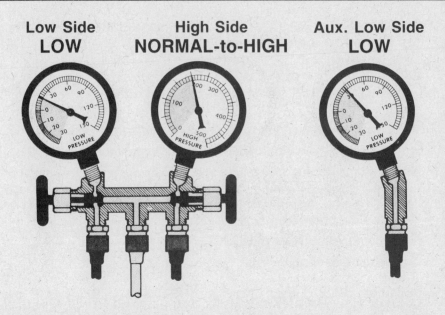

Low Side LOW   **High Side** NORMAL-to-HIGH   **Aux. Low Side** LOW

Diagnosis: The Evaporator Pressure Regulator (EPR) is stuck open

Solution:
    Same as solution for "EPR stuck closed".

STV/POA valve stuck closed

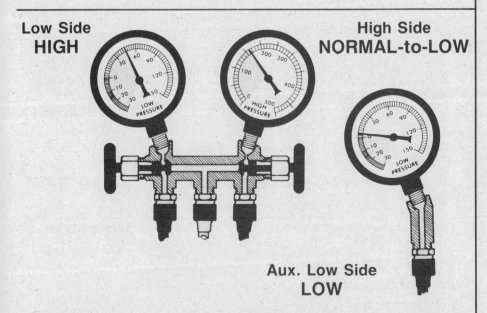

Low Side HIGH   **High Side** NORMAL-to-LOW

Aux. Low Side LOW

Note: *The following two conditions apply only to Ford and General Motors vehicles equipped with a Suction Throttling Valve (STV).*

System pressure:
    The low side gauge indicates high pressure.
    The high side gauge indicates normal-to-low pressure.
    The auxiliary gauge indicates low pressure.

Symptoms:
    The evaporator outlet pipe is warm.
    The discharge air is warm.

Heating and air conditioning

STV/POA valve stuck closed
(continued)

Diagnosis: The STV/POA valve is stuck closed; there's a restriction in the low side of the system

Solution:
Adjustment (Suction Throttling Valve [STV] — 1962 through 1965 General Motors systems)

1 Detach the vacuum line at the vacuum diaphragm fitting.

2 Loosen the locknut on the vacuum diaphragm mounting sleeve.

3 Rotate the vacuum diaphragm and sleeve counterclockwise (out of the valve body) to lower the pressure indicated on the low side gauge until it's within the normal range. **Caution:** *If the valve is rotated completely out of the body, immediate system discharge will occur.*

4 Tighten the locknut securely.

5 Reattach the vacuum line.

Replacement (Pilot Operated Absolute [POA] STV valve — 1965 and later models)

1 Discharge the system.

2 Detach all lines from the STV.

3 Remove the STV. **Note:** *If the STV is an integral component of a combination assembly (such as the Ford system, for example), it may be necessary to remove the combination assembly to gain access to the valve.*

4 Install a new STV. Make sure the replacement unit is the exact same model as the old unit.

5 Replace the receiver-drier, then evacuate the system.

6 If STV failure has caused the superheat switch to cut off compressor operation (on a General Motors system, for example), check the thermal limiter fuse (refer to the fuse guide in the owner's manual). Replace it if necessary.

7 Charge the system.

8 Operate the system and check its performance. If necessary, adjust the STV (older type only) to obtain the proper pressures.

Suction throttling valve (STV) stuck open

System pressure:
The low side gauge indicates low pressure.
The high side gauge indicates normal-to-high pressure.
The auxiliary gauge indicates low pressure.

Symptoms:
The evaporator outlet pipe is very cold.
The low side gauge indicates vacuum when the blower is disconnected.
On General Motors vehicles equipped with a superheat switch, the compressor may have ceased to operate.

Diagnosis: The Suction Throttling Valve (STV) is stuck open

Solution:
Adjustment (STV valve — 1962 through 1965 General Motors systems)

1 Disconnect the vacuum line at the vacuum diaphragm fitting.

Low Side **High Side** **Aux. Low Side**
LOW **NORMAL-to-HIGH** **LOW**

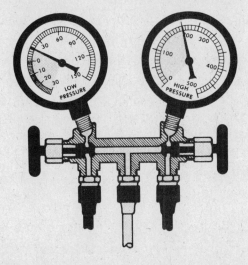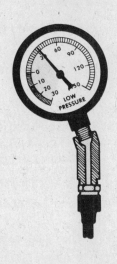

2 Loosen the locknut on the vacuum diaphragm mounting sleeve.

3 Rotate the vacuum diaphragm and sleeve clockwise (into the body) to increase the pressure indicated on the low and auxiliary gauges. Continue turning until the indicated readings are normal.

4 If the valve cannot be adjusted to the correct setting, replace it (see "STV stuck closed" above).

Replacement (Pilot Operated Absolute [POA] type STV — 1965 and later models)
This design is not serviceable. If it's faulty, replace it (See "STV stuck closed" above).

Low Side **High Side** **Aux. Low Side**
HIGH **LOW** **HIGH**

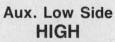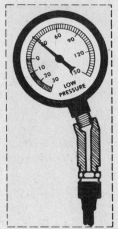

Compressor malfunctioning

System pressure:
The low side gauge indicates high pressure.
The high side gauge indicates low pressure.
The auxiliary gauge indicates high pressure.

Compressor malfunctioning
(continued)

Symptoms:
The compressor is noisy (if the compressor is not noisy but the above gauge readings are indicated, the problem may be a loose or worn compressor drivebelt).

Diagnosis: The compressor is malfunctioning

Solution:
1 Discharge the system (or isolate the compressor, if equipped with stem-type service valves).

2 Remove the compressor cylinder head and inspect it.

3 Replace the reed valve plate assembly if necessary.

4 Install the cylinder head. Use a new gasket.

5 Check the compressor oil level.

6 Replace the receiver-drier, desiccant or accumulator if:
   a) The system has been previously opened.
   b) The system has been operated two or more years with the present unit.
   c) Compressor inspection reveals desiccant particles (very fine, brown or gold in color).

7 Evacuate the system (or the isolated, stem-type compressor).

8 Charge the system.

9 Operate the system and check its performance.

Condenser malfunction or overcharge

Low Side HIGH	High Side HIGH	Aux. Low Side HIGH

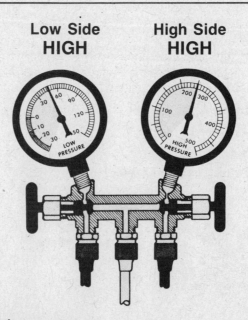 

System pressure:
The low side gauge indicates high pressure.
The high side gauge indicates high pressure.
The auxiliary gauge indicates high pressure.

Symptoms:
The discharge air is warm.
The high side lines are very hot.
There are bubbles visible in the sight glass.

Diagnosis: The condenser is malfunctioning or the system is overcharged

Solution:

1 Make sure the fan is working. Like the radiator, the condenser won't work well when the vehicle is at rest without the fan.

2 A slowly turning (clutch type) fan will also affect condenser performance. Inspect the fan drivebelt for loose adjustment and wear.

3 Inspect the front of the vehicle for a clogged bug shield or grille or any other obstruction that could prevent air from flowing through the condenser.

4 Check the clearance between the condenser and the radiator. Inspect the condenser mounting hardware, particularly any rubber bushings, for wear. Make sure all hardware is tight and in good condition.

5 After making the above inspections and necessary repairs, operate the system and check its performance.

6 If the indicated pressures are not lowered and/or the symptoms have not disappeared, inspect the system for an overcharge and correct as follows:
   a) Discharge refrigerant until a stream of bubbles appears in the sight glass and the pressures indicated on both the high and low side gauges drop below normal.
   b) Add refrigerant until the bubbles disappear and pressures return to normal, then add another 1/4 to 1/2 pound.

7 Operate the system and check its performance.

8 If the gauge readings are still too high:
   a) Discharge the system.
   b) Remove and inspect the condenser to ensure free passage of the refrigerant. Back flush it if necessary. Replace the condenser if flushing doesn't remove the obstruction(s).

9 Replace the receiver-drier, desiccant bag or accumulator.

10 Evacuate the system.

11 Charge the system.

12 Operate the system and check its performance.

System pressure:
The low side gauge indicates high pressure.
The high side gauge indicates high pressure.
The auxiliary gauge indicates high pressure.

Symptoms:
The discharge air is warm.
The evaporator is sweating or frosting.

Diagnosis: The expansion valve is stuck open

Solution:

1 To verify that the expansion valve is stuck open (or that the temperature sensing bulb is stuck open): **Note:** *This test may not be*

Expansion valve stuck open

Heating and air conditioning

**Expansion valve
stuck open**
(continued)

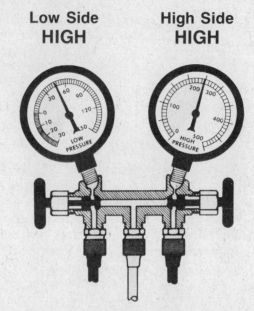

**Low Side
HIGH**

**High Side
HIGH**

**Aux. Low Side
HIGH**

possible on systems with an inaccessible sensing bulb.

a) Set the air conditioner controls for maximum cooling and operate the system for several minutes.

b) Spray liquid refrigerant onto the head of the valve or capillary tube and note the pressure reading indicated on the low side gauge. It should drop into a vacuum. If it doesn't, a stuck open valve or improper installation of the bulb is indicated.

c) If a low side vacuum is indicated, warm the expansion valve diaphragm chamber with your hand, then repeat the test.

2 If the expansion valve test indicates that valve operation is satisfactory:

a) Clean the contact surface of the evaporator outlet pipe and the temperature sensing bulb, then clamp the bulb securely in contact with the pipe and recover with the proper insulation tape.

b) Operate the system and check its performance.

3 If the expansion valve test indicates that the valve is defective:

a) Discharge the system.

b) Replace the expansion valve. Make sure that all contacts are clean and secure.

c) Evacuate the system.

d) Recharge the system.

e) Operate the system and check its performance.

**Ford fixed orifice
tube (FFOT)
system
troubleshooting**

The best way to troubleshoot an FFOT system is to analyze the clutch "cycle rate" and the refrigerant pressures, which vary between the lowest and highest points during the clutch cycle. (One complete cycle is equal to the time that the clutch is on plus the time that it's off.)

After noting and recording the system pressures and clutch cycle rate, simply compare your observations with the correct chart to determine whether the observed values correspond with the normal values.

To obtain accurate clutch cycle timing for the FFOT system, the following conditions must be met:

In-vehicle temperatures must be stabilized at 70 to 80°F.

The air conditioning system must be operating in the maximum cooling

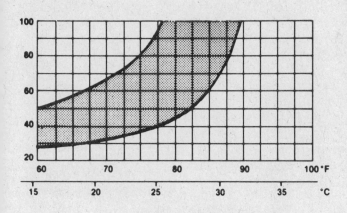

SECONDS — **TOTAL CLUTCH CYCLE TIME — SECONDS**

AMBIENT TEMPERATURES

THESE CONDITIONAL REQUIREMENTS FOR THE FIXED ORIFICE TUBE CYCLING CLUTCH SYSTEM TESTS MUST BE SATISFIED TO OBTAIN ACCURATE CLUTCH CYCLE TIMING

- Stabilized in Car Temperatures @ 70°F to 80°F (21°C to 27°C)
- Maximum A/C (Recirculating Air)
- **Maximum** Blower Speed
- 1500 Engine RPM For 10 Minutes

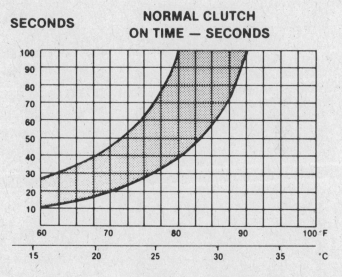

SECONDS — **NORMAL CLUTCH ON TIME — SECONDS**

AMBIENT TEMPERATURES

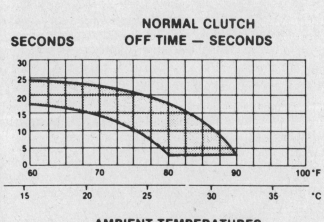

SECONDS — **NORMAL CLUTCH OFF TIME — SECONDS**

AMBIENT TEMPERATURES

mode (recirculating the air).
The blower speed must be at the highest setting.
The engine must be running at 1500 rpm for 10 minutes.

The lowest pressure recorded on the low pressure gauge (observed when the clutch is disengaged) is the low pressure setting of the clutch cycling pressure switch. The high pressure setting for the switch is the pressure recorded when the clutch engages.

It should be noted that compressor clutch cycling doesn't normally occur in ambient temperatures above 100°F, and, in some cases, above 90°F, depending on local conditions and engine speed. In other words, the compressor just keeps running. Clutch cycling also doesn't usually occur when the engine is operating at curb idle speed.

Also, if the system contains no refrigerant or is extremely low on refrigerant, the clutch will neither engage nor operate. If the compressor cycles rapidly, it usually indicates the system is low on refrigerant.

Refer to these charts to determine the normal clutch cycle rates and times for a Ford Fixed Orifice Tube (FFOT) system — Tempo/Topaz, Escort/Lynx shown — others similar

Heating and air conditioning

Note: *Once a problem with the system has been corrected, repeat the following test procedure to make sure the problem has been eliminated.*

1 If insufficient cooling is noted and the vehicle's engine cooling system isn't equipped with an electric cooling fan system, proceed to step 2. If the vehicle is equipped with an electric cooling fan system, verify that the compressor clutch engages.
   a) If it doesn't, check the clutch electrical circuit.
   b) If it does, verify that the cooling fan operates when the compressor clutch is engaged.
       1) If the fan doesn't operate when the compressor clutch is engaged, check the cooling fan circuit.
       2) If the fan does operate when the compressor clutch is engaged, proceed to the next step.

2 Inspect the compressor drivebelt. Make sure that it's not loose or deteriorated.

3 Inspect the compressor clutch wires and connectors. Make sure they're not frayed or otherwise damaged. Look at the electrical connectors. Make sure they're not loose or unplugged. Be sure the resistor assembly is properly connected.

4 Check for blown fuses.

5 Make sure the blower operates properly.

6 Check all vacuum hoses and connections.

7 Make sure all vacuum motors and temperature doors move freely and open all the way.

8 Inspect all dashboard control head electrical and vacuum connections.

9 If cooling is still insufficient even after all the above items have been checked and, where necessary, repaired, the FFOT system must be examined more closely using the following pressure-cycle time charts.

10 Hook up a manifold gauge set, set the selector lever to the Maximum position, turn the blower switch to the highest setting and put the temperature lever at the coldest setting. Close all vehicle doors and windows.

11 Install a thermometer in the center vent (the one closest to the evaporator) and check the discharge temperature. Record the measurement. Also note and record the ambient (outside) temperature.

12 Run the engine for 10 to 15 minutes at approximately 1500 rpm with the compressor clutch engaged.

13 Measure the compressor clutch cycle time (on and off time) with a watch. Record the measurements and compare them to the accompanying charts.

   a) If the compressor cycles very rapidly, proceed to step 14.
   a) If the compressor cycles slowly, proceed to step 15.
   c) If the compressor doesn't cycle at all (runs continuously), proceed to step 16.
   d) If the compressor cycles normally, proceed to step 17.

14 If the compressor cycles very rapidly (1 second on, 1 second off), bypass the clutch cycling switch with a jumper wire. The compressor should operate continuously. Now feel the evaporator inlet and outlet tubes.

NORMAL CLUTCH CYCLE RATE PER MINUTE

CYCLES/MINUTE

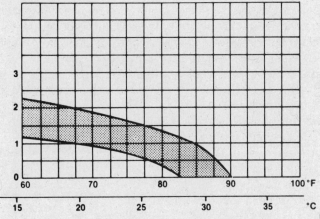

AMBIENT TEMPERATURES

NORMAL CENTER REGISTER DISCHARGE TEMPERATURES

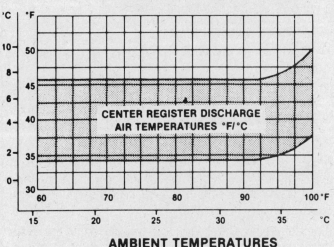

AMBIENT TEMPERATURES

THESE CONDITIONAL REQUIREMENTS FOR THE FIXED ORIFICE TUBE CYCLING CLUTCH SYSTEM TESTS MUST BE SATISFIED TO OBTAIN ACCURATE PRESSURE READINGS.

- Stabilized in Car Temperatures @ 70°F to 80°F (21°C to 27°C)
- Maximum A/C (Recirculating Air)
- Maximum Blower Speed
- 1500 Engine RPM For 10 Minutes

NORMAL FIXED ORIFICE TUBE CYCLING CLUTCH REFRIGERANT SYSTEM PRESSURES

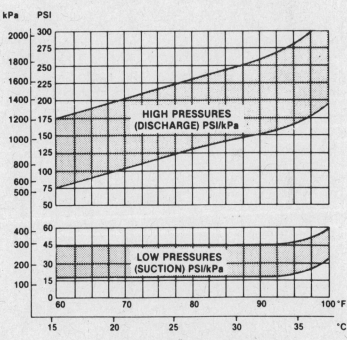

AMBIENT TEMPERATURES

a) If they feel about the same temperature, replace the clutch cycling switch and retest the system.

b) If the evaporator inlet tube is warm, or if the outlet tube feels colder downstream from the orifice tube, leak-test the system, repair any leaks, evacuate, charge and retest the system. If no leaks are found, add about 1/4-pound of refrigerant to the system and feel the inlet and outlet tubes again.

c) If the evaporator inlet tube is colder, add 1/4-pound of refrigerant and feel the inlet and outlet tubes again. Continue to add refrigerant in 1/4-pound increments until both tubes feel about the same temperature (within a range of 28 to 40°F).

d) When the inlet tube feels about the same temperature as the outlet tube (about 28 to 40°F), add another 1/2 to 3/4 pounds of refrigerant and measure the discharge air temperature. It should be about 50°F.

Refer to these charts to determine normal Ford Fixed Orifice Tube (FFOT) cycling clutch refrigerent system pressure/temperature relationships — Tempo/Topaz, Escort/Lynx shown — others similar

187

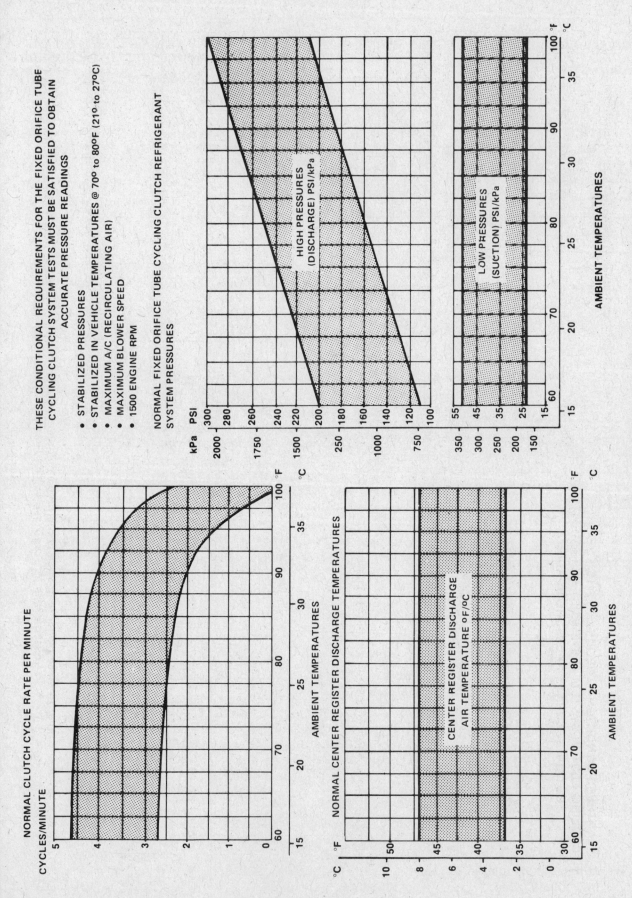

THESE CONDITIONAL REQUIREMENTS FOR THE FIXED ORIFICE TUBE CYCLING CLUTCH SYSTEM TESTS MUST BE SATISFIED TO OBTAIN ACCURATE PRESSURE READINGS

- STABILIZED PRESSURES
- STABILIZED IN VEHICLE TEMPERATURES @ 70° to 80°F (21° to 27°C)
- MAXIMUM A/C (RECIRCULATING AIR)
- MAXIMUM BLOWER SPEED
- 1500 ENGINE RPM

NORMAL FIXED ORIFICE TUBE CYCLING CLUTCH REFRIGERANT SYSTEM PRESSURES

HIGH PRESSURES (DISCHARGE) PSI/kPa

LOW PRESSURES (SUCTION) PSI/kPa

AMBIENT TEMPERATURES

NORMAL CLUTCH CYCLE RATE PER MINUTE

CYCLES/MINUTE

AMBIENT TEMPERATURES

NORMAL CENTER REGISTER DISCHARGE TEMPERATURES

CENTER REGISTER DISCHARGE AIR TEMPERATURE °F/°C

AMBIENT TEMPERATURES

Refer to these charts to determine the normal clutch cycle rates and times and pressure/temperature relationships for Ford Fixed Orifice Tube (FFOT) system on F-100 through F-350 trucks and Broncos

THESE CONDITIONAL REQUIREMENTS FOR THE CYCLING CLUTCH SYSTEM TESTS MUST BE SATISFIED TO OBTAIN ACCURATE PRESSURE READINGS.

- Stabilized Pressures
- Stabilized in Car Temperatures (≈ 70° to 80° F (21° to 27° C)
- Maximum A/C (Recirculating Air)
- Maximum Blower Speed
- 1500 Engine RPM
- Compressor Clutch Engaged

NORMAL CYCLING CLUTCH REFRIGERANT SYSTEM PRESSURES

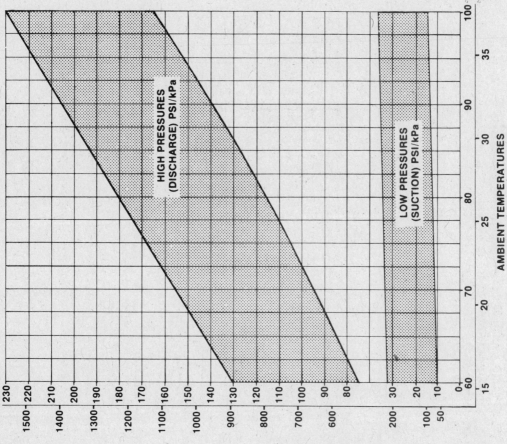

HIGH PRESSURES (DISCHARGE) PSI/kPa

LOW PRESSURES (SUCTION) PSI/kPa

AMBIENT TEMPERATURES

NORMAL CENTER REGISTER DISCHARGE TEMPERATURES

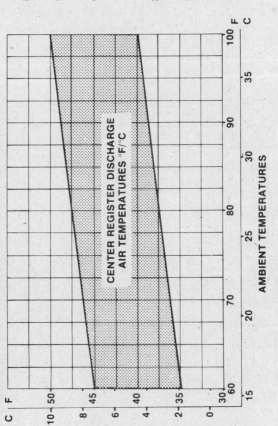

CENTER REGISTER DISCHARGE AIR TEMPERATURES °F/°C

AMBIENT TEMPERATURES

Refer to these charts to determine the normal clutch cycle rates and times and pressure/temperature relationships for Ford Fixed Orifice Tube (FFOT) system on Econoline vans

189

15 If the compressor cycles slowly, feel the evaporator inlet and outlet tubes.

a) If the inlet tube is warm or if the outlet tube is colder downstream from the orifice tube, perform step 14 (disregard part a), to restore the system to its proper charge level.

b) If the inlet and outlet tubes feel the same temperature (about 28 to 40°F), or if the outlet tube (downstream from the orifice tube) feels slightly colder than the inlet tube, check the system for normal pressure.

b) If the inlet and outlet tubes feel the same temperature (about 28 to 40°F), or if the outlet tube (downstream from the orifice tube) feels slightly colder than the inlet tube, check the system for normal pressure.

16 If the compressor does not cycle at all (runs continuously), disconnect the blower motor wire and verify that the compressor cycles off between 21 and 26 psi (low side pressure). Note: Under some conditions (ambient temperatures above 80°F, or slightly lower, depending on humidity), it's normal for the compressor to run continuously.

a) If it does, the system is okay. Reconnect the blower motor wire.

b) If the pressure falls below 21 psi when the blower motor wire is disconnected, replace the clutch cycling switch and retest the system.

17 If the compressor cycles normally, the system is okay. If it cycles on at high pressures (above 52 psi) or off at low pressures (below 21 psi), replace the clutch cycling switch and restest the system.

18 For further information regarding troubleshooting of the FFOT system, refer to the accompanying troubleshooting chart.

INSUFFICIENT OR NO A/C COOLING — FIXED ORIFICE TUBE CYCLING CLUTCH SYSTEM

TEST STEP		RESULT	▶	ACTION TO TAKE
A1	VERIFY THE CONDITION			
	• Check system operation.	System cooling properly	▶	INSTRUCT vehicle owner on proper use of the system.
		System not cooling properly	▶	GO to **A2**.
A2	CHECK COOLING FAN			
	• Does vehicle have an electro-drive cooling fan?	Yes	▶	GO to **A3**.
		No	▶	GO to **A5**.
A3	CHECK A/C COMPRESSOR CLUTCH			
	• Does the A/C compressor clutch engage?	Yes	▶	GO to **A4**.
		No	▶	REFER to clutch circuit diagnosis in this section.

INSUFFICIENT OR NO A/C COOLING — FIXED ORIFICE TUBE CYCLING CLUTCH SYSTEM — Continued

TEST STEP		RESULT ▶	ACTION TO TAKE
A4	CHECK OPERATION OF COOLING FAN		
	• Check to ensure electro-drive cooling fan runs when the A/C compressor clutch is engaged.	Yes ▶	GO to **A5**.
		No ▶	Check engine cooling fan circuit.
A5	COMPONENT CHECK		
	Under-hood check of the following:	OK but still not cooling ▶	GO to **A7**.
	• Loose, missing or damaged compressor drive belt.	Not OK ▶	REPAIR and GO to **A6**.
	• Loose or disconnected A/C clutch or clutch cycling pressure switch wires/connectors.		
	• Disconnected resistor assembly.		
	• Loose vacuum lines or misadjusted control cables.		
	Inside vehicle check for:		
	• Blown fuse/proper blower motor operation.		
	• Vacuum motors/temperature door movement — full travel.		
	• Control electrical and vacuum connections.		
A6	CHECK SYSTEM		
	• Check system operation.	(OK) ▶	Condition Corrected. GO to **A1**.
		(OK̸) ▶	GO to **A7**.
A7	CHECK COMPRESSOR CLUTCH		
	• Use refrigerant system pressure/clutch cycle rate and timing evaluation charts.	Compressor cycles very rapidly (1 second on) (1 second off) ▶	GO to **A8**.
	After preparing car as follows:		
	1. Hook up manifold gauge set.		
	2. Set function lever at max. A/C	Compressor runs continuously (normal operation in ambient temperature above 27°C (80°F) depending on humidity conditions) ▶	GO to **A9**.
	3. Set blower switch on high.		
	4. Set temperature lever full cold.		
	5. Close doors and windows.		
	6. Use a thermometer to check temperature at center discharge register, record outside temperature.		
	7. Run engine at approximately 1500 RPM with compressor clutch engaged.	Compressor cycles slow ▶	GO to **A8**.
	8. Stabilize with above conditions for 10-15 minutes.		
	• Check compressor clutch off/on time with watch. Refer to charts for normal clutch cycle timing rates.		

TEST STEP	RESULT ▶	ACTION TO TAKE
A8 CHECK CLUTCH CYCLING PRESSURE SWITCH		
• Bypass clutch cycling pressure switch with jumper wire. Compressor on continuously. • Hand feel evaporator inlet and outlet tubes.	Outlet tube same temperature approximately −2°C - 4°C (28°F - 40°F) or slightly colder than inlet tube (after fixed orifice) ▶	REPLACE clutch cycling pressure switch. Do not discharge system. Switch fitting has Schrader Valve. GO to **A9**.
	Inlet tube warm or (after fixed orifice) colder than outlet tube ▶	GO to **A10**.
A9 CHECK SYSTEM PRESSURES		
• Compare readings with normal system pressure ranges.	Clutch cycles within limits, system pressure within limits ▶	System OK. GO to **A1**.
	Compressor runs continuously (normal operation in ambient temperature above 27°C (80°F) depending on humidity conditions). ▶	GO to **A11**.
	Compressor cycles high or low ON above 359 kPa (52 psi) OFF below 144 kPa (21 psi). ▶	REPLACE clutch cycling pressure switch. Do not discharge system. Switch fitting has Schrader valve. CHECK system. OK — GO to **A1**. NOT OK — GO to **A10**.
A10 CHECK SYSTEM		
• Leak Check system.	Leak found ▶	REPAIR, discharge, evacuate and charge system. System OK, GO to **A1**.
	No leak found ▶	Low refrigerant charge or moisture in system. Discharge, evacuate and charge system. System OK.
A11 CHECK CLUTCH CYCLING		
• Disconnect blower motor wire and check for clutch cycling off at 144 kPa (21 psi) (suction pressure).	Clutch cycles OFF at 144-179 kPa (21-26 psi) ▶	Connect blower motor wire. System OK, GO to **A1**.
	Pressure falls below 144 kPa (21 psi) ▶	REPLACE clutch cycling pressure switch. Do not discharge system. Switch fitting has Schrader valve. System OK, GO to **A1**.

Preliminary inspection

Before attempting to troubleshoot the CCOT system, check the following components:

1 Inspect the compressor drivebelt. Make sure it's not loose, damaged or missing.

2 Inspect the air conditioning system wiring. Make sure that no wires are frayed or broken. Look for loose or unplugged electrical connectors. Check all fuses and make sure none of them are blown.

3 Verify that the temperature door strikes both stops when the lever is rapidly moved from hot to cold.

4 Verify that the engine cooling fan runs continuously in all air conditioning modes.

Preliminary test

5 After making the necessary repairs, turn on the engine and the air conditioning system and note whether the system is cooling effectively.

6 If the components listed in steps 1 through 4 are working properly but the system is still not cooling effectively, put the temperature lever at the maximum cold position, move the selector lever to normal mode, set the blower switch in the high position, open the doors and hood and warm up the engine at about 1500 rpm.

7 Watch the compressor clutch and see if it engages:

  a) If the clutch doesn't engage, proceed to Step 10.
  b) If the clutch "cycles" (alternately engages and disengages), feel the liquid line before the orifice tube.
    1) If the tube feels warm, proceed to Step 8.
    2) If the tube feels cold, inspect the high side tubes for a frost spot. Open the system and repair the restriction. Evacuate, charge and retest the system.

8 If the vehicle is equipped with a Harrison DA V5 compressor, proceed to "Troubleshooting systems with the Harrison DA V5 compressor."

9 If the vehicle is equipped with any compressor except the Harrison DA V5, feel the evaporator inlet and outlet pipes:

  a) If the inlet is colder than the outlet, inspect the system for leaks and repair any found, evacuate and charge the system. If no leak is found, proceed to Step 15.
  b) If the outlet pipe is colder, or the pipes are both the same temperature, proceed to Step 16.

Compressor clutch test

10 If the clutch did not operate, check the condition of the wire harness to the clutch and the adjustment of the throttle or vacuum cut-out switches. Connect a fused jumper wire between the positive battery terminal and the compressor clutch.

  a) If the clutch doesn't operate, proceed to the next step.
  b) If the clutch operates, proceed to Step 12.

11 Connect a ground wire from the clutch to the engine block. If the clutch still doesn't operate, remove and either repair or replace it.

General Motors cycling clutch orifice tube (CCOT) system troubleshooting

Heating and air conditioning

General Motors
cycling clutch
orifice tube
(CCOT) system
troubleshooting
(continued)

12 If the clutch operates but cooling is inadequate, operate the clutch for a short time and check the low side pressure at the accumulator fitting.

    a) If the pressure is above 50 psi, proceed to the next step.

    b) If the pressure is below 50 psi, proceed to Step 14.

13 Connect a jumper wire across the pressure switch connector.

    a) If the compressor operates, the switch is faulty. Replace it and test the system.

    b) If the compressor doesn't operate with the jumper, look for an open or short circuit between the switch and the clutch.

14 Check the pressure on the high side.

    a) If the high side is above 50 psi, discharge the system and inspect the orifice tube and the high side for an obstruction.

    b) If the high side is below 50 psi, the charge is lost. Leak test the system, make the necessary repairs, then evacuate, charge and retest the system.

System charge test

Caution: *When conducting the system charge test, keep an eye on the gauges for any indication of overcharging (excessively high discharge pressures, for instance).*

15 If cooling is insufficient, add one pound of refrigerant, then check the clutch cycle rate.

    a) If the clutch cycles more than 8 times a minute, discharge the system and check for a plugged orifice tube.

    b) If the clutch cycles less than 8 times a minute, feel the accumulator inlet and outlet pipes.

        1) If the inlet pipe is warmer, or if both pipes are the same temperature as the inlet pipe, add another pound of refrigerant.

        2) If the inlet is colder than the outlet, add another pound of refrigerant. Feel the inlet and outlet pipes again.

            (a) If the outlet pipe is colder or the same temperature as the inlet pipe, add another pound of refrigerant.

            (b) If the inlet pipe is still colder than the outlet, discharge the system and check for a plugged orifice tube.

Pressure switch test

16 If the inlet and outlet pipe temperatures are okay but cooling is insufficient, verify (with a gauge set) that the clutch cycles on at 51 to 51 psi and off at 20 to 28 psi.

    a) If the clutch is cycling correctly, proceed to Step 17.

    b) If the clutch cycles at excessively high, or low, pressures, replace the pressure cycling switch.

    c) If the clutch runs continuously, unplug the evaporator blower motor connector. The clutch should now cycle off between 20 and 28 psi.

        1) If it doesn't (pressure falls below 20 psi), replace the pressure cycling switch.

        2) If the clutch does cycle off, proceed to Step 17.

Performance test

17 Slide the temperature lever to the coldest position, put the selector lever at the maximum mode, and turn the blower to the highest setting. Close the doors and windows, run the engine at 2000 rpm and place an auxiliary fan in front of the grille. Stick a thermometer in the dash vent nearest the evaporator and check the temperature. It should be between 35 and 45°F (assuming an ambient temperature of about 85°F).

18 If the outlet temperature is too high, check compressor cycling time.

  a) If the clutch runs continuously, discharge the system and check for a missing orifice tube, plugged inlet screen or other restriction in the suction line.

  b) If none of these conditions are present, the system has been over-charged. Evacuate and recharge it.

  c) If the clutch cycles on and off, or remains off for a long time, discharge the system and check it for a plugged orifice tube. Replace the tube, then evacuate, charge and retest the system.

Troubleshooting systems with the Harrison V5 compressor

1 Complete the preliminary checks (Steps 1 through 7 in the previous section) first.

2 Connect a gauge set to the system, if you haven't already done so. Connect a fused jumper wire around the cooling fan switch. Put the selector lever in the normal mode and the blower switch in the highest position. With the engine idling at about 1000 rpm, measure the discharge air temperature at the center vent.

  a) If the temperature is no greater than 60°F, proceed to Step 4.

  b) If the temperature is greater than 60°F, check accumulator pressure.

    1) If the pressure is below 35 psi, proceed to Step 3.

    2) If the pressure is between 35 and 50 psi, proceed to Step 4.

    3) If the pressure is greater than 50 psi but less than 160 psi, proceed to Step 5.

    4) If the pressure is greater than 160 psi, proceed to Step 6.

3 If the accumulator pressure is below 35 psi, add one pound of refrigerant.

  a) If the pressure is now more than 35 psi, leak test the system.

  b) If the pressure is still low, discharge the system and inspect the orifice tube for restrictions or plugging. Replace the orifice tube, evacuate, charge and retest the system.

4 Move the selector lever to the Defrost mode. Disconnect the engine cooling fan. Allow the compressor to cycle on the high pressure cut-out switch.

  a) If the compressor makes a knocking noise as it engages, the system oil charge is high. Discharge the system, flush all components, charge the system and add fresh oil.

  b) If the compressor does not make a knocking noise during engagement, set the selector lever to Maximum cooling, adjust the blower to the low setting and allow the engine to idle for 5 minutes at 1000 rpm.

Heating and air conditioning

Troubleshooting systems with the Harrison V5 compressor (continued)

1) If accumulator pressure is between 29 and 35 psi, the system is okay.

2) If accumulator pressure is less than 28 psi, discharge the system and replace the compressor control valve. Evacuate, charge and retest the system.

3) If the pressure is more than 35 psi, discharge the system and replace the compressor control valve. Evacuate, charge and restest the system. If the accumulator pressure is still more than 35 psi, replace the compressor.

5 If the accumulator pressure was greater than 50 psi but less than 160 psi in Step 2, discharge the system and check for a missing orifice tube.

6 If the tube is still there, replace the compressor control valve. Evacuate, charge and retest the system. If the high pressure condition persists, replace the compressor.

7 If the accumulator pressure was greater than 160 psi in Step 2, the system is overcharged. Discharge, evacuate and retest the system.

NORMAL CCOT SYSTEM OPERATING PRESSURES

Model year	Low side psi	High side psi
1973 through 1978	20 to 28	185 to 235
1979 through 1981	24 to 35	150 to 220
1982 on		
Front wheel drive	22 to 29	165 to 205
Rear wheel drive	24 to 30	130 to 190

Glossary

Absolute humidity — The mass (actual amount) of water vapor present in a unit volume of moist air

Absolute pressure — Pressure measured from a starting point of 0 in a perfect vacuum. When measured by the absolute pressure scale, atmospheric pressure is 14.7 psi or 29.92 inches of mercury (in-Hg)

Absolute temperature scale — Also called the absolute scale Temperature as measured on a scale in which the hypothetical lowest limit of physical temperatures is assigned the value zero. The Kelvin scale is an example of the absolute temperature scale.

Absolute zero — The point at which there is a total absence of heat, approximately minus 459 or 460 degrees Fahrenheit

Accumulator — A refrigerant storage device used on General Motors and Ford systems that receives vapor and liquid refrigerant from the evaporator. The accumulator, which contains 'desiccant,' performs a function similar to that of a receiver-drier: it separates liquid from the vapor, retains the liquid and releases the vapor to the compressor. Always located on the low side of the system.

Air conditioner — A device which controls the temperature, humidity and air movement, and sometimes the air purity, in an enclosed space

Air conditioning — A system or process for controlling the temperature, humidity, air movement and sometimes the purity of the air in an enclosed space

Air inlet valve — An adjustable door, often vacuum operated, in the plenum blower assembly that permits selection of outside or inside air for automotive heating and cooling systems

Air outlet valve — A vacuum operated door which directs air flow into the heater core or ducts, usually located in or near the plenum blower assembly

Ambient air temperature — The temperature of the surrounding air

Ambient sensor — A device which samples and detects changes in the temperature of the ambient (surrounding) air

Ambient switch — An outside air temperature sensing switch which prevents operation of the compressor and the recirculating air mode below an outside temperature of 40° F

Ambient temperature — See 'Ambient air temperature'

Amplifier — A device which increases the strength of an electrical or vacuum signal

Aspirator — The air intake of a sensor

Atmospheric pressure — The pressure exerted by the earth's atmosphere at any given point, and altitude, above or below sea level. The atmospheric pressure is calculated by multiplying the mass of the atmospheric column of the unit area above the given point and of the gravitational acceleration at the given point. It's also

Heating and air conditioning

the common term used to denote a value of standard or normal atmospheric pressure equivalent to the pressure exerted by a column of mercury 29.92 in (760 mm) high.

Auxiliary gauge — The gauge which indicates compressor inlet pressure on older Chrysler Corporation vehicles with an Evaporator Presssure Regulator (EPR) valve; also used to measure evaporator pressure on some Ford vehicles with a Suction Throttling Valve (STV)

Axial compressor — A compressor characterized by the unusual piston arrangement. The pistons are arranged horizontally around and parallel to the crankshaft axis or centerline.

Back-seat — A term which means to rotate a service valve counterclockwise all the way down until the valve is 'back-seated.' When referring to a 'stem type' service valve, the term has a more specific meaning: in the back-seated position, the valve outlet to the system is open and the service port in the valve is closed (its normal operating position).

Bellows — A sealed, accordion-type chamber (gas-filled or vacuum) which expands and contracts in accordance with temperature changes. Used as an air conditioning control device on many systems

Bi-metallic sensor — Also known as a bimetal sensor. Consists of a 'thermocouple,' an arm made of two dissimilar metals with different rates of thermal expansion, that flexes in accordance with temperature changes. Used as a temperature sensor.

Blower fan — An electric motor-driven fan which forces air through the evaporator and duct assembly, then forces the cooled air out of the duct work and circulates it through the vehicle passenger compartment

Boiling point — The temperature at which a liquid converts to a vapor. In physics, this point is defined as the temperature at which the vapor pressure of a liquid is equal to the pressure of the atmosphere on the liquid, which is equal to 212° F (100° C) at sea level.

Bowden cable — A cable or wire inside a metal or rubber housing used for remote control of a valve or other device

British Thermal Unit (BTU) — The amount of heat required to raise the temperature of one pound (0.4 kg) of water one degree Fahrenheit. Commonly used as a measurement of heat quantity. 1 BTU = 778 pound feet or 252 calories.

Bulk charging — Using large containers of R-12 to charge the system. Commonly employed with 'charging stations' to perform complete system charges.

Bulk refrigerant drum — Large (for example, 10 lbs, 25 lbs, 30 lbs) container of refrigerant generally used in professional air conditioning service shops which employ charging stations to perform complete system charges

Capacity — A measure of the theoretical maximum amount of refrigeration-produced output, measured in tons or BTUs per hour

Capillary tube — A tube, usually gas-filled, with a precisely calibrated length and inside diameter, used to connect the remote bulb or coil to the expansion valve or thermostat

Celsius — Also referred to as Celsius scale or Centigrade. Uses the freezing point of water as 0° and the boiling point of water at 100°. Celsius temperatures are computed from Kelvin values by subtracting 273.15 from the latter.

Centigrade — See 'Celsius'

Change of state — Rearrangement of the molecular structure of matter as it changes between any two of the three physical states: solid, liquid or gas

Charge — A specific amount of refrigerant by volume or weight

Charging hose — A small diameter hose constructed to withstand high pressures. Connected between the air conditioning system and the manifold set

Charging station — A usually portable unit equipped with a manifold gauge set, charging cylinder, vacuum pump, refrigerant supply, auxiliary gauges, various valves and the plumbing necessary to hook everything together. Used for servicing air conditioning systems.

Check valve — A one-way, in-line valve that permits flow of liquids or gases in one direction only. Used to control flow of vacuum, refrigerant, coolant, etc.

Clutch — An electrically operated coupling device that connects or disconnects the compressor pulley and compressor shaft

Glossary

Clutch cycling switch — A device that turns the compressor on and off in response to changes in pressure or evaporator temperature

Clutch field — A clutch part, consisting of hundreds of windings of wire, that creates a magnetic field when current is applied, pulling in the armature to engage the clutch

Clutch pulley or rotor — The clutch part turned by the drivebelt. The pulley or rotor 'free-wheels' until the clutch is engaged. On rotors which contain the field, the electrical connection is made through brushes similar to alternator and starter motor brushes.

Coefficient of expansion — The fractional change in length, area or volume per unit change in temperature of a solid, liquid or gas at a given constant pressure. For example, an aluminum bar stretches 13 millionths percent of its original length for each degree Fahrenheit rise in temperature. Also referred to as 'expansivity.'

Cold — The relative absence of heat

Compound gauge — Another name for the low side gauge, because it can indicate both pressure and vacuum

Compression — Reduction in volume and increase in pressure and temperature of a gas caused by squeezing it into a smaller space

Compressor — An air conditioning component which pumps, circulates and increases the pressure of refrigerant vapor

Compressor cut-off switch — A device used by some manufacturers to prevent compressor operation. Some typical examples: the wide open throttle (WOT) cut-off switch, low pressure switch and high pressure switch.

Compressor discharge switch — A device that shuts off the compressor when refrigerant pressure is low. The switch is wired in series between the compressor clutch and the control panel switch.

Compressor shaft seal — A seal, surrounding the compressor shaft, that permits the shaft to turn without the loss of refrigerant or oil

Condensation — The act or process of reducing a gas or vapor to a liquid or solid form

Condenser — The air conditioning system heat exchanger that turns refrigerant vapor into a liquid by removing heat from the vapor

Conduction — The transfer of heat between the closely packed molecules of a substance or between two substances that are touching, caused by a temperature differential between the two molecules or substances

Contaminants — Anything other than refrigerant or refrigerant oil in the system

Control head — The dashboard mounted assembly which houses the mode selector, the blower switch and the temperature control lever

Convection — The transfer of heat by the circulation or movement of the heated, or cooled, parts of a vapor or liquid

Corrosion — The eating or wearing away of a substance, such as metal, usually caused by chemical decomposition brought about by an acid

Cycling clutch orifice tube (CCOT) system — The General Motors system that utilizes an accumulator (instead of a receiver-drier). The system uses a fixed orifice tube located at the evaporator outlet, instead of an expansion valve. A thermostatic switch or a pressure sensing switch cycles compressor operation off and on in accordance with system status.

Cycling clutch system — Any system that conrols compressor clutch operation as a means of temperature control.

Dehumidify — To remove water vapor from the air

Density — The weight or mass per unit volume of a gas, liquid or solid

Desiccant — A drying agent (silica gel or a similar substance) used in refrigeration systems to remove excess moisture from R-12 vapor

Diaphragm — A rubber-like piston or bellows assembly which divides the inner and outer chambers of back-pressure regulated air conditioning devices

Dichlorodifluoromethane — The chemical substance (CCl_2F_2) used in earlier automotive air conditioning systems to absorb, carry and release heat. A member of the fluorocarbon family. Usually referred to as refrigerant, or R-12. See 'Fluorocarbon,' 'Refrigerant-12.'

Discharge — To bleed some or all of the refrigerant from a system by opening a valve or connection to permit refrigerant to escape slowly

Heating and air conditioning

Discharge air — Air conditioned air forced through the vents (ducts) into the passenger compartment

Discharge line — The line which connects the compressor outlet to the condenser inlet

Discharge pressure — The (high side) pressure of the refrigerant being discharged from the compressor

Discharge side — The part of the air conditioning system under high pressure, extending from the compressor outlet to the thermostatic expansion valve/tube inlet

Discharge valve — A device used to check high side pressures. Usually referred to as the high side service valve.

Drier — A device located in the liquid line, contains desiccant to absorb moisture from the system. Usually combined with the receiver.

Drive pulley — The pulley attached to the nose of the engine crankshaft. Drives the compressor clutch pulley, usually with a V-type drivebelt.

Drying agent — See 'Desiccant'

Electro vacuum relay (EVR) — A combination solenoid vacuum valve and electrical relay which locks out blower operation and closes the fresh air door in cold weather, and switches the system to the recirculating air mode during maximum system use

Equalizer line — A line or connection used to operate certain control valves. Little or no refrigerant flows through the line.

Evacuate — To pump the air, moisture and foreign material out of the system with a vacuum pump

Evaporation — A change of state, at the surface of a liquid, from a liquid to a vapor. Evaporation can occur at various temperatures, depending on the liquid and the pressure.

Evaporator — An air conditioning system component through which cool, liquid refrigerant is pumped at a reduced pressure. When heated by the warm passenger compartment air being forced through the evaporator, the refrigerant evaporates, drawing heat from the air as it passes over the cooling fins.

Evaporator equalized valve in receiver (EEVIR) — The EEVIR unit is similar in design to a valve-in-receiver type, except that it has an equalizer port on the expansion valve that allows for faster reaction time

Evaporator pressure regulator (EPR) valve — An evaporator temperature control device regulated by back pressure. Used on older Chrysler Corporation systems. Located in the compressor inlet. A system using this device is referred to as an EPR system.

Evaporator temperature regulator (ETR) valve — The ETR valve is a temperature-regulated evaporator temperature control device used on some early model Chrysler Corporation systems

Expansion tube — A device that converts high pressure liquid refrigerant into low pressure liquid refrigerant (thus lowering its boiling point) before it passes through the evaporator. The expansion valve replaces the thermostatic expansion valve. It's also referred to as a 'fixed orifice tube.'

Expansion valve — A device consisting of a metering valve and a temperature sensing capillary tube and bulb which meters refrigerant into the evaporator according to cooling requirements. Formally referred to as a 'thermostatic expansion valve.'

External equalizer — See 'Equalizer line'

Fahrenheit — A temperature scale which designates the freezing point of water as 32° and the boiling point of water as 212°

Fan clutch — A viscous (fluid) drive coupling device which permits variable engine fan speeds in relation to engine speeds

Feedback potentiometer — A variable resistance device which monitors the position of the shaft to which it is affixed and reports the position to the control head

Filter — A device used either with the drier or as a separate unit to remove foreign material (contaminants) from the refrigerant

Flooding — A term which refers to overcharging the system

Fluid — Any liquid or gas that is capable of flowing and that changes its shape at a steady rate when acted upon by a force tending to change its shape. A term used to refer to any substance having the above properties

Fluorocarbon - Any of a class of compounds produced by substituting fluorine for hydrogen in a hydrocarbon and characterized by great chemical stability. Fluorocarbons have numerous industrial applications, but the chemical form dichlorodifluoromethane, known as R-12, is the form discussed in this book.

Flush — The removal of solid particles and sludge, such as metal flakes or casting flash, dirt or oil by running a pressurized cleaning solution through components and refrigerant lines

Foaming — The formation of bubbles in the oil and refrigerant caused by a rapid boiling out of the refrigerant dissolved in the oil when the pressure is suddenly reduced. If noted in the sight glass, this condition indicates a very low refrigerant level.

Ford Fixed Orifice Tube (FFOT) system — The FFOT system utilizes an accumulator instead of a receiver-drier and an orifice tube instead of an expansion valve. The accumulator is located at the evaporator outlet. A pressure sensing switch cycles compressor operation.

Freeze-up — The failure of a unit to operate properly because of the formation of ice at the expansion valve orifice or on the evaporator coils or fins

Freezing point — the temperature at which a given liquid will turn into a solid. The freezing point varies with the pressure and the substance.

Freon-12 - Another name for R-12, a type of refrigerant

Front-seat — A term used to denote the closed position of a stem type service valve to isolate the compressor. The system should never be operated with the valves in this position.

Fuse — An electrical device used to protect a circuit against accidental overload

Gas — A vapor having no particles or droplets of liquid. In physics, a gas is a substance which possesses perfect molecular mobility and, unlike a liquid or a solid, the ability to expand indefinitely.

Gauge manifold or gauge set — The one essential diagnostic tool required for every air conditioning service procedure. A typical gauge set includes high and low side gauges and valves for checking, measuring and controlling pressure and vacuum, and a third valve for controlling discharging, evacuation and charging procedures.

Head pressure — Refrigerant pressure in the lines and condenser between the discharge reed valve and the expansion valve orifice

Heat — The energy associated with the motion of atoms or molecules in solids, which can be transmitted through solid and fluid media by conduction, through fluid media by convection, and through empty space by radiation. All substances with temperatures above absolute zero contain heat.

Heat capacity — See 'British Thermal Unit (BTU)'

Heater core — A finned unit through which coolant from the engine flows and over which air entering the passenger compartment passes

Heat exchanger — A device which transfers the heat of one substance to another. The heater core, the condenser and the evaporator are heat exchangers.

Heat index — A number representing the effect of temperature and humidity on humans by combining the two variables into an 'apparent' temperature. Introduced as a replacement for the temperature-humidity index. For example, a temperature of 90° and relative humidity of 65 percent combine to produce a heat index of 102.

Heat of condensation — The heat liberated by a unit mass of gas at its boiling point as it condenses to a liquid. Equal to the heat of vaporization.

Heat of vaporization — The heat absorbed per unit mass of a given material at its boiling point that completely converts the material to a gas at the same temperature. Equal to the heat of condensation.

Heat quantity — See 'British Thermal Unit (BTU)'

Heat transmission — The flow of heat from one substance to another

Hg — The chemical symbol for Mercury. Used when referring to vacuum as inches of Mercury ('in-Hg').

High load condition — Denotes the condition that occurs when the air conditioning system must operate continuously at maximum capacity to supply enough cold air

High pressure line(s) — The line(s) carrying high pressure liquid and gas from the compressor outlet to the expansion valve inlet

Heating and air conditioning

'H' valve — The term used to denote a type of expansion valve used by Chrysler Corporation

High pressure relief valve — A safety valve located in the discharge line (six-cylinder compressors) or the compressor block (two-cylinder compressors)

High side — Another term for 'discharge side.' The part of the air conditioning system under high pressure, extending from the compressor outlet to the thermostatic expansion valve/tube inlet.

High side service valve — A device, located on the discharge or high side of the compressor, at which high side pressure can be checked and other service operations can be performed

Hot gas — The state of the refrigerant between the compressor and the condenser

Hot water vacuum valve — A vacuum actuated valve which controls the flow of coolant through the heater core

Humidity — The moisture or dampness in the air. Usually refers to an uncomfortably high level of humidity.

Icing switch — A device that cuts off the compressor when the evaporator temperature drops below a predetermined level

In-car sensor — A dual bimetal strip that samples passenger compartment air and controls a vacuum modulator

Inches of mercury — (in-Hg) A unit of measurement which designates the relative amount of vacuum present in a closed system

Inline compressor — Two-cylinder compressor with the pistons arranged side-by-side, like a York or Tecumseh

Latent heat — The heat absorbed or radiated during a change of state at constant temperature and pressure. Called latent because it's 'hidden,' i.e. it cannot be felt or measured with a thermometer.

Latent heat of condensation — The amount of heat given off when a substance changes from a vapor to the liquid without changing temperature

Latent heat of evaporation — The amount of heat required to change a liquid into a vapor without raising the temperature of the vapor above that of the original liquid

Leak detector — Any device used to detect leaks in an air conditioning system (dye, solutions, electronic, propane, etc.)

Liquid line — The line between the drier outlet and the expansion valve. Sometimes, the line between the condenser outlet and the drier inlet is also referred to as a liquid line.

Low head pressure — Refers to a condition of lower-than-normal high side pressure caused by a system malfunction

Low pressure cut-out switch — A device that disengages the compressor clutch when the system pressure drops below a predetermined level

Low refrigerant protection system — A system which interrupts the electrical current to the compressor clutch in the event of refrigerant loss. A typical example is the General Motors superheat switch and thermal limiter.

Low side — Another term for 'suction side.' The low pressure part of the system between the expansion valve outlet and the compressor inlet.

Low side service valve — A device, located on the suction or low side of the compressor, at which low side pressure can be checked and other service operations can be performed

Low suction pressure — Refers to a condition of lower-than-normal high side pressure caused by a system malfunction

Magnetic clutch — A coupling device used to turn the compressor off and on electrically

Manifold — A device which controls refrigerant flow for system test purposes by means of hand valves which can open or close various passageways connected together inside the manifold. Used in conjunction with manifold gauges and service hoses.

Manifold gauge set — A complete testing assembly consisting of a high side gauge, a low side gauge, an auxiliary gauge (optional), a test manifold and a set of service or charging hoses

Glossary

Mercury — Sometimes referred to as 'quicksilver.' A heavy, silver-white, highly toxic metallic element, the only one that is liquid at room temperature. Used in thermometers and barometers. See 'Inches of mercury.'

Mode door — A device which directs the flow of air through the heater/evaporator box

Muffler — A hollow, tubular device used in the discharge line of some systems to muffle the thumping sounds made by the compressor. Sometimes used on the low side too.

Oil bleed line — An external oil line which circumvents the evaporator pressure regulator or bypass valve to ensure positive oil return to the compressor when rpms are high and the system is under a low charge or clogged

Oil bleed passage — An internal orifice which bypasses the evaporator pressure regulator, the bypass valve or the expansion valve to ensure positive oil return to the compressor

Operational test — A check of temperature and pressure conditions under controlled circumstances to determine whether the air conditioner is operating optimally

Overcharge — This term refers to the condition that occurs when too much refrigerant or oil is in the system

Performance test — See 'Operational test'

Pilot Operated Absolute (POA) valve — The POA valve is a suction throttling device used on some General Motors and Ford air conditioning systems. See 'Suction throttling valve (STV).'

Plenum — One term for the air ducts, air valves and blower assembly inside the dash

Power servo — A vacuum-operated or electrically-powered device that actuates the duct doors and switches on systems equipped with automatic temperature control

Pressure — Force per unit area. As used in this book, the term refers to the refrigerant pressure, which is expressed in pounds per square inch (psi).

Pressure drop — The difference in pressure between two points in the system, usually caused by a restriction device

Pressure sensing line — Also referred to as a capillary tube. Connects the remote bulb to the expansion valve.

Pressure sensing switch — A device, used on some late model General Motors and Ford vehicles, which cycles compressor operation in accordance with pressure changes sensed at the accumulator

Programmer — The module that controls blower speed, the air mix door, vacuum diaphragms and other devices in a system equipped with automatic temperature control

Propane — A flammable, heavier-than-air gas used in the Halide torch leak detector

psi — The abbreviation for pounds per square inch

psia — The abbreviation for pounds per square inch absolute

psig — The abbreviation for pounds per square inch gauge

Pump down — Another term for 'evacuate'

Purging — Thorough evacuation of the air conditioning system

Radial compressor — A compressor with pistons radiating out from the centerline of the compressor. The Harrison (Frigidaire) is a typical example.

Radiation — The process by which energy (such as heat) is emitted by one body, as particles or waves, transmitted through an intervening medium or space (like air), and absorbed by another body. Also refers to the energy transferred by this process.

Ram air — A term referring to the air forced through the condenser coils by vehicle movement or fan action

Receiver-drier — Also referred to as a receiver-dehydrator. A container for storing liquid refrigerant and a desiccant. Used in Chrysler Corporation and some import vehicles.

Reciprocating compressor — Any positive displacement compressor that has pistons which travel back-and-forth in cylinders

Heating and air conditioning

Reed valves — Wafer-thin metal plates located in the valve plate of an automotive compressor which act as suction and discharge valves. The suction valve is located on the underside of the valve plate; the discharge valve is situated on the top.

Refrigerant-12 - The chemical substance (CCl_2F_2) used in automotive air conditioning systems to absorb, carry and release heat. Usually referred to simply as R-12. A member of the fluorocarbon family. See 'Dichlorodifluoromethane,' 'Fluorocarbon.'

Refrigeration cycle — The complete circulation of refrigerant through an air conditioning system as it changes temperature and pressure, i.e. changes its state from vapor to liquid, then back to vapor

Refrigeration oil — A highly refined lubricating oil which is free of contaminants such as sulfur, moisture and tar

Relative humidity — The amount of water vapor in the air, expressed as a percentage of the maximum amount the air could hold at the given temperature. The ratio of the actual water vapor pressure to the saturation vapor pressure. Usually referred to as 'humidity.'

Remote bulb — A sensing device connected to the expansion valve by a capillary tube. The bulb senses the temperature of the evaporator outlet pipe and controls the expansion valve accordingly.

Resistor — An electronic device that reduces voltage to regulate an electric motor. In this book, the term refers to the blower motor resistor, which regulates fan speed.

Restrictor — A porous device located in vacuum lines to delay vacuum applied to diaphragms

Relay — An electrical switch that transmits impulses from one component to another

Rheostat — A variable resistor used to control blower speeds

Rotary compressor — A compressor which has rotating rotors, or vanes, that compress and pump refrigerant

Schrader valve — A spring-loaded valve, similar to a tire valve, located inside the service valve fitting to hold refrigerant in the system. Special adapters with built-in depressors must be used to attach service hoses to Schrader valves.

Service hose — Specially manufactured hose designed to withstand the operating pressures of air conditioning systems. Equipped with threaded fittings that can be attached to service valves, manifold gauge sets, vacuum pumps, refrigerant containers, etc.

Service port — A fitting, on stem-type service valves and some control devices, to which manifold gauge set service hoses can be connected

Service valve — Another name for either the high or low side service valves. See 'High side service valve,' 'Low side service valve.'

Servo motor — A calibrated vacuum or electrical motor used to position valves or doors in an automotive air conditioning system

Shaft seal — See 'Compressor shaft seal'

Short cycling — A term referring to the condition in which the compressor in a cycling clutch system cycles too frequently

Sight glass — A glass window in the liquid line, the top of the receiver-drier, or a test manifold, for checking refrigerant flow

Silica gel — A highly absorbent drying agent, usually located in the accumulator or receiver-drier, used to remove moisture from refrigerant

Solenoid — An electro-magnetic relay

Specific heat — In physics, the number of calories required to raise the temperature of 1 gram of a substance 1° C, or the number of BTUs per pound per degree F. In air conditioning, the quantity of heat required to change the temperature of one pound of a substance by 1° F.

Suction line — The line between the evaporator outlet and the compressor inlet

Suction pressure — Compressor inlet pressure. Another name for 'low side pressure.'

Suction service valve — See 'Low side service valve'

Suction side — The low-pressure part of the air conditioning system between the orifice/expnsion tube, or expansion valve outlet, and the compressor inlet

Suction throttling valve (STV) — A backpressure-regulated device, used on some Ford and General Motors systems, that controls refrigerant flow to prevent evaporator core freeze-up. See 'Pilot Operated Absolute (POA) valve'.

Superheat — Also known as superheated vapor. A gas or vapor that is not in contact with the generating liquid (steam not in contact with water, for example), that has been heated to such a degree that its temperature may be lowered or its pressure increased without the conversion of any of the gas into liquid.

Superheat switch — A device that is connected in series with a thermal limiter (fuse). Mounted on the rear of the compressor on General Motors systems equipped with low refrigerant protection.

Temperature — The measure of heat intensity or concentration, expressed in degrees. Measured by a thermometer. Temperature is not a measure of heat quantity.

Temperature dial — A calibrated control lever or wheel used to regulate automatic temperature control system modes

Temperature-humidity index — A number representing an estimate of the effect of temperature and moisture on humans, computed by multiplying the sum of dry-bulb and wet-bulb temperature readings by 0.4 and adding 15, with 65 assumed as the highest comfortable index

Thermal — Of, pertaining to or caused by heat or temperature

Thermal limiter — A fuse-like device that protects the low refrigerant protection system circuit on General Motors vehicles. Stops compressor operation when low pressure is sensed.

Thermistor — A temperature-sensitive, heat-activated resistor. Used in air conditioning system sensors.

Thermostatic expansion valve — A component which regulates the rate of refrigerant flow into the evaporator as determined by the outlet pipe temperatures sensed by the remote bulb

Thermostatic switch — A temperature sensitive switch that prevents icing by cycling compressor operation to control system temperature. Bellows and bimetallic switches are typical examples.

Throttling valve — See 'Suction throttling valve (STV)' and 'Evaporator pressure regulator (EPR) valve'

Transducer — Any device that converts an input signal into an output signal. Used to actuate electric or vacuum servo motors in an automatic temperature control system.

Undercharge — A term referring to a system low on refrigerant, resulting in improper cooling

Vacuum — A controlled, contained system, or condition, with lower-than-ambient-atmospheric pressure. Expressed in inches of mercury (in-Hg). A 'perfect vacuum' is 29.92 in-Hg (a vacuum above a column of mercury will support the column to a height of 29.92 inches).

Vacuum motor — A vacuum-actuated device used to operate doors and valves

Vacuum power unit — A device for operating air conditioning doors and valves using vacuum as a source of power

Vacuum pump — A mechanical device used to evacuate an air conditioning system to rid it of moisture, air and contaminants

Valves-in-receiver (VIR) unit — A component used on General Motors systems, in which the thermostatic expansion valve, POA suction throttling valve, the receiver-drier and, if equipped, the sight glass are all combined into one assembly

Vapor — The gaseous state of refrigerant

Vapor lines — Air conditioning system lines in which refrigerant is normally in a gaseous or vapor state

Variable displacement compressor — A compressor which can change its output in accordance with the conditions

Viscosity — The thickness of a liquid or its resistance to flow

Volatile liquid — A liquid that is easily evaporated

V-type compressor — A compressor with its pistons arranged in a vee-shaped configuration

Water valve — A shut-off valve, mechanically or vacuum operated, for stopping the flow of hot coolant to the heater

Index

Heating and air conditioning

Index

Haynes Automotive Manuals

NOTE: New manuals are added to this list on a periodic basis. If you do not see a listing for your vehicle, consult your local Haynes dealer for the latest product information.

ACURA
*1776 **Integra & Legend** all models '86 thru '90

AMC
Jeep CJ - see JEEP (412)
694 **Mid-size models,** Concord, Hornet, Gremlin & Spirit '70 thru '83
934 **(Renault) Alliance & Encore** all models '83 thru '87

AUDI
615 **4000** all models '80 thru '87
428 **5000** all models '77 thru '83
1117 **5000** all models '84 thru '88

AUSTIN
Healey Sprite - see MG Midget Roadster (265)

BMW
*2020 **3/5 Series** not including diesel or all-wheel drive models '82 thru '92
276 **320i** all 4 cyl models '75 thru '83
632 **528i & 530i** all models '75 thru '80
240 **1500 thru 2002** all models except Turbo '59 thru '77
348 **2500, 2800, 3.0 & Bavaria** all models '69 thru '76

BUICK
Century (front wheel drive) - see GENERAL MOTORS (829)
*1627 **Buick, Oldsmobile & Pontiac Full-size (Front wheel drive)** all models '85 thru '95
Buick Electra, LeSabre and Park Avenue; Oldsmobile Delta 88 Royale, Ninety Eight and Regency; Pontiac Bonneville
1551 **Buick Oldsmobile & Pontiac Full-size (Rear wheel drive)**
Buick Estate '70 thru '90, Electra'70 thru '84, LeSabre '70 thru '85, Limited '74 thru '79
Oldsmobile Custom Cruiser '70 thru '90, Delta 88 '70 thru '85,Ninety-eight '70 thru '84
Pontiac Bonneville '70 thru '81, Catalina '70 thru '81, Grandville '70 thru '75, Parisienne '83 thru '86
627 **Mid-size Regal & Century** all rear-drive models with V6, V8 and Turbo '74 thru '87
Regal - see GENERAL MOTORS (1671)
Skyhawk - see GENERAL MOTORS (766)
Skylark '80 thru '85 - see GENERAL MOTORS (38020)
Skylark '86 on - see GENERAL MOTORS (1420)
Somerset - see GENERAL MOTORS (1420)

CADILLAC
*751 **Cadillac Rear Wheel Drive** all gasoline models '70 thru '93
Cimarron - see GENERAL MOTORS (766)

CHEVROLET
*1477 **Astro & GMC Safari Mini-vans** '85 thru '93
554 **Camaro V8** all models '70 thru '81
866 **Camaro** all models '82 thru '92
Cavalier - see GENERAL MOTORS (766)
Celebrity - see GENERAL MOTORS (829)
625 **Chevelle, Malibu & El Camino** all V6 & V8 models '69 thru '87
449 **Chevette & Pontiac T1000** '76 thru '87
550 **Citation** all models '80 thru '85
*1628 **Corsica/Beretta** all models '87 thru '95
274 **Corvette** all V8 models '68 thru '82
*1336 **Corvette** all models '84 thru '91
1762 **Chevrolet Engine Overhaul Manual**
704 **Full-size Sedans** Caprice, Impala, Biscayne, Bel Air & Wagons '69 thru '90

Lumina - see GENERAL MOTORS (1671)
Lumina APV - see GENERAL MOTORS (2035)
319 **Luv Pick-up** all 2WD & 4WD '72 thru '82
626 **Monte Carlo** all models '70 thru '88
241 **Nova** all V8 models '69 thru '79
*1642 **Nova and Geo Prizm** all front wheel drive models, '85 thru '92
420 **Pick-ups '67 thru '87** - Chevrolet & GMC, all V8 & in-line 6 cyl, 2WD & 4WD '67 thru '87; Suburbans, Blazers & Jimmys '67 thru '91
*1664 **Pick-ups '88 thru '95** - Chevrolet & GMC, all full-size pick-ups, '88 thru '95; Blazer & Jimmy '92 thru '94; Suburban '92 thru '95; Tahoe & Yukon '95
*831 **S-10 & GMC S-15 Pick-ups** all models '82 thru '93
*1727 **Sprint & Geo Metro** '85 thru '94
*345 **Vans - Chevrolet & GMC,** V8 & in-line 6 cylinder models '68 thru '95

CHRYSLER
2114 **Chrysler Engine Overhaul Manual**
*2058 **Full-size Front-Wheel Drive** '88 thru '93
K-Cars - see DODGE Aries (723)
Laser - see DODGE Daytona (1140)
*1337 **Chrysler & Plymouth Mid-size** front wheel drive '82 thru '93
Rear-wheel Drive - see Dodge Rear-wheel Drive (2098)

DATSUN
402 **200SX** all models '77 thru '79
647 **200SX** all models '80 thru '83
228 **B - 210** all models '73 thru '78
525 **210** all models '78 thru '82
206 **240Z, 260Z & 280Z** Coupe '70 thru '78
563 **280ZX** Coupe & 2+2 '79 thru '83
300ZX - see NISSAN (1137)
679 **310** all models '78 thru '82
123 **510 & PL521 Pick-up** '68 thru '73
430 **510** all models '78 thru '81
372 **610** all models '72 thru '76
277 **620 Series Pick-up** all models '73 thru '79
720 Series Pick-up - see NISSAN (771)
376 **810/Maxima** all gasoline models, '77 thru '84
Pulsar - see NISSAN (876)
Sentra - see NISSAN (982)
Stanza - see NISSAN (981)

DODGE
400 & 600 - see CHRYSLER Mid-size (1337)
*723 **Aries & Plymouth Reliant** '81 thru '89
1231 **Caravan & Plymouth Voyager Mini-Vans** all models '84 thru '95
699 **Challenger & Plymouth Saporro** all models '78 thru '83
Challenger '67-'76 - see DODGE Dart (234)
236 **Colt** all models '71 thru '77
610 **Colt & Plymouth Champ** (front wheel drive) all models '78 thru '87
*1668 **Dakota Pick-ups** all models '87 thru '93
234 **Dart, Challenger/Plymouth Barracuda & Valiant** 6 cyl models '67 thru '76
*1140 **Daytona & Chrysler Laser** '84 thru '89
*545 **Omni & Plymouth Horizon** '78 thru '90
*912 **Pick-ups** all full-size models '74 thru '91
*556 **Ram 50/D50 Pick-ups & Raider and Plymouth Arrow Pick-ups** '79 thru '93
2098 **Dodge/Plymouth/Chrysler** rear wheel drive '71 thru '89
*1726 **Shadow & Plymouth Sundance** '87 thru '93
*1779 **Spirit & Plymouth Acclaim** '89 thru '95
*349 **Vans - Dodge & Plymouth** V8 & 6 cyl models '71 thru '91

EAGLE
Talon - see Mitsubishi Eclipse (2097)

FIAT
094 **124 Sport Coupe & Spider** '68 thru '78
273 **X1/9** all models '74 thru '80

FORD
*1476 **Aerostar Mini-vans** all models '86 thru '94
788 **Bronco and Pick-ups** '73 thru '79
*880 **Bronco and Pick-ups** '80 thru '95
268 **Courier Pick-up** all models '72 thru '82
2105 **Crown Victoria & Mercury Grand Marquis** '88 thru '94
1763 **Ford Engine Overhaul Manual**
789 **Escort/Mercury Lynx** all models '81 thru '90
*2046 **Escort/Mercury Tracer** '91 thru '95
*2021 **Explorer & Mazda Navajo** '91 thru '95
560 **Fairmont & Mercury Zephyr** '78 thru '83
334 **Fiesta** all models '77 thru '80
754 **Ford & Mercury Full-size,** Ford LTD & Mercury Marquis ('75 thru '82); Ford Custom 500,Country Squire, Crown Victoria & Mercury Colony Park ('75 thru '87'); Ford LTD Crown Victoria & Mercury Gran Marquis ('83 thru '87)
359 **Granada & Mercury Monarch** all in-line, 6 cyl & V8 models '75 thru '80
773 **Ford & Mercury Mid-size,** Ford Thunderbird & Mercury Cougar ('75 thru '82); Ford LTD & Mercury Marquis ('83 thru '86); Ford Torino,Gran Torino, Elite, Ranchero pick-up, LTD II, Mercury Montego, Comet, XR-7 & Lincoln Versailles ('75 thru '86)
*654 **Mustang & Mercury Capri** all models including Turbo. Mustang, '79 thru '93; Capri, '79 thru '86
357 **Mustang V8** all models '64-1/2 thru '73
231 **Mustang II** 4 cyl, V6 & V8 models '74 thru '78
649 **Pinto & Mercury Bobcat** '75 thru '80
1670 **Probe** all models '89 thru '92
*1026 **Ranger/Bronco II** gasoline models '83 thru '93
*1421 **Taurus & Mercury Sable** '86 thru '94
*1418 **Tempo & Mercury Topaz** all gasoline models '84 thru '94
1338 **Thunderbird/Mercury Cougar** '83 thru '88
*1725 **Thunderbird/Mercury Cougar** '89 and '93
344 **Vans** all V8 Econoline models '69 thru '91
*2119 **Vans** full size '92-'95

GENERAL MOTORS
*829 **Buick Century, Chevrolet Celebrity, Oldsmobile Cutlass Ciera & Pontiac 6000** all models '82 thru '93
*1671 **Buick Regal, Chevrolet Lumina, Oldsmobile Cutlass Supreme & Pontiac Grand Prix** all front wheel drive models '88 thru '95
*766 **Buick Skyhawk, Cadillac Cimarron, Chevrolet Cavalier, Oldsmobile Firenza & Pontiac J-2000 & Sunbird** all models '82 thru '94
38020 **Buick Skylark, Chevrolet Citation, Olds Omega, Pontiac Phoenix** '80 thru '85
1420 **Buick Skylark & Somerset, Oldsmobile Achieva & Calais and Pontiac Grand Am** all models '85 thru '95
*2035 **Chevrolet Lumina APV, Oldsmobile Silhouette & Pontiac Trans Sport** all models '90 thru '94
General Motors Full-size Rear-wheel Drive - see BUICK (1551)

GEO
Metro - see CHEVROLET Sprint (1727)
Prizm - see CHEVROLET Nova (1642)
*2039 **Storm** all models '90 thru '93
Tracker - see SUZUKI Samurai (1626)

GMC
Safari - see CHEVROLET ASTRO (1477)
Vans & Pick-ups - see CHEVROLET (420, 831, 345, 1664)

(Continued on other side)

Haynes North America, Inc., 861 Lawrence Drive, Newbury Park, CA 91320 • (805) 498-6703

Haynes Automotive Manuals (continued)

NOTE: New manuals are added to this list on a periodic basis. If you do not see a listing for your vehicle, consult your local Haynes dealer for the latest product information.

HONDA

351	**Accord CVCC** all models '76 thru '83
1221	**Accord** all models '84 thru '89
2067	**Accord** all models '90 thru '93
42013	**Accord** all models '94 thru '95
160	**Civic 1200** all models '73 thru '79
633	**Civic 1300 & 1500 CVCC** '80 thru '83
297	**Civic 1500 CVCC** all models '75 thru '79
1227	**Civic** all models '84 thru '91
*2118	**Civic & del Sol** '92 thru '95
*601	**Prelude CVCC** all models '79 thru '89

HYUNDAI

*1552	**Excel** all models '86 thru '94

ISUZU

*1641	**Trooper & Pick-up,** all gasoline models Pick-up, '81 thru '93; Trooper, '84 thru '91

JAGUAR

*242	**XJ6** all 6 cyl models '68 thru '86
*478	**XJ12 & XJS** all 12 cyl models '72 thru '85

JEEP

*1553	**Cherokee, Comanche & Wagoneer Limited** all models '84 thru '93
412	**CJ** all models '49 thru '86
50025	**Grand Cherokee** all models '93 thru '95
*1777	**Wrangler** all models '87 thru '94

LINCOLN

2117	**Rear Wheel Drive** all models '70 thru '95

MAZDA

648	**626** Sedan & Coupe (rear wheel drive) all models '79 thru '82
*1082	**626 & MX-6** (front wheel drive) all models '83 thru '91
267	**B Series Pick-ups** '72 thru '93
370	**GLC Hatchback** (rear wheel drive) all models '77 thru '83
757	**GLC** (front wheel drive) '81 thru '85
*2047	**MPV** all models '89 thru '94
	Navajo-see Ford Explorer (2021)
460	**RX-7** all models '79 thru '85
*1419	**RX-7** all models '86 thru '91

MERCEDES-BENZ

*1643	**190 Series** all four-cylinder gasoline models, '84 thru '88
346	**230, 250 & 280** Sedan, Coupe & Roadster all 6 cyl sohc models '68 thru '72
983	**280** 123 Series gasoline models '77 thru '81
698	**350 & 450** Sedan, Coupe & Roadster all models '71 thru '80
697	**Diesel 123 Series** 200D, 220D, 240D, 240TD, 300D, 300CD, 300TD, 4- & 5-cyl incl. Turbo '76 thru '85

MERCURY

See FORD Listing

MG

111	**MGB** Roadster & GT Coupe all models '62 thru '80
265	**MG Midget & Austin Healey Sprite** Roadster '58 thru '80

MITSUBISHI

*1669	**Cordia, Tredia, Galant, Precis & Mirage** '83 thru '93
*2097	**Eclipse, Eagle Talon & Plymouth Laser** '90 thru '94
*2022	**Pick-up & Montero** '83 thru '95

NISSAN

1137	**300ZX** all models including Turbo '84 thru '89
*1341	**Maxima** all models '85 thru '91
*771	**Pick-ups/Pathfinder** gas models '80 thru '95
876	**Pulsar** all models '83 thru '86

*982	**Sentra** all models '82 thru '94
*981	**Stanza** all models '82 thru '90

OLDSMOBILE

	Bravada - see CHEVROLET S-10 (831)
	Calais - see GENERAL MOTORS (1420)
	Custom Cruiser - see BUICK Full-size RWD (1551)
*658	**Cutlass** all standard gasoline V6 & V8 models '74 thru '88
	Cutlass Ciera - see GENERAL MOTORS (829)
	Cutlass Supreme - see GM (1671)
	Delta 88 - see BUICK Full-size RWD (1551)
	Delta 88 Brougham - see BUICK Full-size FWD (1551), RWD (1627)
	Delta 88 Royale - see BUICK Full-size RWD (1551)
	Firenza - see GENERAL MOTORS (766)
	Ninety-eight Regency - see BUICK Full-size RWD (1551), FWD (1627)
	Ninety-eight Regency Brougham - see BUICK Full-size RWD (1551)
	Omega - see GENERAL MOTORS (38020)
	Silhouette - see GENERAL MOTORS (2035)

PEUGEOT

663	**504** all diesel models '74 thru '83

PLYMOUTH

	Laser - see MITSUBISHI Eclipse (2097)
	For other PLYMOUTH titles, see DODGE listing.

PONTIAC

	T1000 - see CHEVROLET Chevette (449)
	J-2000 - see GENERAL MOTORS (766)
	6000 - see GENERAL MOTORS (829)
	Bonneville - see Buick Full-size FWD (1627), RWD (1551)
	Bonneville Brougham - see Buick (1551)
	Catalina - see Buick Full-size (1551)
1232	**Fiero** all models '84 thru '88
555	**Firebird** V8 models except Turbo '70 thru '81
867	**Firebird** all models '82 thru '92
	Full-size Front Wheel Drive - see BUICK Oldsmobile, Pontiac Full-size FWD (1627)
	Full-size Rear Wheel Drive - see BUICK Oldsmobile, Pontiac Full-size RWD (1551)
	Grand Am - see GENERAL MOTORS (1420)
	Grand Prix - see GENERAL MOTORS (1671)
	Grandville - see BUICK Full-size (1551)
	Parisienne - see BUICK Full-size (1551)
	Phoenix - see GENERAL MOTORS (38020)
	Sunbird - see GENERAL MOTORS (766)
	Trans Sport - see GENERAL MOTORS (2035)

PORSCHE

*264	**911** all Coupe & Targa models except Turbo & Carrera 4 '65 thru '89
239	**914** all 4 cyl models '69 thru '76
397	**924** all models including Turbo '76 thru '82
*1027	**944** all models including Turbo '83 thru '89

RENAULT

141	**5 Le Car** all models '76 thru '83
	Alliance & Encore - see AMC (934)

SAAB

247	**99** all models including Turbo '69 thru '80
*980	**900** all models including Turbo '79 thru '88

SATURN

2083	**Saturn** all models '91 thru '94

SUBARU

237	**1100, 1300, 1400 & 1600** '71 thru '79
*681	**1600 & 1800** 2WD & 4WD '80 thru '89

SUZUKI

*1626	**Samurai/Sidekick and Geo Tracker** all models '86 thru '95

TOYOTA

1023	**Camry** all models '83 thru '91
92006	**Camry** all models '92 thru '95
935	**Celica Rear Wheel Drive** '71 thru '85
*2038	**Celica Front Wheel Drive** '86 thru '92
1139	**Celica Supra** all models '79 thru '92
361	**Corolla** all models '75 thru '79
961	**Corolla** all rear wheel drive models '80 thru '87
*1025	**Corolla** all front wheel drive models '84 thru '92
636	**Corolla Tercel** all models '80 thru '82
360	**Corona** all models '74 thru '82
532	**Cressida** all models '78 thru '82
313	**Land Cruiser** all models '68 thru '82
*1339	**MR2** all models '85 thru '87
304	**Pick-up** all models '69 thru '78
*656	**Pick-up** all models '79 thru '95
*2048	**Previa** all models '91 thru '93
2106	**Tercel** all models '87 thru '94

TRIUMPH

113	**Spitfire** all models '62 thru '81
322	**TR7** all models '75 thru '81

VW

159	**Beetle & Karmann Ghia** all models '54 thru '79
238	**Dasher** all gasoline models '74 thru '81
*884	**Rabbit, Jetta, Scirocco, & Pick-up** gas models '74 thru '91 & Convertible '80 thru '92
451	**Rabbit, Jetta & Pick-up** all diesel models '77 thru '84
082	**Transporter 1600** all models '68 thru '79
226	**Transporter 1700, 1800 & 2000** all models '72 thru '79
084	**Type 3 1500 & 1600** all models '63 thru '73
1029	**Vanagon** all air-cooled models '80 thru '83

VOLVO

203	**120, 130 Series & 1800 Sports** '61 thru '73
129	**140 Series** all models '66 thru '74
*270	**240 Series** all models '76 thru '93
400	**260 Series** all models '75 thru '82
*1550	**740 & 760 Series** all models '82 thru '88

TECHBOOK MANUALS

2108	**Automotive Computer Codes**
1667	**Automotive Emissions Control Manual**
482	**Fuel Injection Manual, 1978 thru 1985**
2111	**Fuel Injection Manual, 1986 thru 1994**
2069	**Holley Carburetor Manual**
2068	**Rochester Carburetor Manual**
10240	**Weber/Zenith/Stromberg/SU Carburetors**
1762	**Chevrolet Engine Overhaul Manual**
2114	**Chrysler Engine Overhaul Manual**
1763	**Ford Engine Overhaul Manual**
1736	**GM and Ford Diesel Engine Repair Manual**
1666	**Small Engine Repair Manual**
10355	**Ford Automatic Transmission Overhaul**
10360	**GM Automatic Transmission Overhaul**
1479	**Automotive Body Repair & Painting**
2112	**Automotive Brake Manual**
2113	**Automotive Detailing Manual**
1654	**Automotive Eelectrical Manual**
1480	**Automotive Heating & Air Conditioning**
2109	**Automotive Reference Manual & Illustrated Dictionary**
2107	**Automotive Tools Manual**
10440	**Used Car Buying Guide**
2110	**Welding Manual**

SPANISH MANUALS

98905	**Códigos Automotrices de la Computadora**
98915	**Inyección de Combustible 1986 al 1994**
99040	**Chevrolet & GMC Camionetas** '67 al '87 Incluye Suburban, Blazer & Jimmy '67 al '91
99041	**Chevrolet & GMC Camionetas** '88 al '95 Incluye Suburban '92 al '95, Blazer & Jimmy '92 al '94, Tahoe y Yukon '95
99075	**Ford Camionetas y Bronco** '80 al '94
99125	**Toyota Camionetas y 4-Runner** '79 al '95

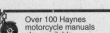

Over 100 Haynes motorcycle manuals also available

2-96

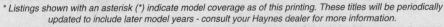

Haynes North America, Inc., 861 Lawrence Drive, Newbury Park, CA 91320 • (805) 498-6703